God: Naked at Last

Debbie Newson

God: Naked at Last

Vanguard Press

VANGUARD PAPERBACK

A CIP catalogue record for this title is available from the British Library.

ISBN 978 1 80016 657 8

Vanguard Press is an imprint of Pegasus Elliot Mackenzie Publishers Ltd.
www.pegasuspublishers.com

First Published in 2024

Vanguard Press
Sheraton House Castle Park
Cambridge England

Printed & Bound in Great Britain

Many people do not want church or religion, but they do want God.

The evolution of Church, Christianity and religion over the last two thousand years have obscured God. We are going to attempt to strip God of this unnecessary religious baggage and reveal what God is like, and what being close to God can be like. The foundations of faith are in awe-inspiring, incredible lifechanging experiences of this God-figure, this being a catalyst for something that was so good the whole world wanted it; Christianity shot around the world and inspired millions to sit at the feet of God and experience all the wonders God had for them. It was totally captivating, yet Church, Christianity and religion have built obstacles around God that have gradually obscured God, making this incredible lifechanging experience unattractive. God might even be tired of being defined by religion, when religion is not what was needed.

These incredible, lifechanging encounters with God are also good for our health and wellbeing. Many of us crave these experiences, but we may have been put off the idea of God because we do not like Church or religion. By stripping away religion, we can discover God afresh for ourselves and express that discovery however we like. We might find the deepest desires of many of us are met, that of God reaching down into the unfathomable depths of our hearts and souls, refreshing those deep, inner parts of our being that may have long been dry. We might just find ourselves transformed, restored, complete.

We will strip God of two thousand years of Christian, Church and religious history, and see what is left. As we do, we may find that our church structures, beliefs and practices crumble, leaving behind only God, face to face.

We're going to try and find God again.

Debbie Newson

Chapter One
Stripping God

It was a beautifully warm evening as we stepped into the little boat in Tamarin Bay, on the island of Mauritius. The sunset was stunning as the local fishermen and I sped out to the edge of the reef amongst the turquoise waters of the Indian Ocean, to dive for lobsters. I was captivated by the scene as we arrived; the moon shining on the water, the waves gently lapping the boat. I'd been travelling for two years, finding it a welcome relief from the struggles of life in New Zealand where I'd grown up.

I dived in, and swam along the reef searching for lobsters. Fish darted around me, while the coral shone brightly in the torchlight. Suddenly, I noticed a strange looking jellyfish. Aware that some could be dangerous, I quickly moved away, but as I turned, I realised to my horror that there was a cloud of them, and I found myself directly in the middle of this swarm.

I could not escape. Suddenly, something hit me on my right arm. A thousand volts surged into me; the pain instantly unbearable. I came to the surface in shock, the pain increasing every second. I gasped for breath, and was terrified. As I tried to move away, more jellyfish tentacles brushed over my skin, again sending agonising shockwaves through my body.

Panicked, I looked for the boat. It was some distance away. I felt I couldn't swim that far; I could hardly move. I called out, hoping my friends would hear me. I tried to move in the direction of the boat but the pain was unbearable. I needed to get to that boat.

Finally, the fishermen still on the boat realised there was a problem. They sped over to me and dragged my painful, blistered body aboard the boat. They realised I had been stung by several deadly box jellyfish, and they knew it wasn't good. They instantly revved the engines and headed as quickly as they could for the shore.

We got to the beach, and they dragged me from the boat and laid me on the sand. Then, to my despair, they sped off to fetch the men who had been left on the reef.

Alone and terrified, the unbearable pain continued to surge in shockwaves through my body. There seemed no relief. Gradually, my breathing became harder. I had to fight for each breath and I knew I needed help.

I tried to get up and walk to a nearby hotel. I was in shock, but so desperate for help I mustered the strength to get up. I dragged myself to the hotel, and collapsed at their door.

A security guard saw me and dragged me inside, calling for an ambulance. In those agonising minutes as I waited, I could see a darkness beginning to creep over me. My bones began to feel cold, and my muscles shook uncontrollably. The agonising pain continued to throb around my weakening body.

Finally, the ambulance arrived. I looked dumbfounded at the old Renault 4 with a stretcher in place of the seats. I was helped into it by the security guard, and off we went. As we drove along, I began to see images of myself as a little boy. I knew I was dying.

Suddenly, I saw a vision of my mother. I heard her speak words to me I knew she had said to me as a teenager. 'Ian, if you are in trouble, cry out to God from your heart, God will hear you and will help you.'

I didn't believe in God. I was an atheist, and I didn't know who to pray to or what to say. I also didn't know that my mother had been woken in the early hours of the morning in New Zealand and heard God say, 'Your eldest son Ian is nearly dead. Pray for him now.' She had been praying for me at the moment I was lying in that ambulance.

The only prayer I knew was the Lord's prayer, learnt as a child in school. As I lay there, pieces of the prayer came to me. I repeated them as best as I could, and as I did, an incredible peace that I had never felt before swept over me. It bought a little relief from my desperate situation.

We arrived at the hospital and I was quickly taken by doctors to the emergency room. I lay there, forcing my eyes open to stay alive. I tried to speak but my lips wouldn't move.

After a short time in the emergency room, I felt myself give a sigh. It was a sigh of relief, and a sense of release came over me. I closed my eyes.

I found myself standing in a dark room. I wondered why the doctor had turned the lights out, and tried to feel my way around. There was a sense of fear in this place. I was cold and afraid, yet alive. I stood there, realising other souls were there too, mournfully wandering around. I cried out to God; I knew I had prayed in that ambulance and so I said, 'I prayed to you for help so why am I here?'

As I prayed those words a brilliant light suddenly shone around me and lifted me up. This light fell all around me, and I was lifted up and into a tunnel, where sparks of light were breaking off and flying around me.

The light got brighter and brighter, and brought a sense of love, peace and joy. I looked at my body and it was transparent, yet full of the light that had been darting around me. It was the most awesome experience of my life.

I then found myself standing beside the source of this light. It was like a mountain of diamonds shining with an indescribably brilliant light. As I stood there, a voice spoke from the light. It said, 'Ian, do you wish to return?' I didn't know where I was, and I didn't know what to say.

I began to think. Why would I return? No one loved me. This was such a beautiful place to be and I wanted to stay. Another wave of light washed over me; I had expected judgment, but instead the wave bathed me in pure, brilliant and cleansing love. As I stood there, wave after wave washed over me, the love penetrating deep inside my being and healing the deepest part of me. I knew this was God.

I hadn't felt love like this before. My mother and father had loved me, but since then I'd known only a harsh world of hurt and pain. Sex bought slight relief from life, but it wasn't love.

I became aware of a figure standing in the middle of the mountain of light, dazzling white robes reaching down to its feet, and the radiant light shining out from its face. I did not feel fear, but freedom, free to stand in the presence of this God-being and enjoy being loved to the very depths of my soul.

Directly behind this figure, I saw a beautiful scene, a crystal clear stream running through a pastureland of perfect green grass, with trees growing either side. There were rolling hills and flowers of all colours, all shining brightly.

I knew this was where I wanted to be, to live here forever. But as I stepped forward, the figure stopped me. The figure asked me again, 'Ian, do you wish to return?'

I said 'No!' But as I stepped forward, a vision of my mother filled the scene, and I realised there was one person who truly loved me. I realised that if I stayed, she would have no idea that in that ambulance I had prayed out to God in my desperation, and that I was here, in paradise, with God. For a second I saw her grief, and knew I had to return. I knew also that I had to tell others what this was like.

But I didn't know how to get back. I didn't want to go through the darkness again. I asked God, 'How do I get back?'

The figure said, 'Ian… open your eyes and see.'

Immediately, I was back in my body. I opened my eyes and found myself looking at a doctor who had no idea I was alive. He looked up momentarily, and as he did our eyes met. He jumped in abject horror as he found this dead man looking at him. I managed to turn my head the other way and saw nurses who had been preparing my body for the mortuary. I had been dead for around twenty minutes.

I was still paralysed, so I prayed for God to heal me. As I did, I felt warmth begin to flood my whole body. God was healing me!

After this encounter, Ian McCormack quickly regained his strength, and returned shortly after to New Zealand where he now lives with his wife.[1]

Many people crave experiences of God. Many wish to experience what others describe as God reaching down and touching their hearts, changing their lives, awakening a part of them that they never really knew existed, God breaking into their lives. Others hope that the whole concept of God would be true, and yet are not quite sure what to believe. Suspecting that there might be *something* that exists, some God-being, but not sure what it is or how to connect with it, we might just be aware of a longing to experience something of God for ourselves. Maybe a previous experience has left us intrigued and we would like to see more, or perhaps the difficulties of life have left us feeling distraught and whilst all other things have let us down, the only hope we have might be in some God-being.

Yet Church can seem so unattractive. Having to adhere to a set of rules, fit the 'Christian' mould, do the right thing, spend every Sunday sitting in a hall with others singing or listening to a sermon when you'd rather be out with family and friends, running through the hills, or relaxing in bed. Many people don't want Church, but they do want God.

At the end of Sunday services at the first church I went to as a teenager, people were often asked if they wanted prayer. Most weeks people would be prayed for and would fall over; it was said they were filled with the Holy Spirit and could not stand up under the awesome presence of God. I used to go forward for prayer at those times thinking it was great, as I loved the game of 'trust' played in youth groups where you fall backwards and people catch you. I would go forward for prayer, fall over, and someone would catch me. I was faking it! I was faking being filled with the Spirit and simply falling over just for fun. I suspect others faked it too… Then one day God showed me, I think with a wry smile, what this was really all about.

I was at a youth conference run by Youth With a Mission, who teach young people the basics of Christianity and theology and take them on overseas trips. The speaker was talking about prayer, and then said he was going to pray for everyone. He asked us to stand up, the chairs were removed, and he started praying at the opposite end of the row to where I was sitting. He placed his hands onto people's heads and one by one, immediately, they fell down. I thought, *I'm not playing this game any more. This time I am not falling over!* I'd had enough of playing around, and I guess I thought it was all fake; that people didn't need to fall over.

One by one the people fell, and finally he approached me. He placed his hands gently on my head, and the most amazing thing happened. A sensation ripped through my body that I cannot explain. A tingling, heavy, powerful sensation that simply took over and that I could not resist. It wasn't sexual, but it was good, like a heavy, soothing, restoring weight laying on you. It felt like I was encountering God face to face, that incredible, raw power surging through my body. I lay there for half an hour, unable to move, not wanting to resist. It was wonderful. And to me, it was God saying, 'This is what it's really like; you've been faking it, but this is it for real!' The same thing happened again the next day.

Something happened that day. Something real. I'd heard about these experiences but never felt it for myself. It was tingly, heavy, powerful in ways you cannot describe. It wasn't a normal sensation, I encountered something physical, a power and love that I'd never felt before. It was physical evidence to me of there being something real in the whole concept of God. This was not religion. This was not the performance of religious rituals that the various traditions of Christianity or religion demand that their faithful followers do. It was real, it was a healing power, it was God close up. What I didn't know at the time was that this experience taught me that the whole weight of Christianity, Church and religion means nothing without experiencing God for yourself.

This is why religion often does not satisfy; there is this amazing, incredible, powerful, irresistible, loving, healing, transforming love and power of God that is so wonderful and so captivating, that when you experience it you are in love like you've never been before, and yet Christianity and the Church have so often reduced it to going to a dark, cold building on a Sunday morning and listening to a rather dull church service. Christianity has managed to exchange this amazing, lifechanging, extravagant connection with God for a series of religious rituals that are not particularly attractive. Often the external husk of religion has been portrayed as the real thing.

The rules, beliefs and practices that Christianity has created often portray God as a being that needs these rules to be fulfilled or you will not be accepted. There is the sense that some are simply not good enough to come and find God, and those that do come have to follow certain rules and conform to the ideal image of a Christian in order to be accepted by God and by Church, and if you don't you may end up in Hell. Yet the concept of God and how God is portrayed, is not necessarily what God is like. It's just what others say they believe about God, what they think the Bible says, what the evolution of Christianity has said. When the building blocks of this image are examined, they crumble, created not by

God but instead by two thousand years of Christianity. It is not surprising that many are not interested in this God, or in Church. Christianity may have got it all very wrong.

We will hear later from Amy, a woman who had a death experience — not near death, because she was actually declared dead for twenty minutes — but the God she saw the moment she died that day was the very opposite of that she had been taught about in her Church upbringing. This is what she saw: 'The "judgmental" God of the Old Testament was nowhere to be found. There was only a vast and eternal presence of love, a being who not only created me and everyone and everything that is, but who was intimately entwined with my evolution. God was also not "male" or a "father" — picture that white-haired pointing guy on the ceiling of the Sistine Chapel — but was both mother and father, my ultimate parent. God loved me even more than I love my own kids — which is enormous! And I was all at once humbled and empowered by being loved so much.'[2]

Many of us dislike the image of God as portrayed by religion. But unless we have experienced God ourselves, we don't really know what God is like. Often we reject the idea of God, when what we might be rejecting is the image of who God is thought to be as portrayed by others, which is often merely their opinion. If I wanted to try an oyster, I would go to an oyster bar and have one. I wouldn't rely on what others told me oysters were like. I would want to try one myself to know for sure if I like them or not. It is the same with God. We can't rely on what others say God is like, because they may be wrong.

The surest knowledge must come from those who have actually seen or experienced God themselves; the stories we explore of those who experienced death found simply extraordinary love and light. Not a male or female, nor a judgmental being, just loving. The experiences of God that many others report say the same, it is simply an incredible, lifechanging encounter that leaves us awestruck.

Some stories we examine will come from the Bible because that's largely what the Bible is; people writing down their experiences of God, not as it is sometimes used, as a weapon to tell others what they should or shouldn't be doing. There will also be first-hand stories of experiences that people have had of God; stories that confirm to those who encounter God, that there really must be something in all this.

It seems that Church, Christianity and religion can so easily obscure God, even if they don't always intend to. Experiencing God can be incredible and irresistible, filled with an orgasmic wonder you may never have imagined, and yet religion has left us instead with scraps of faith that many of us are not interested in. Wonder has been exchanged for tiresome rules and expectations.

We will strip God of Christian, Church and religious history, and see what is left. We will explore the evolution of the structures, beliefs and practices of the Church and Christianity, and see whether they are necessary to connect with God. We will attempt to discover God for ourselves, and we might just like what we find, when all religious debris is swept aside.

There is a new and growing area of study in Christianity; contextual theology. This explores what faith in God looks like in different areas of the world, among those who have cultures very different from one another. It began a few years ago when people started to realise that when missionaries took the gospel message to other countries in the seventeenth and eighteenth centuries, they inadvertently tried to convert people to a white western version of Christianity, thereby taking western cultural norms to others and calling it Christianity. If people converted to Christianity they were expected to look like and do the things that Christians in the west did, when some of those things were totally inappropriate for their culture. Individual cultural expression was disposed of in the belief that the western version of Christianity was the only way to God.

Theological research (the study of God) is now exploring what the essential and universal "nuggets" for faith and knowing God are, whilst advocating that expressions of faith can be different in every culture. Faith should fit the context — the area it is located — rather than a "one size fits all" approach, expecting someone else's expression of faith to fit all cultures and all people worldwide.

Just as contextual theology finds the right expression of faith in God for each culture worldwide, so it can find the right expression for each individual person. What it looks like and how we express faith for each of us might be very different, so your personal way of expressing your faith might look very different to your friends, neighbours or family. We will discover that faith is flexible and personal, and should be right for the individual, because we are all different. We can all discover God and express that discovery however we like.

Many of the things Christianity has said are necessary in order to know God are in fact cultural practices and beliefs, required certainly by Church, but not by God. In short, God might not care whether we do them or not. God doesn't need religion in order to have an amazing relationship with all people, regardless of their life preferences.

I do not wish to criticise the church. I have gained so much by being part of a church since I was thirteen years old. My life was transformed by a church family who took me under their wing, and without them I'm not sure what would have happened in my life. I love the church, and I've had the most amazing times with God through it. I also know millions worldwide benefit from being in church and taking part in church life, the varieties of denomination and types of church meaning you can often find one that suits you. Churches and individual Christians are often incredible, and do substantial amounts of charity work worldwide. Yet the church setting is not right for everyone.

Most people do not need another group to join or another set of behaviours to adopt; we have enough of those at home or work. In addition, many have been hurt by the Church, and it is not a good place for them to be. From terrible child abuse scandals to more minor but just as destructive ill-treatment, many could not bear to be subject again to its systems and beliefs. But although we may reject Church for good reason, we might still wish to find God.

Many do not believe in God and that is not surprising, it does all sound a bit weird and "pie in the sky", if you have never experienced God for yourself. I can empathise with those who struggle to believe in God, or reject the idea totally. I sometimes even find myself awkwardly trying to justify my belief to others because without experiencing it for yourself, the idea of God is a little bit fanciful. There are days when even the most robust Christian will doubt their belief. For many vicars, their belief in God declines the longer they are in the ministry, and new groups of minsters are emerging that feel religion is a human creation.[3]

But then there are those days when we experience something so incredible and real, or feel a peace that really does help us rise above desperate circumstances. The thousands of stories, the feelings we had that day… reignite those nagging thoughts that there might indeed be something real in all this. There is evidence, not proved by scientific study but proved by the millions of people who've felt it, seen it, been changed, been restored by it. Seeing real change in those that need it; the sick healed, the anxious at peace, problems resolved, hope for the hopeless. This is the best kind of evidence you can get.

The evidence of the millions who have experienced this close up, have been blessed by it, had their lives impacted for the better by it, show there is *something* there. Some being, some force, some *thing*. Many will claim to understand it but I don't believe anyone truly does, or maybe we will when we see it face to face after we have left behind the mortal life we now know. It would be great if we could all discover this *something* for ourselves and enjoy it, rather than be put off by other people's rather dry and boring suggestions of what it might be or what they think we need to do to connect with it. For too long, God has been what we needed, whilst Christianity and religion is what we got. It's time to change this.

Many simply want to meet and experience God, finding that unique peace and rest that is found in God's presence, that inexplicable joy in difficult circumstances, to feel God's love bounding into our lives in unimaginable ways. This closeness with God is not found in religious expressions, in rules, doctrine, or strict ways of behaving. Some might find those helpful, but they are not necessary to experience God.

This book will explore how the Church has evolved over its two thousand year history, how the Bible came to have the status of being the "Word of God" and how this has led to many beliefs and practices (and how it is misused), and we will explore what knowing God should, and could, be like. We will strip Christianity back to its bare bones, giving us the choice to discard the outer shell and keep the aspects that help us all connect with God, and perhaps feel for ourselves those lifechanging encounters with this God-being. If that two thousand year history has resulted in a giant religious scrapheap obscuring God, we will sift through the rubble and discard what is not needed, freeing us all to know and experience God.

What will be left is yet unknown… Hopefully it is the ability to connect with this incredible God, to see God, feel God, hear God for the very first time. For lives that need refreshing, to be refreshed, for those who are anxious or suffering with depression to find hope. For those struggling to understand life, to find peace, so that we don't just struggle through our lives, but we truly live and thrive. For us all to encounter and experience for ourselves the wonder and awe of being touched by God.

We will strip God of the religious baggage that hides God from us, but we will also build up what faith can be, how we can find God for ourselves, and how we can express that. We will explore the benefits of this, some of those benefits being remarkable, that faith is actually good for our health. Not attending church or performing the multitude of religious duties, but faith, that heartfelt encounter and intimacy with God.

I have thought much over what to call this God-being because the term "God" can itself put some off. In Arabic it is Allah; in Portuguese it is Deus; in Hungarian, Isten; in Irish, Dia; in English, God. For ease we will use the term God, although I don't believe God is particular about what term we use. Christianity is my area of specialism, but many of the same things could be said of other religions.

I have also battled with giving this God-being a gender. We typically use the male genitive "He", but as far as we know God does not have genitalia, DNA and testosterone levels that would define it as "He". Many who have been hurt by male figures in their lives would struggle to relate to a figure that is portrayed as male, and because convenience or tradition is not a good excuse, I will avoid doing it. However, I have several stories from those who have encountered God; they are told first hand by those people and so occasionally refer to God as male.

I may use the term "Christian" to refer to those in the Church, but in fact no title is necessary in describing those who have a close relationship with God. "Christian" was merely a convenient title given to those first churchgoers in the early days of the Church two thousand years ago. Just as it doesn't matter what we call God, so it doesn't matter what we call ourselves.

We may find that as we strip God of two thousand years of Christian history, that the walls of our churches, our beliefs and practices crumble, and we find ourselves sitting again at God's feet asking what is therefore necessary. As God gently whispers in a divine, powerful, orgasmic voice that nothing is needed except ourselves, we might find that as God restores our souls, and breathes life into our tired hearts, that we experience God as God always intended us to. That we find it is simply us and God, and it is good.

My dream is that through reading this book we will indeed be able to find God, and experience God in new, fresh ways; ways that are right for us. That we will find all the wonders of God for ourselves in a way that refreshes tired eyes, that fills needy lives with love and power, that heals broken hearts. It's time for us to strip away much of the garbage that has for too long obscured God.

It's time for us to find God again.

Chapter Two
The Evolution of Church

It was a dry, hot day in the Roman region of Palestine, in the year 33 AD. The town of Jerusalem had seen upheaval and tension recently, as the supporters of Jesus had seen him tried and convicted in what they believed was a sham trial, and he had been executed. Rumours of odd events had been circulating as some of his friends had reported that they had seen Jesus die, then appear again alive, then, whilst they were on top of a mountain with him, saw him suddenly glow and then disappear into a cloud whilst angels appeared and told them he had gone into Heaven. Jesus' family and those involved had decided to stay together and pray, just as they remembered Jesus telling them to do before he disappeared. Out of desperation they felt this was all they could do.

They were sitting together in the upstairs room of a house in Jerusalem. A doctor who was writing an account of the events describes how there was the sound of a hurricane that caught everyone by surprise. Then, as the sound of the hurricane increased, flames started appearing. But it wasn't a fire — it was God. The Holy Spirit began to touch everyone in that building. As the Spirit landed on people's heads, they started speaking in languages they had not known before.[4] Hundreds of people encountered God in a powerful and unexpected way. Nothing like this had happened before.

The experience that day in Palestine kick-started the church. After that, the text describes people meeting in each other's houses to sing songs, pray, eat together, and share their possessions. Every day thousands of astonished people joined the Church as they also had incredible experiences of God. Miracles were happening daily.[5] There was a collective excitement; an awe that descended on the area as people began to realise God was doing something new. People joined them in droves.

Life in first century Palestine was difficult and short. With no healthcare system and a short life expectancy for people with health struggles, there was little hope. They lost babies and children and lived a meagre existence with long work days and no rest, often going hungry or without sleep. Suffering was commonplace and need was everywhere. So, miracles would have been lifechanging for people. Nothing else would have come to their aid.

Stories taken from the Bible recount many incredible things happening from that time. A man forced to beg because he was unable to use his legs is healed instantly by a mere command from one of Jesus' disciples. Saul, who was killing Christians, sees God in a dramatic way and is forever changed. Peter has a dream which challenges long held religious beliefs and practices, and opens the way for people, previously separated due to religious beliefs, to eat together and talk about what God is doing — and then experience the same! Peter is later imprisoned for his faith but then freed in dramatic fashion as his chains are shattered in front of him, and he walks out of prison.

Crowds gathered regularly, bringing the sick, and many were healed. Many others had supernatural experiences of God, often described as God "falling on" people. God talks directly to people to guide them to those who need to hear about God and what God was doing so they could also experience it too.

The Bible doesn't record much further on in history, but other records do. Although there was incredible joy and excitement, the times were violent as Roman leaders tried to destroy the Church because they claimed to worship God, not Caesar. Christians were killed and persecuted, and many escaped from Jerusalem. As they fled, they told others what had been happening. People were amazed, especially when they seemed to carry the momentum with them, and people in other places started having incredible experiences of God too.

Thousands would listen as the people would tell of what was happening, and as they spoke, people were healed of diseases in their hundreds. Churches started popping up in people's houses all over the known world. Many believed Jesus had come to save the world; the Greek word (Greek was the common language at the time in this area) for this saviour figure was *Christos*; hence Jesus was referred to as "Christ" and his followers were called "Christians".[6] The name stuck.

People were so changed and so awestruck that they were prepared to die for their faith. Tacitus, a Roman historian records, "Nero… punished with the utmost refinement of cruelty a class… commonly called Christians. This pernicious superstition again broke out, not only in Judea but even in Rome. An immense multitude was convicted, besides being put to death they were made to serve as objects of amusement; they were clad in the hides of beasts and torn to death by dogs; others were crucified, others set on fire to illuminate the night when daylight failed."[7]

Christians were killed for their faith in their thousands, suffering horrific deaths. But it remained irresistible, people were captivated by God; during the persecution in the early fourth century, one Christian woman was killed for her faith using boiling pitch. The Roman solider who executed her was so moved by her faith and her perseverance in death that he became a Christian, knowing this would lead to his death a few days later.[8]

Experiencing God has remained irresistible since then, but persecution continues across the world. Today, thirty million Christians suffer persecution, torture or discrimination worldwide, and that number is increasing. In 2021, 5,898 Christians were murdered for their faith.[9] Even in the face of persecution people will cling to their faith, this being their lifeline. For so many, their connection with God is more important than life itself.

Nothing could stop people in those early days of the Church being captivated by this apparent move of God in their lives. Faith seemed to enable an unquenchable belief that whatever people did to their bodies, they could not kill their soul. The direst human circumstances, even the risk of torture and death, could not quench this movement or the zeal people had for God and for what God was doing.

Anyone and everyone was welcome to experience God, and be part of the church. The church was founded on these awe-inspiring experiences of God; people were awestruck, having incredible experiences of God that revitalised their souls and healed their diseases; thousands of lives were changed, healed and restored. Those without hope found they could laugh again. Injected into their difficult lives was the hope of a wonderful future beyond their current troubles and the ability to survive and thrive in the present.

There were no church buildings, there were no vicars, priests, or rules about how one should behave. In fact, it was a crazy time where anything could happen; people would scream as they were set free from spiritual oppression, jump for joy as they were healed, laugh as they were filled with an inexplicable joy, or be overwhelmed with delight as God touched their hearts and souls. Many Christians today express a desire to return to those days of simply enjoying the presence of God; experiencing God without the complicated structures of Christianity.

These early days of the Church were filled with wonder and awe as people experienced God in new and exciting ways. Life was enormously hard, but encountering God made it bearable. God was transforming people's hearts and lives; people who had been oppressed for too long, seen too many bad things happen, experienced grief as loved ones died too young.

These and more incredible, lifechanging experiences of God were the foundation of Christianity, and this continued as the Church grew and spread across the world with new Churches popping up in most countries, all experiencing these things. Many things undoubtedly happened that have simply not been recorded.

It almost sounds too good to be true. It is difficult to know for sure what life was like then or how events unfolded after Jesus died because ascertaining historical truth from the Bible or any text is fraught with difficulty. History, including Biblical history, is written or recorded by individuals and always contains elements of the writers' opinion and worldview, even if it were inspired by God. It was over one hundred years ago when Tolstoy purportedly said that recorded history could never be a complete and accurate account of events. We have to treat all recorded history with caution. But we can still gain insight from these texts especially when combined with contemporary experience which often corroborates aspects of the historical accounts. This can be useful for exploring what God might do for us today and what our expressions of faith can be like.

Details of early Christianity may be difficult to clarify, but clearly, *something* incredible happened for people to be willing to die for this. Whatever did happen caused people to risk their lives, follow this God-being and start multiple worldwide Churches where people in their thousands came to experience God for themselves. Events were worthy of key historical figures recording it for reference. God was moving dramatically in the world and millions of lives were changed for the better. It must have been incredible. If you could bottle this it would be worth a fortune.

Similar experiences of God are still happening today; stories abound from across the world of people's lives being impacted by God, from the quiet to the more ecstatic. For some it is simply a sense of peace they have not known before. For others it is an overwhelming sensation that knocks them off their feet. It can mean both physical and mental healing, it can mean provision of need. It can mean all sorts of things and it is totally captivating.

A hillside in Wales has seen some dramatic encounters in recent years. A footpath cuts through the grounds of an attractive Christian retreat centre near the dramatic coastline of Pembrokeshire. People began knocking on the door of Ffald y Brenin and asking what was going on there, because they often encountered strange events. Visitors would announce that they didn't know what it was, but they knew they wanted it.

Some guests were out praying in the gardens one day when they noticed the bracken quivering. To their surprise they found a young couple lying in the ferns, hands and feet in the air laughing and crying, tears streaming down their faces. Every time the young couple tried to get up, they fell down again in uncontrollable fits of laughter. After a time, they explained that every time they walked near the grounds of this property they were overcome by an inexplicable joy. They kept coming back for more.[10] Countless people have been blessed in recent years by this place.

Millions of people today carry personal stories of their encounters with God and what this means for their lives, stories that would fit neatly into the pages of the Bible.

Those initial years after Jesus died and the Church began were filled with irresistible and incredible experiences between people and God that changed multitudes of lives. It had been a chaotic but fantastic start.

Chapter Three
The Hijacking of Faith

It did not take long for controversy to begin in the early Church, however. Theological debate started about subjects such as who Jesus was; was he just a man? But there are hints in the Bible writings that he was God, so what was he, man or God? Do the presence of the Holy Spirit, Father and Son mean there are three Gods, or one with three personalities? Questions came up over salvation. What do you have to do to be saved? Is there a Heaven and Hell? Is Hell eternal? What does one have to do to become a Christian, and then what behaviour was correct for a Christian?

These arguments and others, show that the beginnings of Christianity and the formation of the Church, were not quite as smooth as modern Christians might believe it to have been. People did not know what to believe; Christianity at that time represented multiple groups who had differences in beliefs and practices and who met all over the Roman Empire and beyond. The arguments were often fierce and divisive and some have never been resolved, still raging on today. Scholars battled to find the truth, but for those first centuries Christianity was not unified, and it was not functioning as one religion with coherent and consistent beliefs and practices.

Added to this disunity was the ongoing persecution of Christians by the Romans and by others who were suspicious of them and their practices. They were accused of eating the flesh and blood of their God in their services. (The practice of communion even today states that the bread and wine are the body and blood of Jesus.) Many people were trying to physically eliminate this fledgling faith, but the internal disputes and lack of continuity were just as disruptive. One solution came from a somewhat unexpected source.

One day, in an effort to win more territory, the Emperor Constantine was riding his horse into battle wondering which gods he should ask for help, when he saw a vision. Suddenly, in the sky was the symbol of a cross made of light, and the words, "Conquer by this". Constantine was awestruck, as was his entire army who also witnessed it. Constantine won that battle; and was so overwhelmed by his vision of the cross that he became a Christian and instructed his entire empire to do the same, making Christianity the state religion.[11] This ignited a period of time in which the Roman rulers shaped and moulded Christianity. This brought about a sudden transformation of the faith; instead of being a persecuted minority it became a powerful force in the Roman empire.[12] But this move was costly; Christianity was no longer a dynamic movement centred around experiencing God, it was to be shaped into a religion. Many of the influences from the Roman empire became integral to the faith and remain today. The hijacking of faith, had begun.

Designed by the Romans, Not by God

The Romans took this still fledgling faith and quickly shaped it into what they wanted it to look like, a religion that would help serve their political intentions. People were suddenly forced to be Christian, rather than choosing so because of their experiences of God.

By the time Theodosius was emperor in 378 AD, the persecution of Christians had been halted, Christianity had become the state religion, and churches were being built in every town across the empire. Days of the week were originally attributed to celestial bodies, and Sunday was the day of the sun-god. This was also a rest day in Roman culture and Constantine knew more people could attend church if Sunday was made the holy day in Christianity. (Monday was moon-day, Saturday was Saturn's-day, designations given by the Babylonian empire thousands of years before the Romans or Christianity.) It is also possible that 25th of December was given as a day to celebrate Jesus' birth because that was originally a day of celebration of the sun-god *Sol Invictus*, although the origins of Christmas Day are sketchy.[13] Christianity continued to spread across the world and people were still having incredible experiences of God, but officially the Roman Emperor was very much in charge, and was able to shape Christianity as he wanted it to be, to benefit his empire.

The faith benefitted from being made the state religion; persecution had ended and there was money available to build churches. These developments are not necessarily negative; people had to meet somewhere and the idea of creating a religious day had its benefits. But these changes shaped Christianity and many of them remain today, created not by God, but by the Romans and those after them. As order was introduced, these fundamental changes also meant that the spontaneity of the faith and ability to encounter God in new and exciting ways was suppressed.

Church Buildings

Basilicas were important secular public meeting places in the Roman empire. They followed a basic plan: rectangular in shape, with a main hall extending down the entire length, with side aisles separated by pillars. The top end was called the apse; domed with a raised platform, where, if it were used as a courthouse, a judge would sit. Constantine's churches followed this basic plan with one addition, a transept, which was a section crossing the main hall just before the apse, thus making the building into the shape of a cross.[14] Traditional church buildings that are seen in most towns today in the UK and across the world have continued to follow this basic structure.

The Romans had adopted much of Greek culture. It was a belief in this Greco-Roman culture that the gods resided in temples, or they would visit the temples regularly, so if you wanted to sacrifice to your god or go and meet your god you must visit the temple.

In this new wave of faith God had been touching people's lives in many different places; in the fields, in homes, in the rivers. The structuring of the faith meant it was beneficial to the Church and to the empire if people were directed to assemble regularly in these new church buildings, instead of being free to experience God anywhere. Today, there is a residual belief that God resides in these buildings and we must go to them to meet God. Sunday as a religious day also became associated with the traditional idea of a sabbath, and this gained importance because of its place in the ten commandments. These are remnants of this Greco-Roman religious culture that became embedded into Christianity. However, the multitudes of stories of people encountering God anywhere in the world today means we can choose to meet God anywhere and anytime we wish to. Religious buildings are designed to house worshippers, not God.

Holy Places?

There was a lovely area next to a graveyard in a town I once lived in. I always wanted to take my dog for a walk there, but there was a sign on the gate saying dogs were not allowed as this was consecrated holy ground. I began to question what made these places "holy" or "consecrated". Was this a physical phenomenon? Was the area different from any other? How is something made or declared holy? Many would say a church is also holy, and there is a sense that you should behave in a certain way and go to that holy place to worship God; that this is inherently different from all other places. But the early Church met in normal people's houses; any house became a meeting place as the Church flourished in those early days.

They didn't only meet in houses. On a bright sunny day in Malta, the young couple handed their ten euro entrance fee to the smiling, happily rounded, elderly lady sitting on a scruffy wooden chair, the peeling blue paint making its way over time onto the ancient stone pavement. The couple found their own way to the cave entrance, tentatively stepping down into the darkness. It took a minute for their eyes to adjust; dim lighting had been installed but it hardly penetrated the menacing darkness. They had come to see the catacombs; ancient underground burial chambers.

Alone, they stepped through the darkness, finding their way by feel along the dusty walls, each footstep a risk as they could not see what lay underfoot. They found a tunnel, and began slowly moving through it, whispering to each other in this strange and daunting place. They did not feel scared; something compelled them to continue. Suddenly, in a cavity cut into the walls of the tunnel, there lay bones; an ancient skeleton, someone buried here two millennia ago when what lay above was a very different world.

As they stepped tentatively through the tunnel, holding hands as fear began to creep up inside them, more and more skeletons appeared, mostly of adults but some woefully small, these remnants of life revealing the fragility of our mortal bodies. The dusty, grim tunnel continued, twisting and turning, as more and more skeletons appeared, lying in their forever home.

The couple continued, somehow compelled to see what else lay in these tunnels, when suddenly the tunnel opened out into a large room. The lighting was still dim but they could see there were no skeletons here, this was not a grave. Gradually, they were able to make out frescoes on the walls, first some figures, then a cross. As they turned around, they noticed a small altar cut out of the bedrock. This was a chapel! To escape the persecution of the Romans in the first centuries of the Church, people had met in the most unlikely of places; the underground tunnels where they buried their dead. At the awesome sight of this little chapel, the tingling fear that had started to well up inside them disappeared, and an immense feeling of awe and peace flooded them. That connection with those ancient Christians as they sought to meet in the security of this most unlikely of places was a moment to treasure.

The idea of a holy place stems from the Old Testament, and from the practices of those early religions when, thousands of years ago, people went to a temple complex to offer sacrifices to their gods. The Old Testament temple design included a curtain which segregated the presence of God from the people, as God was deemed too holy to come into contact with ordinary people. Jeremiah, a prophet from the Old Testament, said God had told him that one day this curtain would not be needed, as God would come and dwell in people's hearts, not in buildings. At the precise moment Jesus died several hundred years after Jeremiah heard God say this, it is recorded that this massive curtain was torn in two by what was described as God's hand; there was no human involvement. It is likely that this torn curtain represents Jeremiah's prophecy coming true;

the need for holy places where God is separated from people has vanished. Jesus confirmed that after he had died and gone to Heaven, God would dwell inside our hearts, signifying that there was no need to have curtains dividing us from God — or indeed the concept of a holy place at all. This theme of people being God's dwelling place, not buildings, occurs in the Bible and in the experience of millions of people. So, it is great to have a grand place to meet together, but it is likely that church buildings are no more holy than the swimming pools the Romans also gave us.

Leaders

Church leaders, until Constantine, had simply been people who cared for those in their house church. Pastoral, wise and strong in their faith, they were able to advise and care for members, helping them to encounter God and find strength for life. Gradually, as churches increased in number and size, bishops were introduced who would lead services from the front while the people watched; people were now meeting predominantly in these church buildings instead of homes. Having larger buildings was useful; religion was an important part of the culture and many people who would have regularly attended temples dedicated to various gods were now attending church. Because of state sponsorship of churches and the large numbers of people attending, bishops gradually became more like business leaders, employed by the state to serve the purposes of the empire, and managing an array of churches from afar.[15] A congregation of silent observers was easier to control than a church where everyone might take part. It also meant that faith could be used to control behaviour; people could be taught that God required them to behave a certain way and any deviation was sinful, with the threat of hell as punishment.

Core Beliefs

In those early days of the newly-fledged church two thousand years ago as the core beliefs of Christianity were being established, many groups formed that held differing beliefs. Ascertaining truth was difficult. Some highlighted spiritual experiences, and believed it did not matter what you did with your body, it was what was happening with your soul that mattered. Others felt that bodily discipline was crucial to achieve spiritual heights, and would fast almost to death to achieve this. The conflicts could be fierce; one is recorded in the Bible, as Paul is sent to Jerusalem to help solve the problem of what behaviour was demanded of Christians. Some leaders had insisted they follow the Old Testament laws and be circumcised. After much heated discussion, it was decided that circumcision wasn't necessary. Every man since has been extremely grateful for this.[16]

These ongoing disputes within Christianity bought disunity and threatened what was now the state religion; and therefore, the empire. There was no continuity, scholars who were studying the scriptures and trying to ascertain truth argued vehemently. It was as if Jesus wiped the religious slate clean but gave no real guidelines for the religion of the future; something that should inspire questions as to whether we need religion at all in order to experience God. It was subsequent scholars, Church leaders and the fathers of the faith who decided what was right or wrong, and all this under the watchful eye of the Roman rulers.

Constantine, in a bid to bring stability to his empire, wished to put a stop to these disputes. He had given power to the bishops to sort out theological problems but confusion and division continued. So, Constantine took it upon himself to end this disarray. In 325 AD he called a council in Nicaea, now Iznik in modern day Turkey. Several hundred bishops from Asia, Syria, Palestine and Egypt gathered to discuss Christianity, and to ascertain, once and for all, Christian truth. Constantine, dressed in robes studded with diamonds, led proceedings. His agenda was focussed on ending disagreement rather than ascertaining truth, which he asserted at the beginning would please both God and himself, the emperor. And anyone who disagreed with him would be at the receiving end of his anger.

Throughout the discussion there was still much uncertainty, and no reliable way of establishing truth. The main argument was around Jesus; was he man or God, or both? How can he be both? And did this make Mary the mother of God?[17]

Trying to fully understand the being and nature of the immense and unknowable God, even with the knowledge that they had of Jesus, was an almost impossible task. We have the same problem today. To define the undefinable, to describe something you cannot see and cannot fully know is too much to ask, even for hundreds of bishops led by a diamond-encrusted emperor. Where there is uncertainty, an attempt to define may instead limit. It may instead constrict what, until now, had been God moving in incredible and inexplicable ways.

But define is what they did. And it was Constantine himself that came up with the final solution, the Nicene Creed. This brushed over deep theological debate, set Christian belief into stone and is still repeated today by millions. This political move achieved its aim; it stopped debate and conflict over the nature of God and created one creed the whole church could follow — and if they did not, Constantine would see to them.

The Church also began to teach that it held the authority on matters of faith and conduct and that there was no salvation or faith outside the Church. People could not just believe what they wanted, or express their faith in their own way as they might get it wrong, and this increased instability in the state religion and therefore in the empire; they felt some had already crept into heresy and were leading others astray. Of course, it was useful for the state if the Church had sole authority in matters of faith and conduct.

Christianity had become a religion, designed by those in powerful positions to harness and control encounters between God and people. From now on the official practices and beliefs would be dictated from the top; they would be done to suit the Church and the empire, instead of enabling people to simply encounter God for themselves. Many were part of the faith because they had to be seen to be doing the right thing; if you behaved as the church said you should then you were okay, accepted by both church and state. A gradual creeping in of pretentiousness; looking good on the outside but with little depth, had begun to infect the Church. It had been over three hundred years since the time of Jesus. Finally, the Catholic Church was well and truly born.

The Church in the Wilderness

The crooked old sign displaying only a picture of a church pointed the way. It was the beginning of autumn, and the trees were a multitude of colours, golden yellow, bright red, and all shades of brown. It was a quiet, serene place, surrounded by bright green fields and gently rolling hills. Birds sang happily in the trees and the squirrels were using their tiny paws to dig holes, ready to store away their food for the winter. The ancient stone building stood unpretentiously in this beautiful setting, lichens and mosses resting on the stones, the foundations of a much earlier structure still visible. The huge graveyard showed people had been part of this church for centuries, the design and carvings on the gravestones displaying the obvious wealth of some, while others were simple, the owners of course all reaching the same end regardless of status.

I found myself wondering if the lichens and mosses were the only life in this church, when suddenly someone spoke, asking if I had been here before. I replied that I hadn't, the look of mild unease on my face betraying my inevitable anxiety. I had attended many other churches previously, and I was wondering why coming here today made me feel nervous.

I sat on the hard wooden pew, taking in my surroundings. I cautiously opened the service book, hoping it would be obvious what I was meant to say and when. A cobweb, caught on the edge of the book, danced in the air; I was pleased to have something to focus on.

I sat admiring the internal stonework, ornately carved figures watching over us from high up in the roof, whilst holding up the old wooden beams. Brightly painted frescoes adorned the ceiling, telling those favourite old Bible stories so that those who could not read were able to see them.

Suddenly there was a rustling sound, and everyone stood. I quickly unfolded my legs and rose to my feet whilst the vicar strode confidently past, his robes flowing with the movement of air. I couldn't help but wonder if he wore a dress often.

The service began, each of us repeating the words in the book thankfully at the right moments. It was quiet and subdued, with around twelve people attending. They obviously wished for more, the pleasant church warden at the end coming to ask me if I would come again; her expression revealing this was more a command than a question. Their numbers had diminished; even before the Covid pandemic they were reducing, now even more so.

I had been invited to attend this service by the vicar himself, who afterwards was willing to help me understand the meaning of some of the aspects of Church life. I knew Church was hugely important for many, with meaning embedded in so many features of Christianity, and I wanted to understand more.

He had a gentle but powerful voice, a voice of authority. As we talked, I felt a certain sadness. The Church was everything for this profound man, it represented such a lot; he was proud to tell me how the Church had created the first hospitals, the first schools. The term "sister" for senior nurses now in hospitals derived from the nuns who ran those first havens for the sick. The term "doctor" was originally applied to those teachers of theology, learned men who it was felt could teach about God and faith.

The minster proudly showed me the beautiful robes, carefully laid in old wooden draws, taken out at the right time each week. Each had meaning, the white being for times of celebration, the red robes signifying the time when the Holy Spirit is said to have descended on those praying in the book of Acts, the event which kick-started the Church, and to honour those who have died for their faith in the past. Green robes signify hope and new growth, and are worn for more everyday occasions.

I asked what he thought the purpose of the Church is. Among common answers like helping people to come into relationship with God, to serve and to teach, he poignantly said, 'To prepare people for the end of life.' It struck me that this is something we do not do very well in our society and perhaps this is one area the Church could lead the way.

He spoke also of the meaning of the layout of the building, that the church was designed to focus the attention on God and Heaven. The nave where the people sit signifies the world, the word originating from the Latin for ship, the ship having been adopted as the symbol of the Church, signifying rescuing souls from the storms of life and bringing them safely home.

The building narrows where the chancel and choir sit, guiding the eye towards the altar rail and the sanctuary which represents the holy of holies, reminiscent of the temple in the Old Testament. The gaze is directed towards this point, hoping that in life we will always keep our eyes fixed on God.

We had taken communion during the service, and I asked why he had added water to the wine. He explained this represented the two natures of Jesus, God and man. He quietly asserted that, 'If it doesn't have meaning we shouldn't be using it.'

His energy and enthusiasm for his Church was infectious, and it was clear he was torn; knowing things needed to change to make this faith relevant to all today, and yet not wanting to remove or alter this great symbolism. He proudly exclaimed that they had recently taken out a long part of the service to make it shorter for those who found it tiresome; people no longer had to recite such a long piece each service. Memories of an image I had seen a few years ago crept into my mind, of churchgoers feverishly hitting an old pony, the caption reading "flogging a dead horse". I tried to stop myself from thinking I had seen this before, people desperately trying to reshape their churches to tempt people in, their efforts often in vain. It was a truly beautiful place and I felt at peace there. I knew I would visit occasionally, but I also knew I could not express my faith in this way.

There is great significance and depth of meaning in many features of the Church, pointers to God and reminders of aspects of the faith that we may one day need. But they sit buried in the rubble of religion, hidden, along with the God they wish so desperately to reveal.

Choosing Solitude

One of the first people to reject Church life and yet retain their faith was an Egyptian man called Anthony. Prior to Constantine making Christianity the state religion, the Christian life had been marked by total commitment to God and to others, with personal faith being shown in acts of love and kindness. The new influx of the general population into churches bought those who did not care how they lived, they were merely ticking the religious boxes. Constantine himself lived what can be seen as a questionable life; although he transformed the Church and halted the persecution of Christians, he still fought wars and while on a campaign in Rome, allegedly had his son and wife murdered.[18] Christianity was changing, and although it was safer to be a Christian, those with a genuine faith in God were diluted by the many who simply knew they had to do what was expected of them.

Anthony did not settle well into this world. He had a genuine faith in his God, resulting from a vision he had after praying and asking God how he could achieve salvation. He saw an angel who told him to dedicate his life to work and prayer.[19] Disillusioned with society and church, and wanting to surrender himself completely to God, he left straight for the desert. Here he lived for fifteen years, doing what he felt the angel had said; working and praying in solitude. His lifestyle attracted others who also rejected Church and society, and his followers grew. He eventually set up the first community of monks near the Red Sea, their name "monk" deriving from the Greek meaning "alone" or "solitary".[20] The numbers Anthony attracted increased. People wanted to retreat and focus on God in solitude, rejecting the world. They wanted God, not religion.

Anthony was among the first to live his faith in solitude and reject the mainstream Church life. He was certainly not the last. Many did the same, and their lives attracted more and more followers, some who joined them, others who observed enviously from the sidelines.

As Anthony lay dying in 356 AD, a two year old boy named Aurelius Augustinus was living a happy childhood with his Christian parents in what is now Algeria. "Augustine" developed an intimidating composure but had a loving and fun personality. An intelligent man, he did well in his studies but preferred a wild life. His most fervent prayer was, 'Grant me chastity, but not yet.'[21]

Augustine joined a sect called the Gnostics, later branded heretics by the church, who relished their focus on spirituality. After some time he left, wishing to live in solitude and become a monk, but as he was leaving the town of Hippo Regius, now Annaba on the beautiful coast of

Algeria, the people of the town grabbed him and forced him to become their bishop. He eventually accepted the role.[22]

Augustine became a key figure in the development of the Church, and became known as one of the Church fathers. Probably better thought of as church designer, Augustine wrote and developed much Church doctrine and was instrumental in establishing Christian beliefs.

Augustine was a great philosopher and theologian, but preferred Greek philosophy to the Bible, which he felt was not well written. He was a great orator, and his speeches would capture the crowds for hours, and he easily convinced people of his views; which were a mix of Greek philosophy and the so far embryonic Christian theology. His influence on the Church is almost insurmountable. Augustine and his comrades, along with other great thinkers of this era, established much Church belief and practice. These men came along at a time when the Church was desperate to find its feet and establish one unified way of doing Christianity. Their input was needed and was received well.

It is because of Augustine that we have the theory of original sin, a theory which led to the practice of baptising babies, in the belief that baptism removed that stain of primordial depravity. It is likely that he had a view that women were subordinate to men, possibly based on the Roman culture he was part of and his interpretation of the Bible. He wrote much on interpreting the Bible, believing that if a passage were difficult to understand, it must have an allegorical meaning; there must be a hidden meaning waiting to be discovered. This led to some dubious beliefs, and still does today.

The church wasn't quick to accept all his ideas, however; it wasn't so keen on a well-known saying by Augustine, "Love, and do what you will", which reflected a belief that everything we do should be motivated by love.[23] If it is, only goodness and kindness would result. What a world that would be! But loving God gives us a connection with God that ignites an innate belief in what is right or wrong for us. When you're that close to God, nothing else is needed to guide behaviour, including the wealth of all the teaching of the Church.

Many of the features of Christianity are man-made; inserted into the faith throughout the evolution of the Church. Not required by God, but required by the Church. Embryonic Christianity was all about simply experiencing God, but at the hands of people it was shaped into a formal religion. It had been cut from its roots. But those roots survived…

Using God to Fill Your Pockets

Christianity was slowly changing from a personal relationship with God filled with wholesome, lifechanging experiences, to an institution that one attended — and followed the rules of. This institution evolved to become the Catholic Church, one of only two major churches that would exist for the next thousand years. With its headquarters in Rome and the pope as the head, life as a Christian was directed from the top; you were told what to believe and how to act. It was not necessarily a bad thing; life generally remained harsh, and the Church would have given desperate people spiritual hope and solace. But it also took their money, teaching that people should pay their way to Heaven.

The Catholic Church taught that when you did something wrong you had to confess to a priest who, once the fee is paid, offers you purification, which in turn allows you into Heaven at your death. If you did not confess you could still be forgiven, but you would have to do time in purgatory; a kind of heavenly waiting room to make up for what you had done. Those people who were well behaved in life banked extra merit, and this could be given away to others; at a price.[24] For priests that needed extra cash, this was a handy way of raising it; now you could buy your forgiveness. When life was harsh and death confronted people all too easily, these matters were at the forefront of people's minds. They were willing to pay. The belief has been modernised for today's society; if you wish to confess your sins now you can dial the "Line of the Lord" and for a fee, confess by telephone.[25]

This corruption continued and the faithful were exploited for hundreds of years, until in 1483 in western Europe, in what is now the pretty German village of Eisleben, a baby called Martin Luther was born. Luther became a monk and taught at the theological university in Wittenberg.

Luther didn't agree with buying your way to Heaven. He was moved by what he saw; vulnerable, poverty-stricken people who felt they had to give what little money they had to the Church to earn their salvation and get to Heaven. Luther never intended to do anything dramatic,[26] but his next action started a movement that gained momentum and eventually shattered Church life as it was.

Luther wished only to start a debate. He believed the teaching of the Bible and that of the Catholic Church conflicted each other; the Bible taught you did not need to earn your salvation; it was a free gift from God and therefore buying your way to Heaven was unnecessary and wrong. At this time, the printing press had only just been invented; the scattering of handwritten texts of the Bible were only in the hands of the educated few. Luther believed that everyone should be allowed to read the Bible and work out for themselves what it meant, and challenge what was being taught from the pulpit. He posted his views about this on the door of the church; at the time this was how you got yourself heard. Luther believed that the Church would opt to fight against corruption and defend the poor, but in fact it defended its own views and accused him of heresy. The pope had approved the belief in buying salvation, and the pope could not be wrong (and he didn't want to lose his income).[27]

Luther was excommunicated from the Church, denounced as a heretic, and condemned. He didn't care. He truly believed he was right and the Church was wrong. Alongside this, publishers had widely distributed his ideas, and many agreed with him. Priests started leading services in normal clothes, services allowed people to participate and not simply watch, statues and images were destroyed, it was taught that the Bible had greater authority than the church, and it was translated into German for the first time, selling thousands of copies as people wanted to know what it said for themselves.[28]

A movement had begun that could not be stopped. People had known things were not right; it took this one man's bold decision and the courage of others to agree and start doing things differently to alter the course of history. The official Church was still in charge, but those who followed the change eventually became known as Protestants, because they were protesting against the norm. This movement rumbled on like an invisible current; powerful but largely hidden.

In England, it was Henry the Eighth who bought the next big change when he wanted a divorce, something Catholics were not allowed to do. He got what he wanted but had to split the Church to do so, and in 1533 the Anglican Church was born. Henry the Eighth's new church retained the traditions and structure of the Catholic Church, but people were reading the Bible for themselves, and beginning to challenge more and more the structure and teaching of the churches. The seeds that Luther had sown were bearing fruit.

The inspiring, lifechanging and vibrant experiences of God that had characterised the infant Church and had been so refreshing for people's lives, were slowly sucked away over the centuries in the effort to control and manage Church and religious life. People experienced less of the wonder of God, and more of the formality of religion.

Suffocated no Longer

That is, until January 1st, 1901. Students in Texas were sitting in a church service when they suddenly and uncontrollably began speaking in a strange foreign language. Convinced this was God at work, their tutor, Charles Parham, began enthusiastically preaching. Equally convinced was a preacher called William Seymour. He began teaching that God was still in the business of answering prayer and healing people just as in the first century church, and spontaneous meetings started springing up as people eagerly gathered to hear him preach. Social barriers of that era – of gender, skin colour and social class – were torn down in these meetings as people met together, all experiencing the same thing.[29] People were fed up with tedious religion and realised something exciting was happening. They wanted their own experience of God.

It was unstoppable. People soaked up the teaching, staying for prayer for hours as they eagerly awaited God's blessing. Just as in the early Church, people were falling over as they were baptised in the Holy Spirit, people were healed, blessed, changed; addicted to this wonderful move of God; they couldn't get enough. A whole new breed of church had begun. The organised, formal church remained with its grand buildings and sober services, good for those who liked tradition and conventionalism. But for those who wanted to feel God, to experience God first hand, to be free to express the joy they felt and not be suppressed, those who were fed up with dry ceremony and desperately wanted to know God, soaked up this new and exciting move of God.

Christianity had slowly smothered God, replacing wonderful, lifechanging experiences of God with a dry religious institution which hindered people from truly encountering God. But God would be suffocated no longer.

It quickly spread. People began telling others about how wonderful this all was. You didn't need to be a minister to experience it or preach about it. Suddenly normal people were having wonderful supernatural experiences. The Church had taught that only priests could hear from God and they had to communicate what God said to the people. But they had been wrong. Now ordinary people were hearing God speak, were praying for people and seeing their prayers answered, and were captivated by these incredible events.

The new experiences of that day in 1901 unleashed a flood of new types of church. Today there are thousands of them with different expressions, styles and content of services. They will disagree on some theological issues, but the thing that unites them is a focus on experiencing God. These churches, largely called Pentecostal, are growing fast. It is the more traditional congregations which tend to stick to more formal styles whose numbers are shrinking. The Pentecostal Church exists in every country of the world and at the time of writing, 35,000 people a day worldwide become Christians in this type of church.[30]

The Church today drags along with it the heavy baggage of two thousand years of debate on how we can know God and what faith should look like. A religion designed by people, centred around a simple desire to know God. The bricks and mortar of its beliefs and practices have built walls that often serve to obscure the God that is at its heart, from traditional congregations with buildings that retain their Roman design, the singing of accepted hymns, the need for a sermon and Sunday as a special day. The congregation largely silent observers, accepted because they adhere to behaviour and dress codes. Even the more modern churches quickly adopt religious norms. Theological disputes and beliefs continue to shape the faith of millions, advocates all claiming their way is best, yet all different from each other.

It is largely perceived that the Church or religion is the key to God; that to encounter God we must embrace these. But many aspects of these are human constructs, created out of necessity for a given time, by people who were trying to manage this rapidly growing, brand new faith, and which became seen as necessary to know God. People and circumstances have shaped the faith, and in so doing shaped how we can encounter God.

This is not always bad; many people benefit from Christianity and other religions and some appreciate structure and conventionalism. But for many they can constrict faith, us and God, direct faith in one direction while experiencing God is to be found in the other. They define God, and they define those who wish to know God, when definitions need not be given. A charming elderly lady I once met was found in tears one day, saying she had spent her entire life dedicated to her local church, faithfully serving every week. She realised as she approached her twilight years that she had never known God, that she did not feel close to God and therefore could not be sure of her salvation at her death. Sometimes Church can obscure God.

Those who wish to discover God often find themselves wading through a confusing, sticky sludge of structures, beliefs and practices that have been constructed over the last two thousand years around what is simply an incredible encounter between God and us. It's no wonder most don't bother.

Adaptation to Culture — We Learn How to Do Church

Wherever people meet regularly, whether at work, socially or in many aspects of life — in school, in sports, career paths or social groups — they form a culture. If someone wants to come and join that group and be accepted, they have to adapt and learn the cultural norms and rules related to the group in order to fit in. If I emigrate from the UK to Spain, I will want to learn the language and learn how to behave in that culture in order to fit in and be accepted. If you look different, speak differently, or challenge the set culture, you are often excluded. If I wish to join a sports club I must learn the rules of the sport, wear the right kit, and adopt the culture of the club.

It is the same with church. If someone is exploring faith and wishes to find out more about how to connect with God, they might attend a church. There, they will be told about God and faith, but in a way that particular church believes is correct. There are of course different types of church who adopt different behaviours, so there might be differences in the way they prefer to dress, certain ways of worshiping, even their own beliefs on what it means to be a Christian. Often the things that we are told are acceptable for the Christian life and are behaviours that God might demand, are preferences for that church culture rather than things *God* would need or want us to do. Habits and traditions can become established and seen as necessary, but when examined theologically the requirement to do them is found to be in doubt. People are often introduced to church life, not God.

A particular church might say certain things are necessary for the faith and for remaining close to God, but these things are often just cultural preferences. Some are obvious, such as whether drinking alcohol is acceptable, or dancing, or praying out loud; others are less obvious, such as baptism. Some churches will baptise someone as a child, some as an adult. Some will baptise by fully immersing in water, others with just a sprinkle. Some may say baptism is essential for knowing God, for others it may be optional. With such variation in belief it is hard for anyone exploring this to know what is right or wrong.

When we attend a church, we learn that particular church's version of Christianity. People in congregations will hold certain beliefs on a subject not because they might have researched it for themselves, analysed all the evidence and come to that conclusion, but because they are told that is what this church believes, this branch of Christianity believes, or it is what Christians look like or how Christians behave. Pick and choose a Bible verse that agrees with that view and there is even more "evidence" that the viewpoint is correct. We tend not to analyse these things for ourselves thoroughly, but we just accept the view because we want to fit in. Gradually, behaviour becomes ingrained, or becomes doctrine. There are many actions and beliefs that have been labelled as essential for faith and knowing God, but in fact are just religious cultural habits.

The Pentecostal Church insisted for many years that speaking in tongues, the new spiritual language that was seen both at that moment in the early church in Jerusalem, and in the eruption of the Pentecostal

Church in 1901, was evidence of salvation; of being close to God. If one did not speak in tongues, one was not saved. The result was the attempt to force whole congregations to speak in tongues together. Of course, many people just learnt the vocal techniques in order to fit in and be accepted; it is easy to learn and copy sounds. Many Pentecostal churches have since been more flexible on this "evidence" as they called it. There are many such beliefs across all walks of the faith.

Of course, there is nothing wrong with these as expressions of one's faith, it has after all, to look like something. Meeting in buildings is practical, rather than people's homes, when you have several hundred worshippers. Many beliefs and practices across the churches do truly help some people meet with God. But what is questionable is saying this is the only way it should be, the only expression; that people can only experience God in church, or must go to church to find God, or that a particular way of expressing your faith is right or wrong. Faith can so easily be cloaked in cultural preference. But, as we see when we explore the positive impact faith can have on our health, true faith, lifechanging faith, does not need or want cultural or religious clothing. It is the juicy nuts that matter, not the hard external shell.

Because stories exist from the Bible, from other texts from around the world and from contemporary life, of people experiencing God in any setting, whether their home or garden, in the hills or on the seas, we can say that God is everywhere in the world. It doesn't matter where you go to connect with God; a church is no different from a field, mountain or your own house in terms of whether God can be found there or not. We also know that our church buildings merely followed the design of a Roman public building, the sense that they accommodate God is a remnant from ancient religious culture. Yet somehow the sense that we must go to church and follow its beliefs and practices in order to find God, remains.

The Church is Not the Fire, God is!

A common thing Christians will say is that in order to grow as a Christian you should regularly go to church as you will receive teaching and discipleship on how to know God. An analogy often used is that of a fire;

individual Christians are coals in the fire; if you take a coal out of the fire then it goes cold — the thought is if you are not regularly attending church you will easily lose your faith and drift away from God; you go cold.

But the church is not the fire, God is! God lives in our hearts and souls, and is everywhere in this world, as much on our football pitches as in our buildings. The coal analogy is correct, but the church is not the fire, God's presence is. It's God that we need, not church. Church is portrayed by Christianity as necessary for faith and for finding God, and yet many Christians would agree that you can find God anywhere, the setting does not define the encounter. It seems as though the theology and the practice do not match.

God, religion and Church are often seen as one, each integral to the functioning of the others like strands of DNA. Yet if this God-being exists it must be separate from religion because it existed before religion, and people from ancient times to now continue to experience this God-being apart from religion. God is not a tame beast that we chain to our altars. On Dartmoor, a group of monks residing in a beautiful ancient abbey, on a display ask the question, "What is God to you?" hinting that as we explore what God is and how it might be right for us to find God and express that discovery, this may look very different from how it traditionally has done.

Many of the people we will hear from in this book encounter God not in church, but elsewhere. Some are alone, some are in company. Of course God can meet us in our church buildings and many report that God does, but often the most profound experiences of God are whilst alone, often while going about our everyday business, whether it is Paul in the New Testament who had an awesome encounter in the desert, or the characters of the Old Testament such as Moses who was happily tending sheep in the wilderness when God met with him. Or perhaps those whose stories we know from recent history, the monks and other religious characters, or the many ordinary folk who encounter God in their everyday lives, such as Ian, the jellyfish man. These encounters show God can meet with us anywhere, and anytime. God is not stuck inside our religious buildings or institutions.

When life gets tough and when trouble strikes, a religion that is merely something you do because that is what you have always done or you are expected to do, will not be of any use. But if you have felt God's presence powerfully for yourself, have seen God or heard God speak, then faith becomes a rock, an anchor, something to keep you strong in tough times. Paul's experience and his subsequent relationship with God, recorded in the Bible, helped him survive beatings, torture and imprisonment. Paul (his previous name was Saul) had been persecuting Christians in the early Church. Racing along on his horse one evening on the way to capture Christians in Damascus, a sudden and dramatic experience changed his life. A bright light suddenly shone and a voice from the light called out to him, instructing him to stop persecuting Christians. Paul was temporarily blinded, taken to Damascus where God had already told people to help him, and subsequently became the founder of many churches. The religious authorities took a dislike to him because he was so effective in creating new churches, and they imprisoned him on false charges. The story reveals that his encounters with God gave him the ability to cope with extreme hardship. Millions throughout the centuries have found the same.

It is the same with us. Experiencing God today can give us strength to endure difficult times and to survive, where we may previously have been overwhelmed by our troubles.

One Size Does Not Fit All

That is why faith has to be right for each of us. God is in every atom of this world and God gets close to those from every culture and design of people, all those who wish to experience God and know God more deeply. That desire for God that rests inside many of us is the first step in discovering and encountering God in ways that are just perfect for us. There is no "one size fits all" with God, because every culture and every person is different. And it is not only that faith will look different in the middle of Africa or Asia to central London; faith will look different from the person next door, because we all have different needs, desires and life preferences. That is why God does not need or demand a religious prescription, weekly doses of Christianity with all its demands. The Church does, but God doesn't.

For some, the only churches many people have access to are the more subdued, traditional churches. Because of their need for orthodoxy and retaining their traditions they can tend to squeeze the life out of any faith that may exist, resulting in the feeling you have not met with God at all, in amongst the fluff that seems to be necessary for these institutions; the notices, hymns, reading the Bible and preaching. These places do have importance; there are people who benefit hugely from these traditions, but many find it too dull to be tempting to go to, and it is no wonder their numbers are reducing. Even the more vibrant churches can develop indispensable traditions.

Those who shaped the Christian faith over the years have piled beliefs and traditions around those incredible encounters of God, replacing that dynamic encounter with religion. But God is not limited to church, and neither are we. We can strip away these obstacles; we can have wonderfully meaningful times with God without ever setting foot inside a church. For those who desire to experience God, to hear from God, to know God closely, but do not wish to go to church or have a set of religious rules to follow or a Church culture to adopt, our faith can be different. Without the restrictions that religion offers we can truly make our faith right for us and our life preferences. Our faith, when we find it, is ours, and just as the early Church had no boundaries on their relationship with God, neither do we. We can rescue God from this sticky religious quagmire.

Not What God Intended

If God could design faith from scratch, it may look very different. Religion probably wouldn't exist at all. It is odd that the Church was founded on these incredible experiences of God, yet in the desire to formalise, organise and control the faith, it has largely excluded the very thing it was founded on and cut off its life source. Tolstoy, that great nineteenth century author, having discovered faith and gained great benefit from it, began to suspect that the Church was corrupt and that many Christian beliefs actually obscured the true message about God.[31] Many have since thought the same.

Most people don't want church, but we do want God. We can strip away the structures, beliefs and practices built up over two millennia of faith; the need for certain types of buildings, ministers who lead, congregations who sit passively and only on Sundays. Those who wish too can sing as loud as they like, and sit for as long as they like listening to those who wish to speak, but for those for whom this does not ignite our faith and lead us closer to God's awesome presence, there are other ways of finding God.

It's time for a new outbreak of God for those who are desperate to see God, feel God, touch God. It's time for God to do something new. It's time for *us* to do something new, because encountering God can be incredible and lifechanging, and may be just what some of us need.

Chapter Four
Experiencing God

Millie was an only child, an unplanned baby. Money had always been tight for the family, and she didn't help. Mum and Dad both felt the constant pressure from people chasing them to pay bills, working hard to earn very little. Tiredness, stress and feeling there was no chance for a better future left her parents feeling hopeless. When they were not arguing themselves, they took this out on Millie, getting annoyed when she wet her nappy again, when she dropped something and made a mess, when she was making too much noise. They themselves had difficult childhoods, living in poverty and suffering abuse, both physical and psychological. Life was tough.

Millie didn't know any different; to her this was all she had ever known, but because of the abuse and arguing she didn't have the connection and love with her parents that a child should have. She felt alone and confused, and she grew feeling there was no one she could trust; except herself. Her parents had not had the experience to know how to bring up a child, which was not their own fault, but it meant they did not deal with situations properly. Every night she would lie in bed and not a bit of her could be left outside the covers, she was too scared to be exposed. She lay there terrified every single night.

One day, Millie's mum just wanted peace and quiet, yet Millie was having fun running around laughing and screaming. Her mum told her off for making noise, and then to keep her quiet ordered her to go down into the cellar. Millie didn't want to go, it was scary and dark and cold down there, but her mum forced her into that underground room. She sat on the steps, alone and scared, and just waited, for hours.

Years later, Millie was diagnosed with post-traumatic stress disorder. The traumas of her childhood left her so scarred she still suffers today. The years of constant arguing, telling her she was no good, she would never make anything of herself and that she was stupid, all left their mark on her life; she never fulfilled her true potential.

When Millie was thirteen years old a friend took her to an Evangelical church that had recently begun meeting in the town. Millie was reluctant to go because she found church so boring, but as she stepped inside the building, someone gave a her a big smile and a hug. She had never had a hug before; she had never felt loved before, and this little church became her second family. They showed her unconditional love, there were lots of hugs at every meeting and they seemed to genuinely enjoy having her around; something she had never felt before. The message they gave was that God loved her and cared for her, and she quickly became a Christian.

Over time, she came to realise that she wasn't feeling the anger and fear that had always been with her. Instead, she felt so happy she kept finding herself irresistibly leaping with joy. She was still living at home in the same situation, but deep down inside she was now happy. She could cope. She had found something that gave her the ability to rise above her difficult situation. Millie had no doubt that her experience of church and of God helped her cope with life as it was, still in her difficult situation but with the ability to survive.

There are thousands of Millies. The trauma might be different, in some cases much worse, but many of us are deeply affected by the decisions of others. It's particularly hard when those who should be loving and caring towards you instead cause hurt and pain. Such things can leave wounds that never fully heal.

Millie experienced not just church, but a vibrant relationship with God that has continuously helped her through life. She knows her faith has been a support she could not have done without. There are millions of stories worldwide of people encountering God; having an experience of God that halts them in their tracks, opens their eyes to all the wonders of God and totally transforms their lives; experiences that go way beyond normal. Many stories are found in the Bible, centuries old but no less awesome, of God doing incredible things, but events are also happening daily today all across the world.

Yet much of Christianity has largely lost sight of these awesome encounters of Heaven touching Earth. It is burdened by the baggage from two thousand years of history which has dulled its message and made it unattractive; the vibrancy and excitement of those first years have been tainted, replaced by rules and must-dos, and for the majority of churches they simply tick the religious boxes. I once knew a vicar who felt that he had to stifle any spontaneous prayer or worship, or any exuberance in a service, because he didn't know how to control it, he didn't know what to do when it happened. At the heart of Christianity is experience of God, but in the efforts to bring order to those experiences it has suppressed the heart of the beast; and cut off the life source. It was never meant to be a religion; it was meant to be an incredible encounter with God.

One event made a huge difference to a timid young girl called Anne. 'When I was growing up I was completely mad about horses and riding. As a teenager every spare minute was spent at the stables riding and looking after my two horses. So when I discovered you could study equine science (the study of horses) at university that was my future sorted as far as I was concerned.

'However, my riding instructor, who was also my mentor and someone I really looked up to, advised me not to study equine science. She said work with horses is physically tough and low paid. She recommended I get a well-paid job doing something else and keep horses as my hobby. Because I looked up to her so much I took her advice on board and decided not to do equine science. But then the question was what on earth do I do?

'So, I went to a few careers advice sessions at school and did a few personality tests which recommended possible subjects I could study. But nothing really grabbed me. Then I went to the careers library to have a look at some prospectuses. I opened the first one. They were in alphabetical order. Agriculture at Aberystwyth. I saw pictures of students milking cows and looking at crops in fields. *That's it!* I thought. I had always loved the outdoors and been interested in farming. *I will study Agriculture.*

'I went home and told my parents. "But you haven't got a farm," my Mum pointed out, which dampened my enthusiasm somewhat. By that point it was getting close to the deadline to submit our application forms and I still didn't know what to do. I had found something I was really interested in studying but my parents didn't approve as they couldn't see any job prospects in it.

'Then I had a dream. In the dream God came and told me how upset God is to see what people are doing to the planet. Concreting it over, spraying it with chemicals, polluting and poisoning it, killing all the plants and animals. It was really vivid. I can still picture it now. God asked me to help look after it.

'It was a very powerful dream and I wanted to talk to someone about it. So at school I had a chat with our religion teacher. I told him what I had dreamt and asked what he thought it meant. He was quite excited by it and said that it sounded like God was calling me to do environmental work.

'So, I went back to the careers library and looked up environmental science. My parents were very supportive of my new direction as they could see environmental conservation being a growing field. To my delight I discovered there was even a course called "Agriculture and Environmental Science". So that is what we agreed on and what I went on to study, and got a first class degree in.

'After finishing university, I was able to get a job straight away, advising farmers on how to help wildlife and the environment on their farms, which was perfect for me. And ever since my career has gone really smoothly. I read somewhere once that if you do what God calls you to do, God equips you with everything you need, and that's exactly how it has been for me. God had given me the contacts and the opportunities just as I needed them. Sometimes I can even feel an amazing warm glow when I know I am exactly where I'm meant to be, doing exactly what God wanted me to do.

'A few years later I was baptised in the River Windrush in Witney, which is one of the rivers I looked after for my work, and I gave a short speech in front of everybody telling this story.'[32]

Bursting With Encounters of God

Remembering what God did in the past can help us know what might be possible in the future. We have to take great care when reading the Bible because it can so easily be misinterpreted, but the Bible is bursting with these encounters between God and people, all of them incredible stories of how God intervenes in people's lives recorded over thousands of years.[33] Authors occasionally write that God asked them to record events so that these stories about what God has done will continue to be told, and people would continue to learn about God, and about how we can know God. Combine this with contemporary stories of God doing incredible things and you find yourself wondering if nothing is impossible. People's experiences both ancient and modern can give us a taste of what is possible for us, now and in the future. There are many experiences of God waiting to happen, and many stories waiting to be told. For many of us, God hasn't even got started in our lives yet.

The Bible launches with an account of God living closely alongside people, walking with them in the cool of the day, involved in their lives, and enjoying each other's company. Whether or not this is an account of actual events, the story of Adam and Eve and the creation of the world gives us a tantalising glimpse of what it could be like to know God. Who would not wish to go for a walk with God one day and quiz God on some of the big questions of life, and picture God tenderly giving us a sideways glance and a gentle smile as we slowly walk along and ask these important questions?

The Bible ends with an equally remarkable vision; "There was a river, whose crystal clear waters gave life to everything they touched. On each side of the river grew magnificent trees, whose leaves were used as medicine to heal the world. God lives there with all the people, and God completely destroys death, sadness, depression, sickness and pain."[34] Other remarkable events show God rescuing the ancient people of the Bible from slavery, with incredible encounters such as towers of fire leading them at night, and unusual clouds showing the way in the daytime. This echoes the account of Jesus calming a storm on Lake Galilee many years later; to help people God will go to extraordinary lengths.

The overwhelming picture from the Bible is of normal everyday people encountering God, and this encounter changing their lives forever. And these awe-inspiring narratives happen to ordinary people just living their lives, not the super-religious, or the best-looking spiritual models faithfully adhering to religious laws, all religious masks firmly in place. God does not need us to be religious in order to meet with us.

Experiences Matter

These experiences matter. If we *experience* God, if we recognise God impacting our lives and helping us in astonishing ways as some of the stories show, it *means* something; it has an impact on us. I recently took up running, and I knew that I needed a goal in order to make me run otherwise there was no incentive to continue, so I signed up for the London Marathon. I knew I could run eight miles, so I figured I could run 26.2! I had the goal in mind, and when I finally got to run the race in 2019 it was incredible. The crowds cheering, the atmosphere of the day, running through the streets of London with thousands of others, helicopters buzzing overhead. I got hooked; I came home, set up my own running club, and I have not stopped running. The memories of that day will never leave me and I kept running because of it. If I had read a book on running, tried to follow a training plan but had no goal, no experience, and no memories, I would undoubtedly have given up.

Memories have a huge impact on us, and the more striking the events the more we remember them, and our recollection of events can then influence behaviour and decision making. On a personal note, church made a huge difference to my life, and I would not be who I am today without it, it literally saved my life. It was such a positive experience. Because of the memories of the love and acceptance I found in church which made such a massive difference to me, I have always been involved in church life.

Negative memories will affect us in the same way. I chatted to a lovely lady who wished to understand more about God and to encounter God, but would never go to church because when she was a child, a family member had died and the minister of the church had been very dismissive of their grief and had been quite rude to them. She was certainly not going to go to church ever again. Having a bad experience will mean one is unlikely to go to church in the future; once bitten, twice shy. Although churches differ a lot in style and the type of people who attend, this kind of experience is off-putting, and yet common. Sadly, many people have a bad experience of church, or of the people in them, or just find it dull and rather pointless. And yet there are these tales of people having incredible, lifechanging encounters with God. There is a discrepancy here, of what church and religion could or should be compared to what it often is.

Strength to Endure

One day when I had attended a church service, I was sitting in a Bible study that met afterwards. Slightly bored, I suddenly heard a voice. It was not audible to everyone else, but it was a powerful, direct word. I knew it was God; it's common that people will often say they knew it was God speaking to them when they hear that voice. I had just met a person in the church who had recently finished a medical degree and qualified as a doctor. The voice said to me, 'That's the person you're going to marry.' I was shocked — almost visibly — but held it together and kept it to myself. My husband and I have now been married over twenty years, but there are times when things were difficult and I considered leaving. It was the experience of the voice that day that kept me in the relationship. I knew God had said this was the person I should marry, and so I had to stay. In the end this was the right decision, although I know it is not the case for everyone; sometimes relationships need to end. This experience many years before remained at the forefront of my mind and helped me make a decision that was right for me later on.

Here's the testimony of a man in the Old Testament. "I had run away from home after I accidentally murdered someone and did not want anyone to know it was me. I was tending sheep on Horeb Mountain, where some people had previously met with God. I suddenly noticed a bush on fire, but it was not being burnt up, it was surviving the fire. I then noticed what looked like an angel standing there too! I suddenly heard God's voice calling my name. Of course, I responded…

"God said, 'I have seen the misery of my people in Egypt. I have heard them crying out because of their slave drivers, and I am concerned about their suffering. So, I have come down to rescue them from their oppressors and lead them to a better place. So now, go. I am sending you to Pharaoh to bring my people out of Egypt.' And with that, God asked me to go back to the very place I was running away from!

"I started trembling, terrified of what would happen to me. I said I could not do it as I cannot speak well in public, but God told me I would be able to do it with God's power and that God would ensure the work was a success. It was indeed a success, despite my fear."[35]

This is clearly a more awe-inspiring experience of God. But any experience, any encounter, can give us the strength to endure hardship, and can mean the difference between crumbling under the weight of adversity or surviving and thriving.

For every one story we know of, there are a hundred unspoken. Whether from the Bible era or life today, stories of people having an incredible lifechanging experience of God can inspire us and challenge our beliefs. When life gets tough, these encounters are what we hold on to, these experiences give us a glimpse of God and a glimmer of hope. It is these heartfelt, innermost encounters of God that create in us that deep faith that gives us the strength to endure hardship. This faith will remain even if everything else in life fails us.

Miracles…

Incredible miracle stories abound across the world. Daily, people are transformed as they experience the wonderful things God is doing. We don't tend to hear about them in our busy lives, and I guess the media would be reluctant to include miracle stories in the daily news. But it would be fantastic to be able to hear more easily about the amazing things God is doing.

Some people really do have raw, gut wrenching, desperate situations where God breaks in and helps them.

Thérèse was a two-year-old girl living in Congo-Brazzaville with her loving family. Her mother left the home for a short while to take food to a neighbour, and as she returned, Thérèse was crying, and saying a snake had bitten her. Her mother knew the urgency of the situation, so grabbed her daughter, strapped her to her back, and ran to the nearest help; the evangelist Coco Moïse. The problem was that Coco Moïse lived on the other side of a mountainous area, several hours walk away.

Despite this, Madame Jacques, Thérèse's mother, continued. This was her only hope; there were no hospitals in the area. She had a deep faith; she was a member of the local Protestant church, and so on that journey she prayed hard.

After a short time, she checked on Thérèse, but realised she was unconscious. Her pace increased as she knew she had to get to Coco Moïse as quickly as she could. The journey was hard, it was hot, and the dusty, steep tracks she had to travel in her flip-flops made it harder. She also had to be careful to avoid dangers such as snakes and scorpions herself.

She continued, but after a little while longer she checked her daughter again. She was dead. But Madame. Jacques was. not discouraged. She knew what was possible, she had heard stories of this sort of thing before, and had seen miracles herself. She continued her journey.

She arrived, desperate; and Coco Moïse immediately began to pray. They calculated that Thérèse had not been breathing for around three hours, but they were not discouraged. All they could do was pray, and as they did, Thérèse began to breathe.

She recovered quickly, returned home, and today Thérèse has gained her degree and is successfully working for a local church.[36] A remarkable story of God breaking in at those most desperate of times. This story was verified by several witnesses.

Of course, getting objective evidence for miracles is difficult. However, there are countless stories of miracles happening worldwide, often in the more exotic nations, and to assume all of them are either fake or a medical phenomenon would be foolhardy. The evidence for many is circumstantial, but there are also stories of the healing of serious diseases that come from sources that can be verified.

Small but Significant

There are also many important, but less dramatic true stories. Pat, a retired pastor had this encounter: 'It was 1983; I was getting ready to have breakfast when I clearly heard God say to me, gently but insistently, "Take communion" (eating bread and wine to remember Jesus).

'My response was something like, "Oh! Okay. I'll do that after breakfast."

'God said, "Why wait? Do it now!" I did what I was told, and as I finished I heard the phone ring, and I took what must have been the worst phone call I have ever had. My estranged wife was fiercely angry with me and was being quite abusive. Having a deep peace and assurance within me I kept completely calm, quietly answering her every accusation and criticism — and a few minutes later as she was finishing the call she was calm and she was actually apologising. I was rather shaken by the experience but overall simply amazed at how God had prepared me and protected me.'[37]

Another encounter is from Anne: 'I am lucky to have had a few experiences of God over the years. The first one was when I was a teenager, around sixteen or seventeen years old. At that age I was very shy and had a stammer which meant I struggled to say certain words.

'At my school, at break time, we could buy pastries (croissants etcetera) from the window of the school canteen. I went to school in Luxembourg so had to speak French to ask for them. My favourites were pain au chocolat, but that was a word I really struggled with. Every day when I was in the queue waiting to ask for my pain au chocolat, I would get so nervous. I was worried I would get to the front of the queue and then not be able to get the words out, and make a fool of myself and hold everybody up. Some days I would have to order something else at the last minute that was easier to say.

'One day I was in the queue, almost at the front, and feeling nervous as always, when God spoke to me and said, "You can do it." I can't explain how I knew it was God speaking to me, I just knew it beyond any shadow of a doubt. And I didn't hear God's voice out loud, it was in my head, but I heard it very clearly and I knew it was Him. And it gave me such immediate and amazing confidence that I got to the front of the queue and said, "Un pain au chocolat, s'il vous plait," so clearly and confidently and walked out of the queue with a big beaming smile on my face.

'The next day, waiting in the queue, I wasn't worried but was thinking about how amazing it was that God spoke to me and took the time to help me with such a small thing (on the grand scale of things). I was so happy I was smiling to myself instead of worrying. Once again I confidently asked for my pain au chocolat. And from that day on I rarely struggled to ask for my pastry again.'[38]

The story of Millie, the scared, abused little girl, continued. As she grew, she relied upon God who had given her so much; a church family, love, hope and joy that she could not explain. When she needed guidance on what to do with her life, she asked God for it, and always felt God gave her an answer. This help, plus the church family that she had gained, helped her make choices that she now knows made a huge difference to her life. The scars from the past still showed, things were not perfect, but she felt that God has always helped her in everything, and without God in her life things would have been very different.

Millie was welcomed and accepted into the church without hesitation. This is not true for others. I remember meeting a lovely lady in our village who had recently been through a divorce. She had just moved to the village to start a new life with her daughter and she went along to the local Anglican church. On being introduced to others over coffee, she mentioned that she was divorced. Their friendliness halted as the atmosphere turned frosty and she suddenly realised they were not as welcoming to her. She felt excluded and judged, and never returned to that church.

Often Christians or churchgoers have been insensitive and sometimes downright abusive, and the hard thing is separating the behaviour of these people towards us with God's behaviour towards us. Those who attend church, and often the church itself, can frequently get it wrong. Thankfully, God doesn't. How God treats us, and how others treat us can be two very different things. It is incredibly hard for

Christians to separate their own biases from what God might believe, particularly if they can find a Bible verse that appears to corroborate their view. Churches, church-goers and God are thankfully not one and the same.

In a sense this is the crux of this book; many have hidden God with doctrine, beliefs and ideas, believing we have to look a certain way or do certain things in order to be close to God or experience God, when in fact it is acceptance by the church they are experiencing, not God. The predominant image of the ideal Christian is a white, western middle class, married, heterosexual person with children who works hard, dresses smartly and who faithfully adheres to Church teaching. Any deviation from this may be viewed as sinful, or not compatible with knowing God. This makes the job of churches easier, if there are no dilemmas around behaviour. Yet these things are just the outward image, which matters little. It is as if God and Church have divergent beliefs, and often by "Church", we mean individuals in the church; Christians who throw judgments around believing it is what God thinks. Those people may not intend harm, but harm is inevitable.

The divorced person may not be welcome in church because of that particular church's beliefs about divorce, but I truly believe God welcomes them with open, loving arms. Often these errant beliefs are based on dodgy Bible interpretation or doctrines created long ago to suit societies that have long since disappeared. The problem is, because God, Church and religion are so closely entwined in our thinking, people can believe that rejection by the Church is rejection by God.

Thankfully, experiencing God is what makes the difference to us, not experiencing religion. This is Paul, the writer of many of the New Testament books: "I can tell you about visions and revelations I have had from God. I was taken up to heaven, to paradise, fourteen years ago. Whether I was in my body or out of my body, I don't know, but I do know that I was caught up to paradise and heard such astounding things that it is impossible to tell them in words. They are things no human is able to describe."[39]

Who knows what Paul saw? He was probably alone in the desert at the time. Maybe something like that of some of the people who experienced death and met God in heaven, like the jellyfish man or Amy, whose story we shall soon hear. When you experience God in such a way it changes you. It opens your eyes to the wonders of God and you are forever in awe. Many crave such experiences.

This highlights the different ways that we learn. We may learn some information in the classroom, but there are some things that are only learnt by experience. I could study archaeology at university but until I get out on the field and dig, I don't get a rounded experience. I can study medicine, but until I start looking after patients I do not fully understand. I can study religion and Christianity and listen to a thousand sermons, but until I meet God I do not fully comprehend it all. There is something odd here because when you do meet God, people often describe that they are less concerned about the rules so often declared as necessary for the faith; less concerned with portraying the right Christian or religious image. Once you've met God your eyes are opened to a whole new level of understanding where lists of rules and doctrines we have to adhere to are no longer given the importance they once were. Our many religious structures, rules and regulations appear to be shallow substitutes in the light of the real thing.

A pastor who regularly sees miracles happening is Bill Johnson. Working in California, his church is so popular that people travel across the world to attend; they regularly have thousands turn up to services. In his book, *The Supernatural Power of a Transformed Mind*, he describes how one night after an incredible church service where people had been powerfully experiencing God during the singing and prayer time, one of his team members discovered a man in the hallway jumping up and down. This gentleman was eagerly shouting that the cancer he had arrived with had disappeared during the service. He knew this because his trousers were suddenly a few sizes too big for him. He had come to church hoping for a miracle after having been told he had two weeks to live.[40]

The same thing happened to a lady who had oesophageal cancer. During the church service she was powerfully overcome by God, and then turned to her husband and told him God had healed her. They went to see the doctor who initially said this cannot be true, but after examining her she was indeed healed.[41]

These incredible accounts continue. A woman whose arm had been badly damaged in an accident had little use of that arm. She had never been able to properly cuddle her little girl. She asked for prayer, during which she knew her arm was healed. She reached down to pick up her little girl, so happy that they could finally have that precious cuddle. Her daughter was cautious as she believed her mummy should not pick her up, but the big smile gave her confidence. Many tears were shed that night as they shared a very special moment in that church.[42] These kinds of miracles happen so regularly to the team in California that they say not enough books can be written to contain them all.

A similar story is recorded in the Old Testament: "One day as Elisha was passing a woman's home, she called to him, offering him a meal. After that, whenever he passed that way, he would stop for something to eat.

"She said to her husband, 'I am sure this man who stops in occasionally is a man of God. Let's build a small room for him on the roof so that he can stay in comfort whenever he passes by.'

"One day Elisha and his servant returned to the house, and said to the woman, 'What can we do for you in return for your kindness to us?'

"'Nothing,' she replied. 'I have no need. My family is very caring towards me.'

"Later Elisha turned to his servant Gehazi and said, 'What can we do for her?'

"Gehazi replied, 'She is childless.'

"'Call her back again,' Elisha told him. When the woman returned, Elisha said to her as she stood in the doorway, 'This time next year you will be holding your own son in your arms!'

"'No!' she cried. 'Don't torment me and get my hopes up in that way.' But sure enough, the woman soon became pregnant. And at that time the following year she gave birth to a son, just as Elisha had said.

"One day when her child was older, he went out to help his father work in the fields. Suddenly he shouted, 'My head hurts!'

"His father said to one of the servants, 'Carry him home to his mother.' So the servant took him home, and his mother held him on her lap. At midday, he died in her arms. She carried him up and laid him on the bed of the man of God, then shut the door and left him there.

“She quickly saddled a donkey, grabbed her servant and said, ‘Hurry! We urgently need to get to the man of God! Do not slow down.’ As she approached, Elisha recognised her.

“She fell to the ground before him and grabbed his feet. Gehazi began to push her away, but Elisha said, ‘Do not turn her away. She is deeply troubled, but God has not told me what it is.’

“Then she said, ‘Did I ask you for a son, my lord? And didn’t I say, ‘Don’t torment me and get my hopes up?’

“Elisha realised what had happened and said to Gehazi, ‘Get ready to travel; take my staff and go! Don’t delay and don't stop for anyone. Go quickly and lay the staff on the child’s head.’

“But the boy’s mother said, ‘As surely as God lives and you yourself live, I won’t go home unless you go with me.’ So Elisha returned with her.

“Gehazi raced on ahead and laid the staff on the child’s head, but nothing happened. There was no sign of life. He returned to meet Elisha and told him, ‘The child is still dead.’

“When Elisha arrived, the child was indeed dead, lying there on the prophet’s bed. He went in alone and shut the door behind him and earnestly prayed to God. As he prayed, the child’s body began to grow warm again. Elisha continued to pray, walking back and forth across the room. Suddenly, the boy sneezed seven times and then opened his eyes.

“Then Elisha summoned Gehazi. ‘Call the child’s mother!’ he said. And when she came in, Elisha said, ‘Here, take your son!’ She fell at his feet, overwhelmed with gratitude. Her tears could not be stopped.[43]

Wow. Just wow. I cannot read that without tears in my eyes; the story of a helpless woman at the darkest times in her life who encounters a miracle beyond words.

Whether you are needing God’s guidance on a career choice, needing God’s support in a difficult situation, or needing healing from wounds both external and those deep inside that no one sees, the stories that people recall about God intervening and helping them show us that God is there for us, and able to help us no matter how big or small, difficult or traumatic the situation.

Some Dream of Meeting God

Many people wish to have experiences of God, to feel that closeness to God, to hear God's voice, to know God's presence there with them wherever they are. People have often said to me how they are slightly jealous of those who can hear from God or have wonderful encounters with God. These experiences, though, are not just for the privileged few, they are for everyone. God can speak to anyone, whatever your past, whatever your current situation, whatever your beliefs. There is no one outside God's help or blessing. And no, we don't have to be religious!

Although the stories of people's experiences of God might be inspiring, they mean very little unless we can experience them for ourselves. It is only when we know God touching our own hearts and lives personally that it makes sense, that it changes us, that it makes a real difference to us. Without experiencing it for ourselves these are merely nice little stories that we might not believe are true.

This can all be a bit scary for some. Some people do not wish to have extravagant experiences, they might simply wish to feel that deep sense of peace that knowing God can offer, that assurance that God is there with you, perhaps to have an end to a lifetime of the anxieties that may have haunted us. There are indeed tales of the miraculous, but there are also many stories of people who simply feel a sense of peace and the disappearance of the many fears that can plague our lives. Because we are all different, our experiences will all be different. The great thing is that God sees through our many masks, even the ones we don't know are there. God looks deep inside us and knows what we need and what might scare us. God treats us gently, meeting with each of us in a way that is right for us; just what we need, just at the right time.

People are forever changed when they encounter God; when you have seen God, when you have felt the power of God hovering over your body, when you have experienced God's help in remarkable ways, when you have felt the wonder of God for yourself, there is no going back. Life cannot be the same when you have had such wonderful experiences.

Often our experience of Church or religion is of sitting in a dull religious service, repeating traditions that are centuries old, good for some, but tiresome and seemingly pointless for many. Of course, there is a place for quiet contemplation; I have on many occasions delighted in the peace found in grand church buildings and I have encountered God there. But I also find myself talking to God, and God talking to me, when out on a hike, or at home.

Churches have an important role for those who wish to express their faith that way. And of course, when you encounter God, it doesn't matter where you are or who you are with. But some more traditional churches can find themselves clinging so hard to the past that they do not ask what God is doing now, or what is right for the culture they find themselves in. They can often be suspicious of new expressions of faith. Often, their doctrines mean they are pinned to the past by contracts drawn out by their predecessors. But the question is not whether the church is a modern or ancient one, a lively one or a dull one, it is whether people can find God there or not. It does not matter what it looks like as long as God's presence fills the place, whatever that place may be.

Knowing God was never meant to be dull. It was never meant to be a series of religious practices. God wants to walk and talk with us, communicate with us, astonish us into discovering who God is and what God can do. When you feel that feeling, when God speaks, when you see a vision, when you have that urgency in your heart to do something and you know it is God, it is the most wonderful feeling. For some it is healing, for others a peace that goes beyond your understanding, or the captivating presence of God resting on you in a powerful way. For all of us, it is the nourishing experience of meeting with God.

Christianity has swapped this life-giving encounter with God for a set of religious practices and beliefs that can hide who God really is and distract from what God can do in our lives. Stories abound about how God's vibrant presence catches our attention and injects us with new life and purpose. They tell us what God has done in the past, and hint at what God will do in the future. The variety of ways that God interjects, from the quiet to the downright extravagant, show that God is interested not in our religious observance, not in how many times we attend church, not at how good we are at praying. God is interested in us, and will relate to us in a way right for us.

The Unseen You

Some experiences hint that there is a part of a human being that is non-physical. We will call it the spirit, or soul, or inner being. When people give account of their near-death experiences, even though the body is physically dead during a cardiac arrest, something is still living. It seems as though there is another aspect to humans that goes on having an existence after the physical body has died. The existence of a spirit/soul part of our lives whose existence is linked to, but not dependent upon, the physical life in our bodies, suggests there is an existence after death; if we exist, we must exist *somewhere*; there has to be another realm, another place.

We do not fully understand this aspect of being human; it is extremely hard to research or prove. The evidence for a spirit or soul is subjective and inconsistent, and some people rightly need hard evidence. Scientific textbooks will offer scanty information about the existence of a soul or spirit, or any existence after death. The only provable thing scientifically is the biological universe and all contained in it. Yet experts are beginning to see the value of subjective evidence; the evidence of the experiences of people, the aspects of life that are real to those experiencing it, yet difficult to prove by scientific research. For those who have such experiences, that is evidence enough of God, no more proof is needed. It is almost as though having these experiences creates a lightbulb moment and gives us a new mental horizon, opening our eyes to the possibility of what might exist beyond what our physical eyes can see.

The God Religion has Created Does not Exist

I had the opportunity to attend a lecture by Richard Dawkins, the hugely successful and influential scientist and staunch atheist. During questions at the end I spoke about my book, *God: Naked At Last*, and although there was not time to give a sufficient summary of the thesis of the book, I did ask whether he thought that if we could strip away religion and allow people to discover the God that lies beneath, would that be a good proposition? His answer was no, God does not exist, at which the audience erupted into rapturous applause. I wanted desperately to say, 'But the God religion has created does not exist; but *something* exists!'

Richard Dawkins had in his lecture said there is no evidence for God, and beliefs without evidence lead to religious extremism, and on to violence; much of which is seen on our television screens. But, I wanted to say, there is evidence. That evidence is indeed subjective, it is based on people's experiences and feelings, it is personal and it is different for everyone, but it is real for the millions that feel it. For the millions who have had their hearts, minds and lives transformed in some way by God, God is very, very real. The idea of God may seem whimsical or irrational to those who need hard proof, but that is because there is no literal big man sitting on a cloud that scientists can examine. Richard Dawkins has never found any evidence for God, and so believes God does not exist. He did go on in further questions to say there are lots of things in the universe we cannot explain. I would have loved to question him further; has his dislike of religion plus lack of hard evidence led him to the conclusion that God does not exist? But therein lies the paradox: lack of evidence for something is not proof that something does not exist; it is proof the scientist has not found it.

Death Experienced

Here's a remarkable true story relating to this unseen part of us from Amy. Twenty hours after her son Nick was born, Amy died from an eclamptic seizure. Medical records show that she was declared dead for twenty minutes. Amy reports that the time she spent in Heaven standing before God, changed her and her relationship with God forever.

Amy had been brought up a Catholic, and was taught much about God, Heaven, Hell and Purgatory in those strict Californian Catholic schools. She was taught that when we die, we go to a place of judgment. Here, our lives and sins are portrayed before us like on a slideshow. We are then directed to one of three options. If we are good enough and our slate is clean, we are sent straight to Heaven and paradise. If we have any stain of sin still lingering on us, any bad thoughts or immorality we have not repented of and dealt with, our destination is Purgatory where we would have to work for our sins and earn our way to Heaven, much like a minimum-security prison. Once we have been deemed good enough and done our "time", we would be allowed into Heaven. The third option was terrifying; if our sins were too great, too offensive, we would be sent straight to Hell. Enough to terrify anybody into conforming.

But Amy went there. She saw God. She saw Heaven. And what she saw was the opposite of what she had been taught. It was nothing like what she had been expecting, and everything she had needed.

Her soul was not sent to a place of judgment. Instead, she found herself standing before this figure full of light, love and power. As she stood there, she found herself wrapped in love, embraced by God; by power and the source of all life and love.

The Being was not male or female. They seemed to know everything about her, every decision she had ever made, every part of her life. There was no judgment, there was no condemnation, only pure love and acceptance. She was at total peace, a peace she had never known before. It was as if everything she had ever done and believed had been part of the evolution of her soul with the aim of bringing her to this incredible moment of unity and understanding.

She could see that in her many lives, she had fulfilled myriad roles, male or female, rich or poor, powerful or timid, kind or oppressive, gay or straight. It was all part of her unique journey that had led to this point. It was all part of who she was, and it was all okay. They understood, accepted and loved everything about her.

It was a revelation. It was so different to what Amy had been taught. It was incredible, awesome, lifechanging. As she stood there, she realised she was not just an insignificant person, a minion being told what to do and where to go, like a soldier in the vast empire of God's kingdom. She felt important, valued and respected. She also had a choice. She could stay or go.

Somehow, Amy could see her one-day old son Nick and his big sister Chelsea, who was nearly two. Amy could see their future, she could see that Nick would be disabled, and she realised that she wanted to be the one to care for them.

She made a choice.

She began to say to this God-being, 'I want to take care of them,' but before she had finished, she was sucked down a tube of light and back into her body.

The nurse was in the clinical room, and Amy's dead body was covered in a white sheet. When Amy sat up, the nurse purportedly pooped her pants!

The journey to recovery was not easy. Immediately Amy was in incredible pain throughout her whole body. Shortly after she came back to life she remembers asking if she could go back to that wonderful cosmic paradise. She understood at once that this place is hard, and that place is wonderful. But she had chosen to care for her children, and she embraced that choice, and all it meant. She realised she had been given an incredibly rare gift; the gift of living this life but with having had a glimpse of Heaven, a glimpse of eternity and the absolute assurance of her place there.

Many people have not been able to accept her version of events. They want to keep their Old Testament judgmental God, their ideas about Hell and Heaven. They want to retain their powerful religious beliefs about how we get there and what it is like. What Amy experienced, and what Ian, the jellyfish man also found, was that the reality does not fit the religious brief. That we haven't quite got it right down here. That religion is not a patch on the real thing.

Amy knew what lay ahead. She saw a life of suffering and difficulty in a world full of pain and fear. But she chose to return. She chose to be with the people who needed her. She embraced what lay ahead, and she did that for one reason: love.[44]

Much that Amy had been taught about God was wrong. How true for so many more of us. God remains hidden, falsely represented by those who should be so different.

We need God. We don't need the incorrect images of God so often portrayed, just God, naked, stripped of the trappings of religion some have burdened God with. Just God and us. We don't need Church if we do not want it, or religion, or any of the things that go with that to experience God for ourselves. As much as these things can reveal God to some, for many others they can cloud God's true self. Life is tough and a connection with God can give us the ability to get through it, soothing what life throws at us. That heartfelt connection with this divine being can be the difference between just surviving and thriving. This isn't Church and it isn't religion. These things are done because for two thousand years the Church has learnt to do them, not because God *needs* us to; I'm sure God gets fed up with structures and belief systems that focus more on keeping themselves in business than on helping people meet God. God can so easily be obscured by religion.

John Wesley was an eighteenth-century minister who became disillusioned with preaching. Returning from a mission trip to America, their ship was almost wrecked. Facing possible death, John noticed how calm and unflustered everyone on the ship was. He asked them why, and they revealed their faith in God kept them strong. They survived, and shortly after, whilst pondering this event and wishing he had the faith of the other men on that ship, read the Bible verse, 2 Peter 1:4, "And because of God's incredible nature, God has given us awesome and precious promises. These promises enable us to experience God." That same day he heard someone preach from the book of Romans. He simply describes what happened next as, 'I felt my heart strangely warmed.' Not the dramatic experience of some, but it changed Wesley's life, leading him ultimately to form the Methodist Church.[45] His experience happened outside of a church setting and inspired him to form a new way of expressing faith. He didn't intend or wish to start a church, just to help others express and explore their own faith expressions in a new way. There might be many more Wesleys out there, wishing to do something very different, wishing to stretch our wings beyond the dusty, sombre confines of our churches.

Seeking an Encounter

A concept that is a persistent theme in the Bible is that of seeking God, looking for God, searching for God, and that when we do search, we will indeed find God. Some Bible stories show people at their lowest ebb, desperate for help in the great challenges they faced in life. Some cried out to God, saying, 'God, I desperately seek you, I thirst for you, my whole being longs for you, like in a desert where there is no water.'[46] One Bible author puts greater importance on searching for God than searching for life's essentials like food and shelter, knowing that food leaves us hungry again quickly after, but spiritual refreshment lasts a lifetime. How we search, what we find and how we express that discovery will look different for each of us.

But...

There are innumerable stories of God interacting to save people, and giving wonderful lifechanging experiences to many. But there are many other people who endure such suffering and inexplicable trauma that it is hard to comprehend. If there truly is a God and God can intervene and interact with mankind, why doesn't God do this more often? If God can save some lives, why not everyone?

When I told a friend about Amy, the lady who had the death experience, she said, 'But not everyone has them!' Why does this not happen to everyone? I did wonder if it does... but most decide not to come back!

We could not talk about how wonderful God is without mentioning some of the awful things that happen that undoubtedly make us question the existence of a God-figure, or even how truly good this being is if it can allow such suffering. For years I claimed how amazing God is and what wonderful things God does, until my thirty-two-year-old friend died of breast cancer.

The question of why God lets terrible things happen in the world is simply inexplicable, especially when you hear stories such as the ones from Bill Johnson of people being healed. It's true that those healed will one day pass away, they are not given immortality, at least not on this Earth. We have to admit it is an unanswerable question, and often when Christians try to answer it, it can so easily sound trite. For some this is the block that stops us wanting to know God, because God can't surely be good if terrible things happen?

Offering an answer to what is an unanswerable question seems foolish, but I'll try. People often blame God for the evil that they may see, or report that they lost faith in God because of the evil they have witnessed and certainly, many cannot imagine the horrors some have to endure with war and unbelievable suffering raging in some parts of the world. But we cannot blame God if people decide to do evil things to each other. It is not God who commits evil acts, it is people, although they may say they do it for God. There are no stories of God performing evil acts in modern life, although you would have to argue that not acting to save could be evil.

Natural disasters are just as incomprehensible. Incredible stories abound of God saving people from the grip of death, yet there are multitudes of heart-breaking stories where God doesn't save. Whether God set the laws of nature in motion and lets that roll, controls day to day life, or is a passive observer to life on Earth, is as unknown as many other inexplicable things, and no trite answer will do when people's lives are affected in such terrible ways.

For some reason unknown to us, terrible things happen in this life; none of us gets out of it alive. Many, including Biblical writers, put it down to the existence of evil; as God exists and has an entourage of angels, so does an evil force, not equal in power and strength but active and causing havoc in the world. Our conversations with God, however they happen, and our connection with this God-being, supposedly help God tackle this evil, and protects those close to God from it. In the next life after we have died there will be no evil; people from the Bible and from contemporary life that have described their visions of the new life say it is clear that evil is absent. But we do not have full understanding of the existence of evil, how it works, or what influence it can have in the world. We simply do not know why bad things happen, and religion simply cannot answer the question.

The only solace I've found in the agony and suspicion that rightly surrounds the question of why such terrible things happen in life is that of the promise of an eternity with God where these things will be no more. This life is only a glimpse, a snapshot of the life to come. Faith in God can give us the strength to endure hardship and suffering, and a hope that one day it will all be over and we will stand in that wonderful place, face to face with God. It may not be a cure for suffering, but it does act as a panacea. It eases suffering and gives us the inner strength to endure.

This life on average lasts seventy years, whereas the rest, for those who wish to be part of it, will be for an undefined period of time, described as eternity. *That* life is the real thing, this is the pre-amble. We don't fully know what happens to people that have passed on from this life — they really may be sipping G&Ts in paradise. Their terrible suffering may be instantly ended as they are whisked from disaster, to paradise. In the words of Amy, who has been there and seen it for herself, "this place is hard, and that place is wonderful."

This is a debate that will never be resolved in this life. We simply don't know why bad things happen, but we do know that discovering and encountering God can help to get us through. God's help and presence in our lives gives us a new spiritual awakening, a new life and a determination to keep going despite circumstances. We don't know why people do awful things to each other or why there are natural disasters, but to reject God because bad things happen is to cut ourselves off from this much needed help in difficult times. It's like saying that because the doctor couldn't make someone better, I never want to see a doctor again. Yet one day you might need one.

Somehow, disasters in our lives can bring us closer to God. It is as though pain and suffering lead us to explore God, to discover God. We cry out to God because often there is no other option, we see that we cannot escape this ourselves, that we cannot help ourselves. Although all physical bodies will eventually fade, our spiritual self, our soul, does not depend on our physical self for life. They can kill the body, but they cannot kill the soul.

Pool of Strength

There is a pool of determination and strength inside each of us that we can draw on when life gets tough. When life throws curve balls at us, those things that we are often just not expecting and could definitely do without, it takes grit and determination to get through. Those things can be minor irritations, or they can be huge traumas, sometimes leaving us wondering how on earth we will survive.

But that pool of determination and grit is always there. We are stronger than we think. And the great thing is, the more we drink from that pool, the bigger it gets. The more we face, the stronger we get. So don't be overwhelmed by troubles, know that inside each of us lurks great strength and boldness to face life, and to win.

My thirty-two-year-old friend was incredibly close to God and gained great strength from her faith and times with God in her fight with cancer. Others saw this close friendship she had with God and were touched by it, also experiencing the closeness to God she had described. She would have struggled with her disease much more if she had not had her faith.

None of us know what our future holds, but when we know God and are close to God, we know we have a secure, safe being that we can ask for help when we need it. And God will not let us down. God may not always change our circumstances but our fears, anxieties and worries fade when we encounter God. They are replaced by a sense of security, peace, rest, even an unusual joy and happiness. Like a soothing balm on dry, irritated skin, or a lifeboat appearing on the horizon as we are stranded in a storm, God helps us.

All across the world every single day people are discovering and encountering God. When you feel God, see God, hear God, it is flipping amazing. There is often a huge contrast to religion, which, in attempting to regulate God and us, can stifle these incredible encounters, and stop some people finding God at all. But we can choose to explore the concept of God and faith in our own way. Knowing this does not need to involve Church, Christianity or religion frees us to discover God and express that discovery however we like. When you find God, you can easily reject it if you don't like what you see. But I have a feeling when you lay eyes on God you'll fall in love forever.

What religious fluff has built up around faith over the last few centuries to hide this amazing God, and to make God appear unattractive to people desperate for God's intervention in their lives? We certainly have exchanged this awe-inspiring, lifechanging unity with this incredible God-being for a dull, unattractive set of religious beliefs and practices.

And discovering God might even be good for us…

Chapter Five
The Health Benefits of Faith

You have to be careful with health claims. There are many of them and some are dubious to say the least. People can claim anything from drinking urine to cure ills, eating worm eggs for weight loss, or drinking mouse wine; wine infused with two-day old mice and thought to kill several diseases.[47] Cow-cuddling, eating purple foods, or shoving a hose up your backside and turning on the tap have all been claimed at some point to have benefit.

Faith and Health

Medical practitioners have to be incredibly careful not to push any religious views they may have on their patients as people can be extremely vulnerable at times of ill health, and it could be seen as an opportunity by some clinicians to thrust their own views on the sick. However, there is some real evidence that faith is actually good for you.

Worldwide, thousands of studies have been done to assess the impact of faith on health. The general trend shows that those who have faith beliefs are less likely to get sick, generally cope better with illness and have a faster recovery. Some figures are astonishing; faith is linked to a reduction in heart disease, so you are 66% less likely to have a heart attack. High blood pressure and death are less likely after coronary heart bypass surgery, and disability following a stroke is reduced. There are less cancer diagnoses, and where cancer is found, there are less deaths from it. [48] There are reduced disabilities,[49] longer life span, better overall health, improved quality of life, better mental health, a greater ability to cope with life's challenges, especially with ill-health and terminal disease, and people recover from illness quicker.[50] The figures are astonishing.

Mental Health

Faith can have a notably positive impact on mental health. The majority of studies reveal that there is better wellbeing, a greater feeling of happiness and life fulfilment and enjoyment, less incidences of mental ill-health, anxiety and suicide, and less reliance on alcohol or drugs. Where mental illness does occur, there is faster recovery. There is better stability in relationships, and people generally survive bereavement better.[51]

A significant number of scientific studies confirm that having a faith or spirituality improves mental and physical health. The evidence shows that faith can be good for you, and these are studies done by doctors and other health professionals, not church ministers.

One health claim that the Bible contains is the calming effects of prayer. Paul, the writer of many New Testament letters, mentioned it when he wrote a letter to a church in the Roman town of Philippi, now in modern day Greece. Paul said, "Do not worry about anything at all; instead, we can talk to God about our concerns. Simply tell God what we need. When we trust God to help us, then we will experience God's inexplicable peace. It is beyond our understanding, but this peace will protect our hearts and minds…"[52]

Paul travels widely across the Middle East, leaving in his wake a host of flourishing churches to which he wrote regularly. His letter to those in Philippi shows that he is now living in sombre circumstances; Paul is in prison, facing the death penalty for establishing those churches and helping people find God. He has clearly made some enemies. Yet he has also come to be at peace with himself, for in the letter he says, "I have learned how to be satisfied with what I have. I can live and be happy in a survival situation, or with sumptuous luxury. I have found the secret of life; to live in any situation, whether I am satisfied or hungry, whether I am prosperous or experiencing poverty. I can do anything through God who strengthens me."[53] Paul must have been in the worst situation of his life, stuck in a Roman prison for the crime of establishing churches, and yet Paul finds inner strength and peace because of his faith in God. He is able to say, "Do not worry about anything at all…" perhaps revealing that when we have experiences of God similar to that of Paul we will indeed find peace, whatever life throws at us. It was only a short time before, that Paul was describing that experience of being taken up to the third Heaven and seeing things too incredible to be able to describe, something that happened after his awesome experience on the Damascus Road when he was blinded by a vision of God. When you encounter God in such a powerful way it leaves you stronger, and unshakeable.

Faith seems to be able to release positive emotions and improve mental strength in challenging circumstances. This is the experience of many of those whose stories we have heard, and it is my experience too. Encountering God is incredibly nourishing to the soul. One lady, who would say she is not religious at all and rejects religion quite strongly, said she had a wonderful experience as a child where she saw God, and was transfixed. She did not want the experience to end because it was so wonderful, and that feeling and the sense of peace and wonderment it bought has stayed with her throughout her life. She felt she had a glimpse of God. Whilst she dislikes organised religion, she would rather like to see God again.

To encounter God (and that does not necessarily mean encountering church, religion or other Christians) is one of the most amazing life experiences we can have. It gives us something not found elsewhere. Encountering God is captivating, all-consuming, with a vast array of positive emotions released[54] that simply make us feel good — for a long time. Nothing else matters as you experience this most incredible of phenomenon. It is almost indescribable but it is as though eyes in your mind are opened, not physical eyes seeing physical things, but spiritual eyes, seeing things only revealed in that moment to you. When we have witnessed these things, the troubles of life do not affect us as much as they might before. This must surely be the experience of those who have been persecuted and died for their faith. Although troubles may remain in reality, we gain a new spiritual inner strength that is unmeasurable but very real. The difference between experiencing God and finding other great things that make us feel good is that the feeling of encountering God lasts a lifetime.

Better mental health can lead to better physical health, as we experience less angst, less stress, and we are at peace. The body functions better and is less at risk of contracting illness; our immune systems can be diminished when we are stressed, and will function better when our mind is at peace. As we discover and tap into our faith it can become a source of strength and help, a comfort in the face of life's burdens and unsolvable problems, whatever they may be. A former president of the Royal College of Psychiatrists remains dumbfounded because the benefits of faith and spirituality on health and wellbeing have been largely ignored by doctors. He believes that in any other area of healthcare, governments and health providers would be furiously promoting it when presented with the evidence of how good faith is for us generally.[55] However, doctors and researchers are understandably reluctant to promote faith and spirituality for its seemingly proven health benefits, because religion has marred faith and made it unattractive.

Many struggle today with mental ill health. It is a great challenge, and unlike physical illness, you often don't know there's a problem until it becomes a crisis. It creeps up on you, and can hit you hard. It also carries a stigma, and sufferers often feel they should hide their struggles, feeling unable to say they are not okay. In fact, one in three people will encounter some sort of struggle during their life with their mental health, so it's incredibly common. Some symptoms are mild, others more serious, but for each person who suffers in this way, it can be incredibly debilitating. Life is hard, and people are under immense pressure from different aspects of life; from work, relationships or lack of them, financial pressures, and many more. When you reflect on the intensity and busyness of life it is no wonder so many of us are struggling.

This is from Julia, a church minister: 'I love those stories that people tell sometimes of God working dramatically; of miracles witnessed and instant changes to situations. I fully believe that God can and does act like this often, but my experience of God has normally been quite different. I have more often experienced God in the small things, in the quietness and in the way he has been present with me even when the big miracles haven't come.

'There were the times as a young girl — maybe eleven or twelve years old when I was suffering from quite serious anxiety. I was sleepless and fearful of so many things. One night as I was asking God to help me, he filled me with a peace that was beautiful and lifechanging. It was lifechanging not because it healed me of my anxiety, but because God gave me an assurance of his love and comfort that was amazing.

'There were the years when I was single and wondering if I would be 'on the shelf' forever! I prayed and prayed that God would give me a husband. As I wondered why I couldn't have the blessing that seemed to have been given to almost all my peers, I experienced God keeping me going through that lonely time. I knew him in the gift of good friends who would walk the road with me. I experienced a sense as I read the Bible of God asking me to keep trusting him — that he knew what I needed and he would provide for me.

Later as my (long awaited) husband and I went overseas to serve as mission workers we went through hard times of isolation, culture shock and infestations of fleas! Through these times God never miraculously altered our situation that we know of, but he did give us grace to keep going. He was with us in letters from supporters, gifts of mince pies from home at Christmas, tiny glimpses of beauty and the ever-present hope that he was there and that he loved us. For me God's presence has always been a kind of deep knowing within me. I am so grateful for him, for his still small voice and all the blessings he has sent along the way.'[56]

The External Shell of Religion versus Deep Inner Spirituality

A team in the USA researching the effects that faith in God has on those attending the more modern Pentecostal churches found that interaction with God seemed to encourage benevolence, or doing good things for other people. Benevolence, in turn, can have a positive effect on the mental health of the giver.

This wasn't all they found. A remarkable discovery was made by this research team, that there is a vast difference between the "external shell" of religion; religious or Christian practices such as attending services, praying, singing songs, and other customs or traditions, and the "heart" of religion; encountering the love of God.[57]

Other studies have also made the distinction between religious practices and rituals; this external shell, and a heartfelt commitment to

God.[58] It is this internal, deep, soul searching experience of God, this inner, heart and soul encounter that makes a difference in our lives; experiencing God for ourselves, God touching our heart, spirit and soul, a captivating, all-encompassing love experience. It is different for everyone, but faith is an encounter with this powerful love; God is portrayed in the Bible as being made of a powerful love, and so encountering God is like encountering a power, a sensation that is unlike any normal experience in life. This is real faith. This is what changes your life and turns desperate circumstances into success stories. The effect of experiencing God somehow nourishes our whole self. The memories of these experiences keeps us strong in tough times.

Yet the majority of our religious institutions and structures seem to foster the shell, rather than the heart. It appears that Christianity has largely exchanged this all-encompassing, wonderful, orgasmic love of God for a cheap imitation; and sold that as faith. You can be blinded by religion, tricked into thinking religious practice is what is important and instead missing the heart of faith. The Bible hints at the disapproval of those for whom religion acts as a mask, blinding the religious.[59] Some cannot see the wood for the trees. Many cannot see God for religion.

Wellness

In 1971, the king of Bhutan decided he would measure his nation's progress not by wealth or productivity, but instead by happiness. How happy its people were was more important than how much money they earned. National happiness was their aspiration, and they believed the whole world needed to adopt this same goal.[60] Newspapers have long commented on this utopian ideal, and the World Health Organisation took a keen interest in this method of running a country.

Significantly, the spiritual dimension of life is seen as contributing to this overall happiness in Bhutan. Included in the definition of happiness is the spiritual, physical, social and environmental health of its people and its natural environment. The country has suffered environmental and financial stress and many are poor, but they have maintained their focus on being happy. It was written into the legal code that the aim of the government should be to promote happiness among its people.[61] That's a policy that may win elections.

It was in 1946 that the World Health Organisation felt that wellness is not just the absence of disease, but has a more holistic and comprehensive make-up. They defined health as, "Complete physical, mental and social wellbeing and not merely the absence of disease or infirmity".[62] Medicine ever since has focussed on enhancing health and encouraging habits and behaviours that make people healthy, rather than simply healing the sick. Bhutan emphasised four areas, spiritual, physical, social and environmental that contribute to overall health; studies done in the USA found six main areas that contribute to wellness: physical, social, intellectual, occupational, spiritual and emotional.[63] The health of the planet is rapidly becoming an additional component of wellness.

Physical health relates to the body; nutrition, exercise and certain habits. Your emotional or psychological health relates to how you feel and your emotional balance. Occupational health involves being in a job where you feel you are valued, using your skills to the best of your ability, and not feeling unfulfilled or overstretched. Your intellectual health indicates how stimulated you are mentally, your critical thinking and ability to learn. Social health is our relationships and interactions with those around us. Spiritual health relates to an awareness of and connection with the spiritual realm and with a God-being. It does not indicate adhering to a religion or religious practice although for some it may involve those things, but spiritual health is an internal, meaningful, experience led phenomenon.[64] It is important to tailor each area of well-being, including spiritual health, to our life preferences and needs. Our well-being is our own; we nurture each area of our wellness as we wish.

A conclusion of studies done by Christian doctors was that we are not just biological machines, we do indeed appear to have a soul or spirit, a part of us which impacts our physical health and bodies as much as the food we eat and the amount of sleep and exercise we get.[65] Acknowledging this spiritual aspect of our being and nourishing it in the way right for us can form part of our overall wellbeing.

When we think of health we tend to focus on physical health and body image, and we often ignore or neglect other areas. Yet all aspects of wellbeing can contribute to our overall health and if one is lacking, it may affect the others. If we are hungry or without shelter, attention will be diverted to those things. If we are facing a terminal disease, we might be more concerned about spiritual health. If we are carrying psychological burdens such as guilt, worry or regret about past decisions or suffering with anxiety, then our mental health may be our concern. Our focus may change according to what life throws at us, but the many areas of well-being can affect our physical health and may cause disease. If we give each aspect of our wellness the nurturing they need we are likely to be healthier, feel better and less likely to encounter disease.

Life can often leave us wondering why we may be suffering from mental or physical ill health, or why we feel unfulfilled or lacking a passion for life. Often we trawl through our years, time flying past us as we eat, drink, work and have the occasional holiday. We can head towards retirement feeling unsatisfied with our lives, our only enjoyment found in things that prove to be short lived pleasures like our favourite alcohol, cigarettes, sex and television. We might occasionally wish to be healthier, not realising that the answer is not found in another trendy diet, but is found in exploring the mosaic that makes up the entirety of our health and wellbeing. It is found in looking at all aspects of our lives, in discovering more about ourselves and what our life preferences are. We are not just a gathering of cells that survives only on food and water — the complex mental health concerns many of us have proves that — we are whole beings, with desires, needs, wishes, likes and dislikes. We have things we love and hate, things we want to do and things we don't want to do. Some of us love other people, some of us prefer our own company. Some of us love exercise, others prefer a more sedate lifestyle. We are all so very different, and that is why health and wellbeing looks different for us all. This also means that the spiritual aspect of wellbeing will look different for us all.

Creating Inner Strength

When Millie was at school, her home life was chaotic and stressful, and this meant she was unable to learn or achieve. She failed all her exams. She used to work in a store to earn money and would sit, passing everyone's purchases through the checkouts each day for hour upon hour, thoroughly bored. She hated it. She wasn't even very good at it because she was so bored and uninspired, and couldn't achieve her full potential. It was only when she went to nursing college and was inspired to learn and achieve, and was then given responsibility on the wards, that she found confidence, and got the highest mark in her year group. She later gained a bachelor's and a master's degree. People had written her off as being stupid and someone who would never achieve anything, but the truth was her physical and psychological health impacted her intellectual and occupational health, and therefore her opportunities. Those around her even said she was a nasty piece of work and did not deserve to be successful. It was only when she was out of that setting that she realised they were wrong and she could achieve what she wanted. She had not been healthy in some key areas, and this affected her overall wellbeing and opportunities. When those were corrected, she thrived.

There are lots of people in that situation. Often told by others that you are no good, you will never achieve anything, you are not clever enough, you are not worth anything. Put into a school system that probably does not suit your needs and learning preferences, and then told you are a failure because you do not do very well. It is a battle to get yourself out of that situation, but it is possible — just ignore anyone who tries to inflict these lies on you. How can they possibly know anyway? It can be hugely frustrating to feel as though you are capable of achieving your dreams, however big they are, yet be told you can't because you are not clever enough, or you are not good enough. Only *you* know what you are capable of, and if you want something, go out and get it. Ignore the critics, because only *you* know *you.* Your dreams are your own, and that is the great thing with dreams, no one can take them away.

Knowing Our Inner Self

The journey of life is incomplete until we have discovered ourselves. To step inside ourselves and see what lies beneath can help us better understand ourselves and discover our life preferences. Just as when underground rivers rush through the beautiful limestone hills they form huge caverns and networks of tunnels, there is, in our inner being, vast caverns of unfathomable depth. In them lie our feelings, our hurts, our memories. The whole breadth of our psychology, our emotional and mental self, our identity, our character and our ego sit deep within the depths of our being, sometimes imperceptibly. We can so easily rush through life focussing on the outer parts, the bits we can see and easily perceive. Yet what lies inside affects us just as much as the physical.

A concept developed by a sixteenth century nun, Saint Teresa of Ávila, explores the notion of our inner life using the analogy of a castle.[66] Our internal life and being is like a castle with many rooms, and whereas we often pay attention to the outer walls — our bodies — the internal part is just as important. You can visit any time and go as deep as you wish. Some may visit for just a few moments, others for longer. You may visit just once, or make a regular journey into your inmost being; it is up to you.

Exploring Ourselves

For those who wish to, let us try journeying through those rooms of our inner castle. You are about to step inside yourself, into the depths of your mind, the very deepest part of your inner being. This is where your beliefs, your values and your life preferences lie; this is where your inner strength is found. It is also where we store the memories and feelings of our past experiences, good or bad. It might be where you find God too.

You might know and expect some of the things that lurk in those inner rooms, things that you could picture yourself rediscovering. Or you may not know what lies there. For some, the inner self may be a well-ordered castle, the rooms neatly organised, tidy and clean. The décor is just as we would wish, the lamps are lit, the rooms warm and comfortable. Good, nourishing food may be laid out ready for when you visit and wish to dine. For others, you may never have been here before. The rooms may be dusty and untidy, filled with unopened boxes stuffed into the corners, the owner hoping never to have to open them. This castle may be cold, damp and uninviting, and there may be a little renovation work needed to improve things. The inner self can resemble a beautiful, grand towering castle, or a labyrinth, a complicated network of tunnels and caves that wind their way into your inner being, with many secrets hiding in their dusty corners.

As we step inside, perhaps tentatively, we imagine going into that ancient stone doorway, turning that wrought iron handle, and opening the large wooden door. As our eyes adjust to the light, we look around. In that first room does it appear untidy, cold and uninviting? Are there the scattered remains of old carboard boxes, with slightly curling edges and with layers of dust on top? Sometimes it is too hard to open those boxes, too painful to go back and revisit the things we have stored away. We may have a peek inside, and then retreat back, fearful of what we will find. We do not have to deal with things as we find them, just acknowledging their presence is enough; we can deal with them when the time is right. It is a brave thing to revisit them, but it is a journey that is worthwhile.

It is good to acknowledge how we are feeling; are we happy to be here, or scared we might find something we buried all those years ago, that thing that was too painful to look at? We often pack away our unsavoury things because they are too upsetting to fully deal with, things we did or were done to us, things we saw or heard, or things we felt. The brain can hide away our painful experiences so our shallow conscious self does not know they are there; they are stored instead in our inner being, lurking deep inside ourselves. Their presence can sometimes affect us in our daily lives, causing us problems we may not know the cause of. Are we employing a coping mechanism in our life right now that is easier to repeat day after day than to delve into the painful memories and wounds that cause us to need them? We might be aware our wellbeing would be better off if we dealt with those dusty packages that we have hidden away, but they can be unbearable to look at. There may even be something we have suppressed because of a fear that we may not be accepted if we reveal it.

Some things are nice to revisit, reigniting fond memories. Other things it is not so nice to remember. As we might open an old attic in the family home and begin to discover old photographs, mementos of old times, letters from the past, we are reminded of events, old feelings are reignited and memories return — of the good times and the bad.

As we explore our inner self, all the things that we discover help us to get to know ourselves a little better. As we rifle through old memories, previous experiences, emotions, feelings and the battles in our minds, we might find intense emotions and feelings rise up. It can sometimes feel too much to bear, but exploring them and acknowledging how they make us feel is the first step to reducing the damaging effect they can have on us.

We may step back in horror as we first encounter them again, but then the next time we visit, the next time we have those same feelings again, it will be a little easier. Each time we step inside ourself and explore our inner being with all its twists and turns, dark corners and dusty rooms, we find it is a little better; a little more light floods in as some of those dusty boxes are opened and dealt with. Whilst there, we might choose to sweep away more of the rubble from our past, those things that have been a burden to us.

We need not judge ourselves for what we find, nor accept the judgments of others. Even if difficult, this is a good thing to do, and it will form part of our restoration, enabling us to be free to move into our future. Sometimes the hardest and most painful things are the most valuable, and reap the greatest rewards.

We may prefer to forget painful memories, but each experience and memory makes us who we are, each piece of our lives builds us into the people we are, and sometimes the most painful things can be our greatest asset as we turn those bad memories into ammunition to achieve our future goals. Sometimes people or circumstances try to hurt or destroy us, but we can turn those events into our future success as they give us the grit and determination we would not otherwise have. We are in control of this process; we may not have been able to control our past as much as we would like, but our future is fully in our hands.

I remember for days trying to find the source of a bad smell in our house, thinking some shoes had been put away wet, or some food had been left to rot. I hunted everywhere, but could not find it. Then one day I was tidying up the daypacks while organising the cupboards and in an outer pocket I found a doggy poo bag — used — neatly tied up. The source of the smell had been found, thank goodness, and we vowed never to store them away like that on a hike again.

This journey into our inner self is a journey of discovery; discovering our own self, our passions, our desires, the things we like or dislike. We discover what drives us and what is important to us. We can create goals for our lives and then, because they have an importance that goes into the very heart of our being, we have the determination to achieve those goals. To discover more about ourselves means we can identify what we want our well-being and lives to look like. We can tailor all aspects of our well-being to our own preferences. This sets us free to be ourselves and means we listen less to the opinions of others, not letting their criticism of us affect us or our goals. As we start to live in that freedom, we may find we are happier and more content with who we are. If we never discover who we truly are we can never be ourselves. In discovering ourselves, we set ourselves free to be who we truly are.

Sometimes our physical being can do things that may be contrary to what our inner self might prefer. Then we get internal conflict, and this can affect our mental and physical wellbeing. If we value healthy lifestyles but our diet and exercise habits are not in line with those beliefs, or if we value knowledge and educational achievement but are not making life decisions that aim towards that then we may have internal conflict. The same may happen if we love adventure, but feel driven to a career that does not foster exploration.

Sometimes things can be out of our control, so we may need to adjust our dreams accordingly. Even so, dreams and desires lurk within, wishing to be fulfilled. Follow your dreams, desires and deepest wishes, because they might just be telling you, consciously or subconsciously, who you really are. If we are filled with desires to travel, to be alone, to be with others, to climb that mountain or swim that ocean, to follow a career, to study, to write, whatever our deepest wishes and desires, these are often letting us know who we truly are. Even if our dreams lie trapped in our current circumstances, they remain, waiting for an opportune time for their fulfilment.

As we take those initial steps in following our dreams and desires, often they evolve, becoming clearer and more focussed. As we begin to travel, we can often realise that our desire to see the world becomes a yearning for studying ecology and finding out what makes our planet healthy. Or our desire to see justice merges into studying politics. Many a career in healthcare was born through a wish to help others. Follow your dreams and watch them evolve. Step out of your comfort zones. Allow your mind to run wild with your deepest desires and see what your life can become.

The Baby

Sarah was sixteen years old when she met Harry. They quickly fell in love and spent hours talking, walking and just enjoying being together. Their families admired their relationship and felt they were well suited, and their friends were envious of them.

As they grew closer, they knew they wanted to be together forever. Then one evening as they were alone, Harry gently kissed Sarah, and they both knew what they wanted. In that moment they knew that they did not want to resist the passion that had been growing deep inside them.

The moment was incredible. They felt their bodies endlessly pressing against each other, enjoying every second. They lay together for what felt like hours, naked and deliriously happy.

They had both had a church upbringing. Both families regularly attended church and their Christian faith was important to them. And Sarah and Harry knew their parents would strongly disapprove if they knew they had been sleeping together. They had been taught that sex before marriage was wrong, and they knew it would bring shame on the family if they were found out. But they didn't care.

That was until a few weeks later when Sarah realised she was pregnant. Horrified, she panicked. She did not know what to do. She could not tell her family, but knew they would eventually find out. She met with Harry and told him; their distress was mutual. Harry felt he had to insist she have an abortion, that there was no other way out. They simply knew they could not have a baby at this time.

Sarah did not want to do it, she knew she did not feel comfortable with abortion, but equally she could not think of another option. So, she went to see her doctor, and requested her appointment at the abortion clinic.

It didn't take that long. Sarah was home the same day, and after a few weeks her body returned to normal. It was her mind that didn't. She could not forgive herself. She felt she was forced into this desperate situation, and as much as she felt she could not care for a child, she also desperately wanted that child. For the rest of her life, every time the due date came around, every time it was the anniversary of that appointment, she felt that acute mental pain once again.

There are high rates of mental illness related to abortion. Desperate women with no other way out often suffer for the rest of their lives, carrying guilt, shame and sadness, unable to forgive themselves. The things that we hide deep inside ourselves and that we feel are too shameful to share can lie there, hidden, but able to affect our lives and prevent us from thriving.

We need not suffer mental ill health for the rest of our lives because of decisions we made long ago; we can free ourselves from their grip. By visiting them again we can revisit the pain we felt when we knew we had to make those decisions. We can learn to forgive ourselves as we realise that there really was no other way. Often in these agonising situations there is no clear right or wrong, and so we make the decision that is right for us at that time. We did not do wrong; and others will continue to make that same decision in those same circumstances. There are many other situations that may cause us this same mental distress from decisions that we made long ago.

We need not judge ourselves for what we find, nor accept the judgments of others.

Opening those boxes is the first step to freedom, healing and restoration.

We May Discover God

Saint Teresa found that in each room as she progressed through her inner castle, God was there, in ever-increasing intensity. We may find God on our own journey, but that discovery will look different for each of us, and the experience and the response will be our own, just as our wellness journey is our own. We each have our own faith and wellness goals, and so the destination and the journey will be different for each of us.

If we discover that faith is important to us and we want to explore more about God, as we discover more of ourselves, our ideas about what faith is and who God is may change. We may discover God and discover how we want to express our faith. We might even find we catch a glimpse of God that is clearer than before. Faith or spirituality is part of wellbeing but we can design that to be just how we want it to be for our lives.

Could we even imagine ourselves having a wonderful experience of God, seeing God, hearing God speak to us personally, and perhaps impacting a part of our lives we would like help with? What would you want God to do for you today, as we wander through these ancient rooms, discovering things we may wish to be free of? Perhaps this journey does not need to involve God; we just need to discover more about ourselves.

We can stay inside our inmost being for as long as we like. We can visit as often as we like. We can go as deep as we like. This can happen naturally, but it is good to allow ourselves the space and time to navigate this journey. Perhaps it will lead to greater freedom, although we can often benefit from professional help in bringing about further healing from the wounds of our past.

Forgiveness

Forgiveness is an important concept in Christianity but is little understood. Christians will insist that we forgive those who have hurt us based on a few Bible verses that seem to state this. But forgiveness is far more complicated than simply saying a prayer. Christianity generally underestimates and trivialises forgiveness.

Millie was left with mild post-traumatic stress disorder after her childhood. Every day she would re-live painful situations, re-run scenarios in her head, telling her parents how unfair it was, and thinking she would not let that happen again. This made her constantly ready for a fight. If anyone crossed her, challenged her, or criticised her at all, she would be there, fists up, ready to defend herself, because she was not going to let her childhood hurts happen to her again. She had not dealt with the hurts from her past and it was eating her up, stealing her peace and happiness, and her marriage and other relationships. That initial peace she had felt when she first met God had started to fade because the mental trauma was still present. There are many that live with this, and suffer even worse symptoms.

Sometimes these things are very hard to address and trauma can leave us with deep wounds that never seem to heal. It is normal after a traumatic experience for the brain to be unable to deal with what has happened; it can stop us in our tracks, and halt any ability to learn, be creative, or move on in life. It can feel as though we are stuck in the moment the trauma happened. We can't reach our full potential if previous traumatic situations are still at the forefront of our minds; holding on to hurts from the past and re-living the bad experience can cause psychological and even physical problems. By remembering and re-living the hurt, you re-live the emotion, the distress, and you repeatedly get the fight or flight response in the body, which prepares the body for defending itself or running away with a release of adrenaline. If this response happens regularly in the body, it can adversely affect our wellbeing, and this is why it is better for us to release past traumas and attempt to deal with them. We only know they are there as we begin to explore ourselves a bit more.

It is a natural reaction to re-live these traumas in our minds, as if we are punishing the person who hurt us. Yet all that happens is you hold onto what someone else did to you for the rest of your life, and you get two crimes for the price of one. We might feel stressed or anxious, not get the sleep we need, and not be able to thrive and fulfil our potential if we hold on to hurt and pain; it can steal our happiness, freedom and health. Those who have suffered abuse or traumatic events know too well that this kind of thing is not easily dealt with. Someone might not even recognise that they have been abused, and yet the perpetrator can leave scars from their treatment of us that affect us for the rest of our lives. This quagmire of emotions can be detrimental to our health and how we live and thrive. Dealing with it, processing it, and freeing ourselves from it is important for our overall health.

Forgiveness is an important concept for our health, but these kinds of hurts are not dealt with by saying the words "I forgive you" like many Christians are often encouraged to do, as if it is up to you to put right what someone else did wrong. For years I was told to forgive those who had hurt me, and warned that my relationship with God would be affected and I might not be saved, largely because there is one Bible verse that says we must forgive or we will not be forgiven. But with deep emotional hurts that can carve huge crevasses out of our lives and souls leaving deep, festering wounds, we need more than words or a Bible verse thrown at us to be free of these kinds of burdens that weigh us down and prevent us from truly living and thriving in our lives.

If we are struggling to cope with the hurts that continually flood our minds, often a combination of things will help us find freedom. Professional help may be required to free us from the strong grip of past experiences, but sometimes just someone to listen, a cup of tea or our favourite wine, the right medication or that journey you've always wanted to take is needed. A multitude of options are open to us and as we discover more about ourselves and our preferences, the right things may gradually become obvious to us. Some may appreciate God's soothing presence in our lives, taking our damaged souls and letting us rest beside those healing streams in quiet places. God is great at healing and restoration, and taking our battered shells and sculpting something more beautiful than we might be able to imagine.

Taking Control of Our Wellbeing

Wellness looks different for everyone, and we can all interpret health, and the different areas of wellness, in a way that is right for us. Whatever the research says, we all know our own bodies and know how healthy or well we feel. Some can feel extremely healthy and happy, and yet totally neglect one area. Not everyone benefits from being sociable and many prefer their own company, so social health is not going to be a major thing for everyone. In the same way, spiritual health will look different from person to person. So, one person may want to focus on spiritual health as an important part of their lives, others may not, wishing only to touch on this aspect in a small way.

Christians are often urged to live completely for God, giving God 100% of their time, devoting everything they have to God. This is something often preached about in churches, with the belief that God demands this of us. There appears to be an obligation in some Bible verses to work unceasingly for God, such as Philippians 3:12-16: "I press on… forgetting the past and straining forward toward the heavenly goal…" Christians are repeatedly told to give everything to God, including time, effort and money, or risk losing their salvation.

Many have felt pressure from such claims. Busy families have often felt this is something else they have to fit into their week, with people urged to attend church meetings after work, when it might instead be more beneficial to be resting. Samuel, a student, said he used to attend church and would faithfully read his Bible as often as he could. But he felt stressed and anxious from the pressure to give as much as he could to God, and from the demands of his faith imposed by his church. Gradually, Samuel has left his church behind, and although he feels much more at peace by not having to adhere to the demands of his church life, he still retains a remnant of belief in a God-being. Samuel pointed out that sometimes we are highly motivated in one area of health and wellbeing and at other times we may not have the capacity to pay much attention to those areas. Strangely, although I'm really passionate about running and there are times when I could easily run a marathon without training, and other times when it's just too hard to climb the stairs. Equally, I really value a healthy diet, but there are times when I want nothing more than to stuff a massive pasty into my mouth whilst guzzling copious amounts of beer.

We must tailor our health to our own preferences. As long as we are at peace with our decisions and know they are right for us it does not matter what those decisions are. We are not robots programmed by the demands of others. Health and well-being will look different for us all. We can take control of our wellbeing and we can take control of our faith.

If we are feeling under the weather, not healthy or fulfilled and that we might be neglecting some of our deep desires, life goals, or an aspect of our wellbeing, it is worth spending time with ourselves to search our hearts and minds and see if we are living the life we wish to lead.

An Odd Element of Wellness?

It might be surprising to some that spirituality is identified as a key part of wellness. A wellness organisation in Australia describes spiritual health as something you cannot easily describe or give a definition to. It can mean different things, including belief in or a connection with a God-being, a sense of purpose, receiving guidance, or hope, faith and peace. They point out that historically it has meant adhering to a religion, but it does not have to mean that. They maintain that spiritual health can promote greater physical and mental health.[67]

A professor of psychiatry describes how spirituality involves a search for and a discovery of God and a resulting intimate connection with God. Organised religion has many boundaries, whereas faith and spirituality are limitless.[68] It is like a journey, the first steps of which are searching and asking if there really is something there, which may lead to a belief, and on to an intimate connection and experience of this God-being that can only be felt and understood by the person experiencing it. We will return in the last chapter to discovering our own spiritual preferences, and embarking on our own search.

My aim is not to convince anyone to turn to faith or spirituality. I would not wish to coerce. I have just gained such incredible benefit myself throughout life from having a faith and having the most incredible encounters with God, and I know others have had the same. I know lives that have been totally transformed, I know sick people who either have recovered or have died peacefully, safe in the knowledge that they really are going to a better place. I know of the immense joy and elation of knowing God and the feeling when you hear God's voice guiding you, or just letting you know you are loved and cared for. I want everyone to have that feeling! It is so utterly incredible and lifechanging, that I want everyone to share it. I guess this is what the research is showing, that interaction with God makes us feel good. This in turn impacts our general health, because when you feel that good, nothing else matters. If nothing else, I'm a nurse, and so promoting health is my job. If we find something that has health benefits as much as faith appears to, we should be shouting it from the rooftops.

The key, though, is that the spiritual or faith aspect to our lives is not necessarily enhanced by adherence to a religion, or practices such as praying a certain way, reading the Bible, singing certain songs or any other ritual. The buildings, structures, institutions and practices of religion do not always foster the beneficial effects of faith, although some find these a helpful way to express their faith and this is good, but many more will find them tedious and frustrating, perhaps a waste of time. It is what goes on in our heart and soul that can bring transformation, however that is bought about. That heartfelt faith, that internal connection to God, that genuine spirituality is what has the impact on our overall health, not external religious expressions. We don't want the nutshell, we want the nuts. Roasted and salted as well… Those who promote discovering our spiritual side are not advocating that we all march off to church, but instead explore what it means for us to nurture this spiritual aspect of our lives. As we will see, this is a very individual thing and will look different for each of us.

Genuine Faith versus Religious Nonsense

Jesus said the same. This is a heavy theme in the Bible; the condemnation of pointless religion. Take Matthew 15:8-9: Jesus sat in front of the religious leaders of his day and said, "You hypocrites! Isaiah was correct, 'These religious people worship me with words, but their hearts are elsewhere. Their worship is scam, because they teach man-made ideas as instructions from God'." Matthew also mentions a banquet at the end of time but fiercely suggests that the merely religious people will not be invited, while those with a heartfelt connection to God will be welcomed in. The repetition of this theme suggests we can learn that God might not value religious practice if it does not lead our hearts to discover God. Jesus is recorded as saying this a couple of times, no doubt with a wry smile on his face.

The Bible, the tool of the religious, itself condemns the religious. Some preserve religious traditions for the sake of keeping the religion alive, instead of being motivated to simply help people find God. Religion is a solace for some, and some find great benefit in attending religious services; but for those for whom such venues are not the best way of expressing our spirituality, we do not achieve anything by simply going to church and maintaining and propagating religious beliefs and practices. This is great news for those who love to be out in the fields, on the mountaintops, on the beach or in bed on a Sunday morning. It is also great news for those who wish to have a spiritual aspect to their lives but have no desire, nor the time, to attend church or any religious services.

Hope

Encountering God can also give us hope. Hope is difficult to pin down and to define; to have hope means to have an optimistic view of our future even if we cannot see evidence of anything good to come. With hope, our future is always better than our past. This hope and optimism can be of benefit to our health.

Whereas people, jobs, money and life will let us down, we can be confident that God will be with us throughout our lives and experiences, and will secure a future for us in paradise after we have died, just like Ian, the jellyfish man, and Amy described in their death experiences. Hope gives us a positive expectation for the future which can strengthen us in the present. If life leaves us despairing and unable to find happiness, exploring this in our journey with God can bring us to a place of peace. This will look different for everyone, but going on that journey of exploring those painful wounds and our difficult situations in the context of our connection with God can bring us that point of relief and freedom. As we see more of what God does in our lives we begin to trust and desire more. It is only over time and through multiple experiences of God that we can look back and know this hope that grows within us. For some of us, life can be so painful we need all the hope we can get.

Hope is a feature of faith. Paul's prayer at the end of his letter to the Roman church says this: "God has hope, joy and peace in bucketloads to give us all. I ask that God will fill you personally to overflowing with hope, joy and peace because you trust in God. Then you will have confident hope through the power of the Holy Spirit."[69] It would be pretty good if our discovery of God could cause us to be overflowing with joy, peace and hope. In the same letter Paul says how, when we are close to God, "Running into problems and trials helps us develop endurance. Endurance develops physical, mental and spiritual strength, and this strengthens our confident hope of new life in God, now and forever. And this hope will not disappoint. God loves us dearly and has given us the Holy Spirit to fill our hearts to bursting with God's love."[70]

To experience God filling us up with love and power is that lifechanging experience many of us crave. Finding spiritual strength to help with our physical troubles is a great aid.

So, trials develop endurance and character, which can lead to hope. Paul wrote this letter at a time when Christians were persecuted, and he himself was in prison and facing death.

Yet hopes can so easily be dashed in life. When hopes are dashed time after time, it can break you. You end up not trusting hope, you can't hope, because it's too painful, whether it be long term disease, or financial struggle, relationship worries, or the many struggles we face in life, where any hopes we may have for the future are shattered time and again. Some endure lives that many of us would struggle to survive through. Some of those might be the awful scenes seen on our television screens of war, famine or natural disaster, but some of the terrible situations we have to endure are hidden; abusive relationships, crippling debt, even our minds can torture us constantly even in the absence of physical threat. So, when Christians talk of hope it can feel more like a kick in the teeth than something good.

But there's a difference between hoping for something we would really like to happen in our lives, and the optimistic hope that gives us a steely determination to survive and win. I could hope for a new car, a better job, a new relationship, or to travel the world, but those hopes are so easily torn apart. These things can be important to us, but they are shallow in the presence of the hope that we encounter in God. God's hope is a deep confidence, a mental strength, a surety that God will see us through. It is a firm foundation, a stable base through which to live our lives. It is a feeling that whatever happens in life, we will be okay, because God is ultimately in control of everything. It is a certain confidence in God.

This hope grows in us as we endure the trials of life, and as we encounter God. Paul had perseverance when he was in prison and facing death, he had hope and an assurance that whatever happened God was in control and so it would be ok. He was not captivated by the fear that many of us might feel, but was instead strong. He knew his God, he had absolute certainty of who God is and that he would be with God in paradise on the day he died. Let's release those limitless bucketloads of hope, joy and peace that come from God into our lives so we can all have that same reassurance.

Religious Anxiety

Many have spent their lives wracked with guilt about so called sins we think we have committed and an underlying feeling that we are terrible sinners, not good enough for God. For many this stems from a Church upbringing and the emphasis on sin, hell, damnation and purgatory that is often reinforced. Church beliefs and doctrine have contributed to an overwhelming religious anxiety and guilt among many people, but these religious beliefs are not certain; scholars argue vehemently about these issues and there is no consensus. Much unnecessary anxiety has been caused by Church teaching.

Much unhelpful guilt and shame can be caused by those within Church. Rachel found this: 'I worked for a church for five years and after experiencing much heartache and hurt, I haven't gone back. I love God, I love spending time in worship, I go on retreats and love doing reflections on the Bible over a cuppa. I love meeting friends and talking about what God has been doing but I don't like church and I've been feeling really guilty that I would rather be walking the dog or playing with the babies than go and feel uncomfortable, judged and bored.'[71]

Much angst comes because Church teaching has traditionally come down very hard on sexual desire and practices. I'm not calling it sexual sin, because it is a natural human desire, and expressing ourselves in a way that is right for us is part of being healthy. Yet the Church and individual Christians continually condemn the way people express their sexuality, from masturbation to other sexual preferences — unless you're a married, heterosexual person with children; then you're okay.

In fact, people's sexual preferences are no one else's business. Each person is an individual with their own desires and ways they wish to express themselves. We do that in most other areas of life, such as choosing your career or the colour you paint your house, but when it comes to sex, we feel condemned if we don't stick to cultural expectations, and we feel we have to resist any desires we think will be condemned by others. Of course, if an act is against the law or hurts other people then it's not okay, but if not, enjoy it. Christianity has traditionally been quick to judge in this area when it is not Christianity's job to do so. If masturbation was wrong, God would have made our arms shorter.

In a sense it doesn't matter what others think about our decisions. Once we have truly discovered more about ourselves and we live according to our life preferences, our happiness and wellbeing need not be dependent on the approval of others. A dear gentleman who was happily part of his local church and had many friends decided to be open one day, telling his friends he wished to become female. His friends rejected him, telling him the Bible says this is wrong. The gentleman went ahead with surgery, knowing this was his deepest desire, and now lives happily as female. She has to live her faith alone with God, having felt acutely that rejection by her church, and realising that if she is to be true to herself, her faith has to remain just her and God. Rejected by Church, but with a closeness to God. Her friends had been unable to consider the effect their Bible interpretation had on her, and the implications for this person's faith. How many others are unable to be their true selves in faith settings because of these tendencies among people of faith? Our image of the model Christian, acceptable to our churches lurks uncomfortably in the corner...

Stories abound of God communicating with people if there is need. God knows each of us intimately, and knows what our needs and desires are. God cave-dives regularly into our depths, and knows what we hide away in those dusty boxes. And God doesn't care what lies there, God just wants to meet with us and bless us. When we have that intimacy with God, that soul connection, that closeness to God, God will tell us about anything we need to change. If God doesn't say anything, it is probably okay. God will tell us anything we need to know.

This means that Christians need to stop judging people for their sexuality or lifestyle choices. Anyone, whatever their life preferences, who wishes to express their faith by attending church or any religious building or service should be embraced fully as members of churches, capable of performing any role including being ministers.

It actually doesn't make any sense to do it any other way, as most Christians would insist that we are all equal before God, that everyone's so called sins are equal and no one is any better than any other, but if you are seen to be expressing your sexuality in a way the Church does not agree with then you might be judged too sinful for the Church and excluded. Yet Mr Bloggs who has an anger problem, or is fiddling his taxes, or whatever else he does behind closed doors is okay, even though those same Bible verse condemn his actions too. This becomes a massive contradiction in our theology and practice that does not make any sense and needs to stop. Again, it is hard for some Christians to separate their own prejudices from what God might say.

This contradiction stems from the pervasive problem of our chaotic use of the Bible. There are certain verses that, if we interpret literally, we can make them condemn certain lifestyle preferences. Using the Bible to condemn aspects of others' lifestyles that we may not agree with is one major obstacle that Christians frequently place in the way of people getting to know God, and it needs to be removed. We examine the use of the Bible more fully in due course.

Reaching the End of Life

Lucy (not her real name) was a patient in a nursing home, suffering with breast cancer that had spread to her lungs and brain. It was clear nothing more could be done for her, except to give her a peaceful death. She was given any food she requested, enjoying her favourite tipple regularly too. She was given drugs that would suppress any pain she felt, and her other symptoms too. She had a bright, airy room with a view of the gardens, and the area around was peaceful. It was the perfect place to live her last few days.

Yet Lucy was terrified. As part of her nursing assessment Lucy was asked what her religious beliefs were, if she had any. She fiercely denied any belief, and was quite sure she wanted nothing to do with religion or minsters at all. Her anxiety increased, and even the strongest drugs did not fully treat the intense distress she was feeling. She died after a few days, but it was not peaceful.

It is a real privilege to care for people coming to the end of their life, and make this journey as good as it could possibly be for the individual and those close to them. Yet I have seen two types of emotional state in the dying; those at peace, and those not at peace. In some, there is a real distress, a deep anguish, a fear which seems to penetrate to the heart of their being.

Medics call this "existential distress". The phenomenon is not fully understood, but it is a state that seems to be linked to a deep part of us, a part that is aware the end of life is coming, but it somehow is not prepared, and shows itself in physical and emotional distress.

Many experts believe there is a spiritual element to existential distress, and that our spiritual self is integral to our very existence, our very being.[72] It is as though our spiritual self is the real us and our physical bodies are just the shells – then our spiritual self *is* our very being. Like a butterfly emerging from a cocoon, death is then us shedding our outer shell and being free to fly.

How existential distress relates to faith is unknown; could it be that the person might be aware of what lies ahead, as if there is something they can see that they do not like? Maybe there is something that can hinder our spirit from being set free? In these cases, there is often in death very little of the "peace that is beyond understanding" that is mentioned in the Bible.

"Do not worry about anything at all; instead, we can talk to God about our concerns. Simply tell God what we need. When we trust God to help us, then we will experience God's inexplicable peace. It is beyond our understanding, but this peace will protect our hearts and minds …"[73]

Maybe there is something in this after all?

Fear of Death

Here's an encounter from Beryl, who, as a young girl, had an encounter that meant she need not fear death for the rest of her life:

'In the spring of 1938 I was taken ill suddenly with sickness and pain. As I had not been ill for seven years and was a very healthy fifteen-year-old, it was not realised for a few days that I had appendicitis. When the doctor saw me, she at once diagnosed this and had an ambulance take me to Salisbury infirmary. It was Friday afternoon, April 29th.

'I had never experienced any such symptoms before and had ceased being violently sick. The pain had dulled to an ache, so it was decided not to operate but to keep me under observation. During the weekend, I began to feel easier and to look forward to going home.

‘On the evening of Monday, May 2nd at six p.m., I was taken with such a terrible pain that I could not even call out for help. My appendix had burst. Fortunately, a patient across the ward noticed my distress and called the sister to me. She at once put screens around me and sent for the doctor. I was given an injection of morphia which gave me complete relief and I slept.

‘When I woke it was night and I was almost ready to be taken to the operating theatre. My father had been sent for and remained while the operation took place, which was from eleven-forty-five p.m., May 2nd, to three a.m., May 3rd. Later that day my parents met the surgeon, Mr Taylor-Young, and he told them that I could not be expected to live for more than three days.

‘They then came to see me but told me nothing of their meeting with him. I was propped up in a sitting position with many pillows, but I could not see clearly beyond the end of my bed. They sat one on each side of me, holding my hands. I wanted to look at both of them, so my father came round to the same side as my mother and sat on the locker base because I could not keep turning my head. They had been told that I had peritonitis and septicaemia, but they gave me no inkling of how ill I was. They told me that prayers had been said for me in church and that relations and friends were praying for me. I prayed myself, and put myself in God’s hands in complete confidence that I would soon be well.

‘It was during the second night after the operation that I found myself struggling along a deep valley. I was tired and was finding it very heavy going. I looked up and above me was a very high hill, steep and dark, but above it shone a clear brilliant light. As I looked, I was aware of dark figures climbing the hill, and as they disappeared over the top they were silhouetted against the light. I started to climb too to reach it, but before I could get to the top, I suddenly found that Jesus Christ himself was standing before me in a radiant light.

‘I was sitting up in bed propped up looking at him. His feet were on a level with the foot of my bed and his height was that of a tall man. I leaned forward saying, “Jesus,” and stretched out my arms to him, but he just smiled at me and shook his head slightly. I tried again, but once more he shook his head and looked at me with a wonderful expression in his eyes.

‘I sat back and gazed at him. The love and compassion in his face are indescribable. I had never seen such total love before or since. We looked and smiled at one another for a long time and then he went, the light began to dim and then disappear. As it went, I became aware of the few small lights that shone out over beds where the patients were having attention, and then I slept.

‘When my parents came the next day, I told them all about it; also my vicar, the Reverend W. Mauleverer, was told. The doctors and nurses were amazed that I continued to live, particularly as within a week my wound had become gangrenous. After four weeks my abdominal problem was still as acute and I developed pneumonia and pleurisy. The first signs of returning health began after six to seven weeks and after just over ten weeks of illness I was able to go home in a wheelchair. After this I spent three weeks in a convalescent home.

‘My case was considered to be a miracle in the hospital. The doctors had been afraid to re-operate to try to remove the abscesses they knew must be there, because they did not think my heart would stand it. I have always been so grateful for the nursing and care I was given in that hospital ward. This illness brought me the greatest experience of my life. Through it, I can say quite definitely “I know that my redeemer liveth” and that he cares for all that put their trust in him.’[74] Mrs Beryl Hutchesson lived a long and happy life, and died at age ninety-seven.

Fear of death is a real thing for many people. Anything from the news that one may have a life limiting illness, to the act of dying, and then to what might happen afterwards, can cause real fear. It’s related to the unknown, being afraid of what we do not fully understand and are not in control of. We often only fully realise this fear when we face death.

There are no simple answers but ignoring fear of death won’t make it go away. Ignoring it and not exploring our beliefs about faith, God and our spiritual life may even lead to existential distress on our deathbed. This is something we can explore as part of the journey into ourselves and as part of the discovery of who we truly are. Those who have had an experience of God may find that quiet confidence, that hope, that they will be enjoying a new life in paradise after they have died, but not everyone feels so sure.

If we want that hope, if we want that quiet confidence in God, it is there for the taking. God does not play games with us; if we have a real fear of this then we can talk to God about it, ask God to show us something of this new life, ask God to give us that hope, that confidence. Heck, like a divine estate agent, we can ask God to show us a glimpse of Heaven.

Humans often don't do death very well. We don't talk about it and we don't prepare for it, and yet it is something that happens to us all. That dear minister in the Church in the Wilderness that day said he felt this should be a role of the Church, to help prepare us, to help us explore our beliefs before it is too late, before we reach that point when we may not have the capacity or the time left to explore it for ourselves.

It makes sense that we will have less fear of death if we know we are going to have a glorious eternity with God in a place better than this physical planet. Life threatening illness or death would not be so scary for the patient or others around them. Faith can become a harness clipping us securely onto the zipline of life, giving us purpose and the strength to endure when life gets hard, ensuring we do not fall, and delivering us successfully to the end of the slide.

There are many reasons why we may feel frazzled by life. Sometimes it can feel that we are expected to give out to others constantly, with no one giving back to us. When this happens day after day it can be draining, and for some this is the norm; there might be no days off from our duties. The awful things people do to us can leave us reeling, suffering sometimes for the rest of our lives. Things happen to us that are often no fault of our own; loved ones leave us too early, illness or accidents take away our freedom and health, the burdens of our career or job can become too much to handle, or we just get so sick of the stresses and strains of life that we want to escape.

We also find that other people do not truly understand us and the fact that who we are and the things we do sometimes results from the many things we may have experienced in life. Sometimes people endure terrible suffering at the hands of others, and these experiences can stay with us forever and affect our whole lives; many will have found that they end up in destructive behaviour patterns or are left with a residual anger. Often these things lead to negative consequences and are seemingly out of our control. The psychology of how and why life experiences affect us the way they do, and affect some people more than others, is little understood, but it can be hugely disabling, and hinder us from achieving our full potential.

Whilst others may not understand us, faith offers a God-being who loves us without judging us, understands us, and cherishes us despite what we believe about ourselves, or who we are, or our history. To have this support can be a real comfort. We do not need to strive any more, to try and change ourselves, or be different. We do not need to worry about what people think because what God thinks is all that matters, and God just simply loves us. Amy's experience of standing before God after she experienced death showed her that God understood who she was; God knew her and knew why she did certain things; God understood everything from the past to the future, and did not judge her. The angry, judgmental God that she had been taught about from her church days was absent, instead there was only love. Things she thought had been sinful in fact were swept aside by a torrent of love. The Church teaching she received had been wrong. There are people who believe God would never love them because they just don't feel good enough, but the truth is God cannot resist loving each of us unconditionally. We are all invited to share in this incredible experience of knowing God, with no restrictions — it just isn't true that you have to be good enough to discover and know God. With that news, let's all grab it with everything we've got.

This data on wellbeing is taken not from religious texts, but is from scientific studies. Many of the doctors, scientists and researchers state they are amazed that not more research is done, and that faith and spirituality is often not discussed with patients, given the amount of data confirming the benefit faith seems to bring to overall health and wellbeing. It is sad that we have stigmatised faith because there is evidence it can improve health and quality of life. This stigma means there is less investment in research and less enthusiasm among scientists to engage with research on this topic.

It is left instead to theologians and church ministers; yet along with their contribution comes the push to engage in church or religious activity, which many do not wish to do. This is a hindrance to those for whom faith in God might be of great benefit. We throw the proverbial baby out with the bathwater, as we reject the aspects of faith we don't like, but also those which are good.

This impasse is not helped by the fact that it is difficult to obtain hard data on faith. Unlike objective scientific studies which provide proof that is beyond reasonable doubt, and so we know which antibiotic will kill which bacteria for instance, data from studies on faith and religious belief is subjective and influenced by a number of factors. Religious belief is complex, you are also measuring something with no physical manifestation, God is not a physical being you can dissect in order to see how God works and what God is. Neither is faith belief; you can measure how often people attend church and what they may do there, but not the feeling a person has when they have a lifechanging encounter with God.

Although it is hard to obtain and interpret data relating to the effects of faith on health, what is consistent is that faith has a positive impact on life and health. Faith is good for us. God is good for us. But as we shall discover, this may look different for us all.

This is a journey of discovery, as we embark on that venture of finding God. It's a journey of inner sensations you did not know you could have. It is peace, joy, happiness and wonderful tingling sensations. It is uncontrollable laughing in the absence of jokes. It is mind-blowing realisations about you, about God and about life. God can catch you at any moment and speak to you, prompt you, give you success where you believed only failure was possible. It is awesome, and it is worth it. And like many who have taken the challenge, they find that much of what they believed and had been taught about God, is simply wrong.

But to do this we have to blast the obstacles away because many of us have been led to believe we are not good enough for God, or that God is not full of love and passion and is instead judgmental and evil. People have throughout the centuries preached their own views as God's word.

Things that have been labelled as sinful in the eyes of God are actually man-made lists of offences, often defined based on cultural preference or dodgy use of the Bible rather than truth. Many truly believe they have done wrong and will be condemned by God, when all along, when we examine our definitions of sin, we find in fact we have little idea of what sin actually is. Much angst has been felt by those who feel condemned by so called sins. It is religion that causes this unnecessary torment, not God.

God knows us inside and out and loves us just the way we are. We occasionally hear this being said in church, but often the opposite rings out from our pulpits and our garden parties; what many people teach about God, and how God is in reality, are often two very different things. The church often hinders people accessing this lifechanging relationship with God that can give great health benefits, instead hiding God with the fluff of various beliefs and practices that we are told we have to do to make ourselves good enough to meet with God. Christianity has dictated what a person should look like and should do before they dare approach God, and in the process has put more and more obstacles in the way. God is ready to get out a divine sledgehammer and knock those walls down.

Faith is good for us. Not religion or performing religious tasks, unless they contribute to our own faith goals. There is real scientific evidence that those with a heartfelt faith, an inner spirituality, a connection with this God-being, are healthier mentally and physically, get better from illness quicker, and are likely to thrive, rather than be swallowed up by the troubles of life. There is real benefit in exploring and nurturing our spiritual self.

Ant Middleton, the SAS soldier who presents the television programme *SAS: Who Dares Wins*, realised there are some people who endure real struggles in life and are able to cope with them, but there are others who are swallowed up by their trials.[75] Let's be the ones who survive and thrive. Let's go deep inside ourselves and discover our inner being, and all that lies within. Let's discover ourselves again, and begin to like ourselves and find value in every fibre of our being, every part of us that makes us who we truly are. Let's discover for ourselves what we truly believe and let's get as much of God as we can handle. Let's live life to the full now, but when that day comes, let's die well, with the confidence and hope we are taking a one-way trip to paradise.

Faith is not magic, but it is a flipping good help in times of need.

Chapter Six
What is God Really Like?

'The "judgmental" God of the Old Testament was nowhere to be found. There was only a vast and eternal presence of love. The being was not male or female, they seemed to know everything about me, every decision I ever made, every part of my life. There was no judgment, no condemnation, only pure love and acceptance. They understood, accepted and loved everything about me. God loved me even more than I love my own kids — and I was all at once humbled and empowered by being loved so much.'[76]

Amy saw a pure and brilliant love. John, the writer of Revelation, saw this…

"The city shone with the glory of God, as if God's light was reflecting off a thousand diamonds. There was a figure; dressed in gold and white, and the light shone from its eyes as if it were on fire. It spoke, and its voice was like thunder. Yet I was not afraid. It spoke lovingly, as if it understood me, as if it knew everything there was to know about me. The figure smiled and gently touched my head, and as it did I felt love and power flow through my body. I could not take my eyes off this person; it was stunningly beautiful and yet full of love and power. I had never known such love.

"There were other people there; but this figure made it clear that each was precious to it. As we stood there, it opened its arms and said, 'Come! Let anyone who wants to, come; and let those who wish to, take the free gift of life.'"[77]

Finding out what God is like is difficult, with no physical manifestation, no dissectible being. The philosopher Philo knew the human languages are largely inadequate in describing the deep mysteries of God and spirituality.[78] We are trying to describe the indescribable. Yet many people have seen, felt or heard something of God, shown in stories either in the Bible or from modern life. These encounters of God offer hints of what God might be like; they can give us a glimpse of this God-being.

You can also understand a little about a person from their house and garden.

The Concept of Paradise

We get the concept of paradise from limited texts in the Bible, from experiences and visions people have had, and from our own innate desires, but such things are subjective; we may not be able to ascertain facts from the Bible or from contemporary reports. But the concept persistently crops up. It is likely that if this God-being does indeed exist, it must exist somewhere, and the stories we heard from Amy and the jellyfish man describe a paradise scene they saw as they experienced that post-death moment. Whilst Jesus' life ebbed away that day over two thousand years ago, according to reports, he said to the man on the cross beside him, 'Today you will be with me in paradise.' Yet we will not have full understanding of the concept of paradise until we get there ourselves, and it seems very few of us return to tell others what it is like.

The place John saw and recorded in Revelation was so incredible, the only way he could describe it was as a stunning place, full of light and colour, studded with precious stones, paved with gold; and filled with palpable love. Paul also saw something incredible as he was whisked into paradise and heard things that were so awesome they could not be told to mortals on earth.[79] What secrets are to be discovered the day we get to experience this awesome journey?

Whatever experiences these people had, they saw *something*; and as much as it could have been a dream, or some unknown medical phenomenon, the likelihood is there is something somewhere, some place, some realm where God dwells, and to which we will go after this life, when we are set free from our cocoons.

It is consistently recorded in biblical descriptions of this place that there is an absence of evil, suffering, pain or sorrow, reflecting perhaps how God feels about the terrible things that affect our lives; God detests it. Its absence in God's home — some call it Heaven — shows that evil, pain and suffering do not originate with God, but somewhere else. God's home is a healing place, keeping those in it safe and providing restoration. That feeling when you are exhausted but you arrive at your holiday destination and suddenly find a beautiful beach where you can relax, rest and play. That feeling of stress dissipating, when there are no more responsibilities, nothing more you need to worry about or do. You can simply rest. And this holiday goes on for eternity.

The concept of paradise can be a source of strength to some. In the 2021 London Marathon I was running alongside a gentleman who was running for a hospice charity that had been a great help to him whilst his wife was dying. As he and his wife held hands for the last time, they promised each other that they would meet again in paradise. This one promise has been a great source of strength for this gentleman in his grief. He fervently said that he totally rejects religion and Church in any form, and in fact does not believe in God. But when I asked if he believed that there may be *something* out there, some God-being, or power, or energy, or force, he said he did indeed believe a God-being existed in some form, he was just not sure what. He certainly rejected traditional images of God, but he was certain he would see his wife again in paradise. I asked if he felt his belief in this God-being and his hope of paradise gave him inner strength? He said yes, this gave him enormous strength that enabled him to keep going in the worst of times.

Perhaps this realm is similar to our planet but without being tainted by millennia of war, pollution and destruction? But for now, whilst life continues to present its many challenges to us and we cannot easily visit this paradise and enjoy its pleasures, our only solace is to enjoy God's presence enhancing our current lives. When you have felt God permeate your soul, mind, body and situation this is paradise itself, as much as we can have it in this life. God's presence and power captivating our minds and hearts is so good you never want that feeling to end. There is something deeply irresistible about this God-being. When you experience it, you never want it to stop; you want to go back for more. When you meet God it changes everything.

God's garden is just as beautiful.

"It was a magical place, a tropical paradise. Birds flew energetically through the trees, twisting and turning, their feathers displaying their stunning colours. It seemed as though they were playing together, coming down to rest on our shoulders. They would pick fruit, then come with the fruit in their beaks as if taunting us and showing us what they had found. Families of bears wandered along with their cubs, enjoying the feast of good fruit on offer. Streams trickled along with crystal clear water, gathering in pools deep enough to swim in. We walked along enjoying the beauty and the coolness provided by the trees, with occasional patches of sunlight that gently warmed our skin, a crystal-clear blue sky above us. When we felt hungry, we would see what fruit there was around us. We found juicy, ripe mangoes in the trees or sweet pineapples on the ground. The animals would sometimes come and share what we were eating, interested to see what we had chosen. At night we would make our bed from the leaves and grasses we found, and often a family of bears would come and join us, keeping us warm. It was a place of peace and we felt gloriously happy."[80]

This is not the stunning tropical rainforests of this beautiful planet, this is Eden. There are two descriptions of creation and of the garden in the book of Genesis, one in chapter one, and the other in chapter two. Both are poetic writing and differ in detail, and just as you would not take poetry literally, these texts are not meant to describe how everything happened exactly as it says. They offer instead the hope of every person and the vision of some: a future paradise.

It may have been a serene sight; the scribe, resting on a convenient stone with an animal skin over for comfort, a papyrus scroll to write on. Feather quill in hand, he sits hunched over his work, concentrating hard. The cave is cold but there is a fire in the entrance to keep him and his family warm, and keep intruders out. The rain trickles down the mountain outside, bringing much needed moisture to the dry earth. It is a good sound; in such a dry land water is precious and very welcome. Our scribe has been feeling that nudge in his soul the last few days, that unmistakeable prompt; God has been gently encouraging him to write. His subject? The beginning of the world.

Perhaps he had a vision, perhaps he heard the voice of God, perhaps he felt God kindle his creativity, inspiring his words. Perhaps as he wrote he was carried away by the scene, the flow of creativity unstemmed by crying children. Perhaps he was inspired by stories of old, carried down through the years by passionate storytellers.

The result was a piece of writing that would give generations after him a glimpse, a tiny bit of insight into this largely unfathomable God. The concept of paradise where God dwells and provides everything nature and people need continues through the Bible, and the idea evolves to become the paradise we dwell in after we have died.

Juicy Roast Lamb and the Finest Wine

Not only will we dwell in safety in this paradise, but when we get there, there might be a feast to welcome us. Vegetarians and vegans look away, because there is mention of a luscious meaty feast when we reach paradise.

"God will prepare a feast of rich food for everyone, a banquet of fine wine, delicious roast meat and the finest produce. God will destroy evil, death and fear forever. Sadness will be replaced with a glorious happiness."[81] Provision will not only be made for physical need, but also those wounds within us that no one can see.

Admittedly written in a culture where such luxuries would have been rare and so something to look forward to in a future paradise, it gives a glimpse of what people over the centuries have felt the concept of a heavenly paradise might include.

I look forward to a place where you can drink as much wine and eat as much red meat as you like, and not get liver failure and heart disease.

A friend of mine used to keep tropical fish. It was a time-consuming hobby; he would spend hours creating the perfect environment for the fish to live in, knowing that his hard work would mean they would live happily and have everything they needed. They looked stunning, with beautiful colours and shapes; the scene was eye-catching. He would make sure he created the perfect environment for them to live in before he put them in the tank, knowing if he didn't, they would die. In the same way, biblical and contemporary descriptions offer an image of God creating a perfect environment for people to live in, providing everything they need. Poetic, of course, but with hints of a future reality.

Needs are Not Only Physical

God knows what we need to live and thrive, but many people do not have those things in their current lives. Many suffer terribly in all sorts of ways, some more obvious, such as not having the right food or shelter, but some suffer internally. The demons in our minds can torture us beyond what we feel we can bear, and this suffering is just as hard as being deficient in food or other essentials.

We don't just need food, water and shelter, we also need repairing. Life can treat us harshly and events can leave us reeling, struggling on through life scarred and battered, lots of baggage in tow, weighing us down. Descriptions of paradise reveal trees, majestically standing alongside a river, intended for the healing of the nations, and for all who wish to dip their toes in God's river of life. The river that feeds the trees comes from God, God is the source of life and the source of healing in these descriptions. It's pictorial, but it conveys an essence of reality. Some describe how when they experience God in their physical lives, their troubles seem to fade. Imagine existing in that place where you can stand face to face with God—our troubles simply would not stand a chance of ever being seen again.

Healing, restoration and provision of the things we need is not only for a future paradise. Many experience that now.

Millie, the abused little girl, suffered with anxiety, fears and worries, and a total lack of ability to trust others or believe in herself. She carried the baggage of abuse for years after her torment. Many post-traumatic stress disorder sufferers will know the same; thoughts that continue to haunt us and spring that fight or flight response on us at any moment. There was little that eased Millie's emotional and psychological torment, but the times when she felt close to God, she at last felt peace. God became her only solace.

"There was a river with crystal clear water, flowing from God through a magnificent city. On the banks of the river grew enormous trees that bore delicious fruit every month. These were not normal trees; their purpose was to bring new life and healing for all people and all nations. There was nothing bad in this place, evil could not be found there."[82]

The need for trees that bring healing perhaps shows that God knows how tough life will be for some of us.

Diane writes, "After an emotional farewell to a dear old friend, I sat quietly in the lovely church in Brailes, near Shipston-on-Stour, for a while trying to find some comfort and peace; the shot was still ringing in my ears. My beloved horse, Kildare, at the age of twenty-five, was being buried on the side of Brailes Hill.

"I took a break in Devon to spend a few days with friends and then moved on to the tiny hamlet of Culbone in the woods near Porlock. Other friends ran a retreat there and visits always produced a feeling of relaxation, peace, wellbeing and being part of something.

"My friend was taking me through a meditation, when suddenly I saw a vivid image of Christ standing there with his arm around Kildare's neck. Christ said gently to me, 'Don't worry, I am looking after him. He's okay.' Suddenly all the grief I had felt came flooding out, but the tears no longer meant sadness and distress, they were tears of relief, of knowing that God had this all in hand, that I could trust Christ with my dearest friend."[83]

The story of creation was written thousands of years ago, but the principle remains the same today. God knows what you and I need to live and thrive. The beautiful imagery is of life, health and security. There is no *need* in this forever paradise, no one wants for anything. Everyone has enough, and it is all provided by God. Not only that, but descriptions show unlimited access to God, to walk, talk and just exist in God's presence. That irresistible desire to meet God can be fulfilled. This is Eden, and the echoes of the same concept in the middle of the Bible in Ezekiel and at the end in Revelation suggest Heaven will be our Eden, a perfect paradise to dwell in safety once our bodies have died. It is a wonderful scene that in our stressful, challenging lives we can only crave. The writer of Psalm 23 said the same:

"God is my guide; I have all that I need.

"God lets me rest in green meadows; and leads me beside peaceful streams.

"God renews my strength and guides me along right paths. Even when I go through the most difficult and fearful of times, I will not be afraid because You are close beside me.

“You protect and comfort me. You give me the nourishment I need.

“You love to meet with me and bless me. I am precious to You.

“My life overflows with blessings. Your goodness and unconditional love will accompany me throughout my life, and I will live in the house of God for eternity.”

A comfort indeed for all those who have lost someone dear; or fear they themselves will be lost.

I have never had a vision such as the one John had in Revelation. I have never seen God or Heaven, but I have on several occasions known God’s help and support in difficult times, experienced God’s power and loving intervention in my life, and the sense that I matter to God. There are many times I have not known what to do in a situation, or needed help in making an important decision. I have found God to be a comforter, healer, provider and many other things.

This is when the whole inexplicable conundrum of suffering leaps in, for the wounds have to be there for God to heal them. The sick have to be sick for God to heal them. We have to experience death before we can have a full revelation of God and what this is really all about. Sometimes it is as if suffering creates the way for our spirit to connect with the heart of God. In this way, we can sift through our sufferings and our trials and discover the enormous treasure that lies within.

The Ogre

But a God who is all love, power and passion is not how God has traditionally been described. God is often portrayed by Church and religion as judgmental and harsh, forcing people to behave themselves and act rightly with the threat of hell for those who don’t conform. People are labelled as “sinners”, with Christianity offering the solution to this sinful state, but to receive it we have to mould ourselves to fit the perfect Christian image; what Church culture says we should look like and be like. The emphasis is often on sin and what we must do to pay for our sins, to make ourselves good enough for God (and for Church).

This image of God that is often portrayed is what people and the Church over the centuries have said about God. But were they right? Like

I wanted to say to Richard Dawkins that day, "The God religion has created does not exist; but *something* exists!"

The whole concept of God is so vast and complex, and information sometimes comes from an unreliable source; it has been very dependent on how Church fathers interpreted the Bible and allowed that interpretation to steer Church thought and beliefs. Those interpretive skills may have been found wanting. There is a high chance they emphasised certain aspects of God's nature over others — over the most important. And as much as the Church may have inaccurately portrayed God, it may have got sin wrong too; we soon suggest that we may not really know what sin is.

There are some rogue ancient texts in the Bible where God is portrayed as an angry God, harshly punishing people, but the origin and meaning of these texts is a matter of great contention. The stories we have heard and the majority of stories in the Bible reveal a God who is bursting with love for all of us, and has an all-inclusive eternal party waiting for us in paradise. And to get there, we may not have to jump through as many religious hoops as we have previously thought.

But how do we know? How do we know what God is like? The dream of paradise seems too good to be true — pie in the sky or wishful thinking as we travel through life, sometimes enduring hardship that makes us unable to comprehend the idea of a loving, caring God.

But they are mentioned repeatedly from reports in the Bible or from contemporary life where people have either seen this in a vision or say they have experienced it in some way. We cannot determine *details* from these descriptions and stories, that is not what they are there for, but the concept is the same throughout: a stunning place where evil is absent, the needs of all people are provided for — including, if it's our thing, fine wine and sumptuous roast lamb, and we can meet with God face to face.

I'm sure many of us would choose to grab this opportunity and run with it if we knew it to be true. This is why it is vital to experience God for ourselves, not go on second hand information, even if it is the full weight of the Church saying it. We might have heard oysters are delicious (and have other benefits...) but we won't just rely on other people's stories of what oysters are like, we'll have one ourselves.

Oysters are there for everyone who wishes to partake. So is paradise. Anyone who wishes to be there is welcome. And religion is not the key to the entrance gate.

Describing the Indescribable

Over the centuries God has been described in many different ways, but all are ways of describing something that is largely indescribable. Often terms use analogy; the use of words that compare what someone is like with something in everyday use, to make it easier to understand. These analogies also reflect the era in which they were used. In the society in first century Palestine where rich landowners were called lords, it was appropriate to refer to God as Lord, as that title afforded God the importance it was felt God should have. Shepherd was a title appropriate for a farming society, where people knew all about sheep and what a perfect shepherd would be. Father is another analogy, of God being the perfect father, with children loved, cared for and protected. This can also be a perfect example of an imperfect way of describing God; for those who have not had a good experience of a father figure in their lives, calling God Father can cause great distress. The attribution of male titles reflects the patriarchal society the Bible was written in, not physical truth about God's gender.

People describe God as strong, trustworthy, faithful and good. God is portrayed as a lion (Isaiah 31:4), an eagle (Deuteronomy 32:11), a light (Psalm 27:1), fire (Hebrews 12:29), a fountain (Psalm 36:9), a rock (Deuteronomy 32:4), a hiding place (Psalm 119:114), a tower (Proverbs18:10), a shield (Ps. 84:11), life partner (Isaiah 54:5), parent (Deuteronomy 32:6), protector (Psalm 121), just and righteous judge (Isaiah 33:22), healer (Exodus 15:26), all representing what people experienced or how they might describe God. There are many more. Fascinatingly, as Amy saw God in her death experience, she describes God as 'they', not it or him/her. It may be that if we had the chance to see God it may demolish commonly held views of what God is like.

Just as people in the ancient world referred to God in ways relevant for them, so today we can refer to God in ways that are helpful to us. So, if we want to call God lover, friend, music idol, film star, rescuer, we can. Imagine an SAS soldier with huge, pulsating muscles coming to rescue us from a war zone, or a fireman running towards us to save us from a fire, or a gorgeous doctor saving our life, or that teacher at high school we had a crush on. So that we can understand and know God we must use language that we understand today. The many ways God is described in the Bible were powerful titles in that culture; God is not actually a lion, or a shepherd or a king, but people used those analogies to make this indescribable God understandable for them. It is the same for us, we don't need to use those ancient titles to describe God, we can create our own, ones relevant for us today. God is what we need God to be, and it has always been that way.

God can morph to become exactly what we need, in any context. When you need to know that God is strong, you will find strength. When you need understanding and loving, God is exactly that. To the widow God is a husband, to the orphan, a parent. To the employee, the best CEO. The best manager, leader, instigator, team player. God can be your life coach, counsellor or psychologist. God can be the pinnacle of our innate desire for love, affection and understanding that we often cannot find in life.

The stories of God interjecting into people's lives in profound and relevant ways hint that God knows us better than we know ourselves, so our experience of God will be what we need it to be, even if we do not know what we need or if we are in such a difficult situation that we cannot see a way forward. Another image is of an eagle, and us sitting under the shelter of the eagle's wings, protected, safe and secure when danger comes. It is, of course, only an image, but it represents the idea of God shielding us, protecting us, giving us shelter and security when life goes awry. The images of God in the Bible are always positive and helpful for those who cry out to God for help. God always responds. Many have experienced God descending upon their bodies and lives with a powerful love when they are in need. Sometimes we stand astonished, in awe that this awesome God-figure would help us. Our troubles can fade to insignificance when we touch the heart of God.

When we feel helpless, when we do not know where to turn and there appears to be no hope, wherever we are, however we wish, we can cry out to God. Imagine God is there beside us, ready to help. We can ask for whatever we want, and then wait for God to respond, and just see what God does.

These images portray how God has the ability to reshuffle our lives, demolish the many walls we build around ourselves, throw upon us an experience of God that blows our minds and gives us a new perspective that makes our troubles seem less significant. They show how God relates to us, how God reaches out to us, wishing to be close to us and to help us live our lives to the full; to experience all the wonders God has for us, and all the amazing blessings that come from knowing God. Who knows what wonderful experiences are yet to come, and they might be different from anything anyone has experienced so far. There are many stories waiting to be told.

Tower of Strength

People have always built towers. A convenient way of watching out for enemies, towers were built into castle structures from the tenth century onwards as part defence, but also as shelter if the castle were besieged. The tower, or keep, would have been the last resort where inhabitants could seek shelter in times of attack. You would need your tower to be strong, able to keep you safe and prevent the enemy getting in, but also provide for your needs while being besieged; you need water, food, warmth and ammunition. In a world where no one would come to your rescue if the enemy attacks, you need your place of shelter to be your only defence. It had to be strong, trustworthy, and secure.

God is described in Proverbs 18:10 as a strong tower: "People run to God and are safe." God is described as a place to turn to in times of need or distress that is strong and can help the situation and provide for our needs. Yet God is not bricks and mortar; this is an analogy that portrays how we have a place we can run to in a spiritual sense, but which can also give us real physical help in time of need. Thousands have sought solace in God's protection over the centuries and gained great benefit from it. There is that lovely old hymn that is perhaps twee in places and employing older language, but nonetheless meaningful for some:

What a friend we have in Jesus,
All our sins and griefs to bear!
What a privilege to carry
Everything to God in prayer!

Oh, what peace we often forfeit,
Oh, what needless pain we bear,
All because we do not carry
Everything to God in prayer!

Have we trials and temptations?
Is there trouble anywhere?
We should never be discouraged—
Take it to the Lord in prayer.

Can we find a friend so faithful,
Who will all our sorrows share?
Jesus knows our every weakness;
Take it to the Lord in prayer.

Are we weak and heavy-laden,
Cumbered with a load of care?
Precious Savior, still our refuge—
Take it to the Lord in prayer.

Do thy friends despise, forsake thee?
Take it to the Lord in prayer!
In His arms He'll take and shield thee,
Thou wilt find a solace there.

Blessed Savior, Thou hast promised
Thou wilt all our burdens bear;
May we ever, Lord, be bringing
All to Thee in earnest prayer.

Soon in glory bright, unclouded,

There will be no need for prayer—
Rapture, praise, and endless worship
Will be our sweet portion there.[84]

Of course, we could not move on without exploding the common ideas about prayer. Traditional images of prayer and liturgy can be useful for some, but prayer can be what you want it to be. You can talk, whisper, think, write, draw, type, meditate, dance around the kitchen singing along to Abba or Simon and Garfunkel. You can do anything you like, as often as you like, for as long as you like. The word prayer conjures up a typical image, but I prefer to see it as a communication or contact, a way of us chatting to God. It could be mindfulness. It can be whatever we need it to be. Sometimes we are so exhausted we don't have the strength to communicate, and then a mere thought is enough.

The poetic nature of many of the descriptions of Heaven and God mean they should not be taken literally. But poetry is not fake news. The detail may be uncertain but the concept is there, that of God being a source of strength and help in time of need, of paradise welcoming us after we finish this life, and death not being the awful thing we think it is, but instead being the start of a new, unlimited, everlasting and beautiful life with God in paradise. Death is obviously distressing and something many of us fear, but as we approach the doors of death it is eased by the hope of something better; our dream holiday. The night he died, an elderly friend got out of bed and walked unsteadily across the room. His carer gently asked where he was going. He replied, 'To Heaven.' He died later that night. His response was a huge solace for his loved ones.

The physical shelter and provision of basic needs are one thing, but the unlimited presence of God is something much greater than any of us can imagine. This alone is paradise, it is all your needs met in one go, it is wonderful. Yet it is not limited to that time after the doors of this physical life have closed on us; it is real help now, to get through life and not only survive, but thrive.

One remarkable example of how this God-being can look after us is that of Julie and Glen, who had been sailing around the world for five years and were in Thailand. They wanted to spend Christmas with other sailors who lived on their boats, on the stunning beaches near Phuket. However, Glen had been having trouble passing urine for some time, and just a few weeks before Christmas, as they pulled into the Thai bay where they were planning to stay, Glen began peeing blood. Realising they had to get back to the USA quickly for medical treatment, they searched for a place to leave their boat. However, all the marinas were full. At this time of year every sailor in the area had planned to celebrate Christmas in these stunning bays, and there was no spare mooring for them.

Desperate, they were told of a small marina up a narrow boggy creek, used by locals for fishing. With few services and little security for boats it was not ideal, but they realised it was their only option. They had to put their precious boat, their only home, in this unsatisfactory place and fly off to the USA.

Once back in their home country, things quickly escalated with Glen's medical treatment. He was told he had bladder cancer, and needed months of treatment. They settled in for Christmas, and for the foreseeable future.

It was on Boxing Day that the shock came. Woken at dawn, they were told by a relative that a tsunami had hit the area where their boat was stored, and that the news was unlikely to be good. It was 2004, and an earthquake out at sea had sparked a tsunami, and caused widespread devastation and much loss of life. Assuming their boat was gone, Julie and Glen were struck with the realisation that if Glen had not had his health concern, they would have been on that boat, and most likely lost themselves.

After some time, they were able to locate friends who went and checked the marina their boat had been on. They were amazed to find that the narrow boggy creek they had so disliked, had protected their boat. The marina was untouched, and their boat was safe. If they had been able to get space in their chosen marina before Christmas, their boat and all their possessions would have been lost. That boat was their only home and everything they owned was on board.

Julie and Glen were not religious people; they did not attend church or express an overly extravagant faith. But they did have a subtle faith, a discreet sense of a God-being that exists, and that helped them that day. After realising how close to death they had come, they held their heads high and quietly whispered a little, 'Thank you.'

That thank you got much louder when after Glen's cancer treatment failed, he was given the bad news that a scan showed he must have major surgery. A second scan was needed to ascertain how big the surgery would be. They prayed hard. Then, as they attended an appointment to receive the result of this second scan, they walked in to a beaming doctor who happily told them they were not quite sure what had happened but Glen's cancer did not appear on that second scan at all; he was cured, and his cancer had gone.

They returned to their boat and helped with the clean-up effort after the tsunami. They remained humbled by the events that had unfolded, grateful that they had been saved, but also aware of the great loss of life from the events that Boxing Day. They have since dedicated their lives to humanitarian aid work. You can read of their sailing adventures in Julie Bradley's exciting books, *Escape from the Ordinary*, and *Crossing Pirate Waters*.[85]

Feeling the Love

If you were to describe Mother Teresa, you might say she loved all people unconditionally. She reached out to those who literally had nothing, and helped them. She exuded love, as though it were her essence. Or imagine a huge vat of chocolate in a chocolate factory. Lots of components go in, but the result is a delicious blend of yumminess that is chocolate. If you pour it, it pours as sumptuous chocolate.

We know this because we know about Mother Theresa and others like her, and we know what chocolate is, or the best wine, or Michelin star delicacies. We devour juicy steaks with a delicious Merlot in the company of our favourite people, or soak in the hot sun beside golden beaches with the crystal clear ocean lapping the shore. We don't just eat, we don't just bathe, we *experience* them; a whole series of emotions is behind each one of our favourite things.

In the same way, God *is* love. This is a concept that runs throughout the Bible and is consistent in people's experiences, and so we can surmise that God's physiology somehow has a large component of this powerful love. When I felt God resting on my body as I lay on the floor as a damaged teenager that day, it felt like a phenomenal, powerful, healing force. It was God, and it was incredible. This love is a power, a force, a knowledgeable trustworthy strength.

This love is unfailing. It does not stop or choose to suddenly dislike someone for what they do, so all those so-called sins may not be as important as we have been led to believe. It lasts for eternity and nothing can separate us from it. God loves us with a radical, unstoppable, powerful love, a love that forces God to reach out to us and bless us. A love that makes God desperate for us to be close to God and experience life with God once we have died.[86]

"This love surpasses knowledge… May you experience the love of God, though we cannot fully understand it. Then you will be filled with all the life and power that comes from God." These words come from Ephesians 3:19, and suggest that although we may never fully understand God's love, we can certainly experience it, although it is something you cannot easily describe or understand until you have experienced it. Experiencing God is an incredible phenomenon and the memory of it never leaves you. It is this memory that gives us inner strength. We need this stamina and vitality in our lives.

Life with God is presented in these texts and the experiences of many as an exciting love story, but I am not convinced we have ever fully grasped this aspect of God's character. Church and religion seem to portray a different God, one that needs us to follow the rules or we are all doomed. Yet my experience, and the experience of many thousands of others, suggests knowing God is an exciting and lifechanging, powerful experience. It is far better than any human lover who might decide you are not right for them, or never exist at all. This is how others across the centuries have described God's love, but when we experience it for ourselves, we tend to find our own descriptions. Imagine a divine fist smashing through the church roofs and reaching down to touch the hearts of those within, those desperate to know this awesome God but who may be trapped by the shell of religion.

Other texts suggest God *pours* love and blessings on those who are close to God.[87] This *pouring* suggests an image of a gushing stream of love, pouring like an uncontrollable gushing torrent continuously from God's being, like a majestic waterfall. You get a glimpse of the love of God in those moments when you see your child and feel that rush of love towards them. When you first meet your lover, and feel that tingling excitement for them. When you hold your puppy, when you stand on a mountain and see the vista of wonderful landscapes all around you. It's when a nurse has compassion for their patient, the teacher sees a child doing what they have been trying to teach them, when a troubled soul finally feels they like who they have become. It's like when you feel you love someone so much you would die for them. And yet these things are only a glimpse of the love of God. The feelings you get when you experience God for yourself in a fresh way is a hundred times more exiting and fulfilling than any love we might experience from, or for, others.

Experiencing God is experiencing this love, washing over us, cleansing, restoring, healing every part of us. Many of us carry deep wounds that have little hope of being fully healed. We can find we are held captive by our past, with no amount of therapy proving effective in bringing relief. For the wounded and the hurt, experiencing God's love pouring onto our shattered lives may be the only hope of comfort.

Yet love is an odd term to use for God. It doesn't fully describe what is going on. It's not a feeling like human love, it's more like a physical force; a power. The feelings people experience when God touches their life, those feelings of joy and peace, the overwhelming feeling of God taking over is this release of love. It's like dipping your finger in that vat of chocolate and then realising its so good you dive right in. God is bursting with love. Because God is love, when we encounter God, we encounter love and we encounter power. It's an overwhelming force that can knock us off our feet and change us forever. The day that happened to me, I lay there under what felt like a heavy, restoring power, a presence, God literally resting on me, God's power filling every fibre of my being and captivating my mind and heart forever. It was so good I didn't want it to end.

Yet this is why it is so frustrating when religion tries to define God and define the way to discover God. The structuring of religion and the harnessing of God has made many of us not want God. But in truth religion has not even scratched the surface of what is possible and what God can do. It is indescribably amazing. Anyone who felt God touching their lives would be instantly addicted.

Do We Believe What Others Say?

Many have believed things they have been taught about God by church and religion, when those things may not be accurate. We might have said we do not like God, yet we may never have actually met or experienced God. What we are actually saying is we do not like what we are *told* about God and about what God is like. We mean that we do not like how God is portrayed; because unless we have experienced God for ourselves, we are only going on someone else's words, someone else's opinion. So, we don't like their opinion of God, what they say about God, what they say God is like. But what if they are wrong? How do *we* know that *they* know what God is truly like? Do we trust other people's opinions, when if they are wrong, we may miss out on a wonderful experience of God?

We cannot physically dissect God or analyse God's being. We only have the subjective knowledge of what people describe of God through their experiences — what they have found God to be like — but this knowledge is better than several thousand years of theological discussion and debate, especially if our experiences prove them wrong, just as Amy found out in her death experience when she went to Heaven and met God.

These experiences and encounters people describe might conflict with some Church or religious teaching and therefore show us a God we may never have met before. Faith that makes a difference to our lives has to involve experiencing God in a way right for us, and so we really cannot go on other people's words or experiences. In order to know truly what it is like we have to experience it for ourselves, and then of course if we do not like it, we can reject it. At least then we know what we are rejecting.

Justice

A strong, persistent theme in the Bible is God's hatred of injustice. Stories suggest that God hates to see people treated wrongly, especially if it means they go without things that are essential for life. Today, it's hard to imagine dying from hunger, and yet every year around nine million people die from starvation worldwide,[88] often because of the actions of others. Injustice leaves us feeling mistreated and bitter, and often the person who has wronged us can seem to get away with it. Many of us face injustice in our lives, whether it's a crime that goes unpunished, or hurts that go unresolved.

Sadly, injustice is common. It can eat you up and leave you feeling helpless. Trying to get anyone to listen to your version of events can be exhausting, expensive, and get you nowhere. That feeling of injustice is like an urge that you cannot satisfy, a feeling of helplessness and desperation that you have no way of easing. It is the feeling of a mother who has watched her child starve to death while others throw food away. It is the feeling of an abused little child, wondering if anyone loves them. It is the widowed partner who has no access to the inheritance because they were not married; the churchgoer, abused by the minister and yet hearing them preach in front of many on a Sunday morning; the occupants of a car in an accident which was not their fault but the insurance company will not pay out; the family that loses their home due to financial problems that were not their fault; or people treated differently because of their skin colour. An ex-lover who keeps criticising you to others, or worse, to the courts; a parent who abused you as a child who now wants your love and care, and your reticence to give that love means they complain about you to others. A family feud that means you do not get the inheritance you are due, and so desperately need. Attacks that go unpunished, or worse still, murder, where bodies of loved ones have never been found, and no one bought to justice. The person for whom school was not the right learning environment and so they "failed" and were told they were not good enough, yet given the right environment they thrive. The worker who does a good job that goes unnoticed, whilst being pulled up on a minor mistake.

Many of us encounter inexplicable and often heart-breaking struggles in our lives, and this is why this all matters to all of us. This is why we need to explore, discover and embrace all we can about God, faith, life and our well-being. This is why we must sweep away the debris that hides God and stops us from benefiting from all God has for us.

It may be comforting to know God notices and is passionate about the unfair things that happen to us, especially if it seems the perpetrator has got away with it. When no one will listen and justice seems far away, we can offload it onto God, asking God to deal with it. What we need is to be free of the tension and stress that feelings of injustice will bring, feelings that can affect our wellbeing. However terrible the situation, the comfort this can bring can release us from the feelings of anger, hurt and bitterness which can swallow us up. We cannot move on from something if we are weighed down with feelings of unfairness and bitterness and these can sometimes affect us for the rest of our lives. Thankfully, God offers to lift these burdens from us and set us free from their grip. This can be a great comfort when there seems to be no way to get the justice we feel we deserve. We just might never find out exactly how God deals with it.

Jesus is What God is Like

There's something really significant about Jesus. Jesus is the centre of Christianity and is vitally important to the religion and to Christians. To find out more you have to turn to the guys who recorded what happened when Jesus was born and what he did through his life. The stories are quite remarkable; before he was born people recorded that God told them Jesus was going to open the way to God and enable everyone to be close to God, that Jesus' birth was a really significant thing and he was going to change the world. Ever since then, people have studied and analysed the person and work of Jesus to understand more about God, how we can interact with God, and what this all means for us.

In a similar way to humans, God is described as having a Spirit, mind and body; although this concept may also be an analogy, a way of describing something the human mind cannot comprehend. In basic form, Christian theology teaches that Jesus was the body, but wanted to reach everyone on Earth, and the impracticalities of doing that with just one man, meant that once Jesus died, He handed over to the Holy Spirit who can be everywhere, and who continues the work of helping us encounter God and live our lives. So today, when we encounter God in our lives it is the Spirit part of God we are communicating with. When people talk about God coming to dwell in your life and body, this happens via the Spirit. For some reason Jesus had to be born the way He was, and did what He did on Earth in order for us to encounter God freely. The innumerable accounts and stories from people who experience the palpable presence of God and encounter God in all sorts of ways, would not be possible if Jesus hadn't come. It is said that Jesus somehow made it possible for us to be close to God, and for us to encounter God today.

We Don't Need to Understand Jesus or the Trinity in Order to Benefit from It

Although all this had to happen in order for us to be close to God, have encounters with God in our lives, and have a future with God in paradise, *we do not need to understand this or grasp it in any sense, in order to benefit from it.*

The Church would teach that salvation and getting close to God is only possible through Jesus, and this may well be true, but I do not believe we need to say the name Jesus or understand what Jesus did, who Jesus was or is now, or how the three parts yet one God works, in order to benefit from it. It is largely incomprehensible anyway, and gleaning the full understanding of God's nature and character is impossible in this life.

If we want to understand more about Jesus and the Trinity there are reams of books we can read, but many people do not have time or the will to study such complicated theologies. Many of us just want to receive God's help in our lives. It is possible to be close to God without understanding the intricacies of God's being. In fact, even the best theologians and those who have studied this at great depth for years will admit they do not fully understand it. Many experts in these fields of academia will disagree on God's nature. One controversy that began in the early church nearly two thousand years ago and still rages on today is over the nature of God. It is likely that no one has ever grasped God's full nature, and our current theories, beliefs and practices on who or what God is and how God works may be incomplete or wrong. The Bible cannot give us full understanding and the only other way of getting the information is through experiencing God yourself, and I doubt one would gain a thorough appreciation — you would be too awestruck to be concerned with such details when standing before God.

This almost sounds too simple, but Jesus is God, and so if we pray to God we are praying to Jesus. It doesn't matter what we call it, the experience is the same. Jesus is not a magic word that allows us to encounter God.

It is useful to get a glimpse of what God can do by looking at stories of what Jesus did on earth two thousand years ago. What is recorded is only a small amount of what he actually did. John says at the end of his book that Jesus did so many things that if every event were recorded, the entire world could not store those books. The reports give us a tantalising glimpse; but perhaps that is all we need.

Superman or Supergod?

To be honest, if you had been one of Jesus' followers two thousand years ago, it would have seemed bonkers. Here is a snapshot of what he did with some contemporary comparisons showing that this incredible stuff is still happening today:

At a funeral where a widow had lost her only son – and in that society that meant your support and provision in old age – Jesus commands the man to come back to life, and he does. The woman, her son and the whole town are in awe. Comparing that with the story of Madame Jacques whose daughter Thérèse died from the snake bite enables us to see this is not just for the history books; it is possible today.

Jesus and the men with him were crossing a huge lake in a boat. A storm comes over them, and they are at great risk of sinking and drowning. At a mere word, Jesus calms the storm, and saves them. In awe the men wonder who on earth this person is, that he has power over the weather.

When John Wesley had that profound encounter during a storm where he nearly lost his life, he no doubt felt the same.

As Jesus is on a journey, a woman who had suffered for years with bleeding secretly approached him. She knew he could heal her, but it would be forbidden in that culture for a woman who was bleeding to touch such a person; women were seen as unclean when bleeding. This woman had been a prisoner of her illness for 12 years. She reached out quietly to touch his robe, knowing that was enough to receive her blessing. She is instantly healed, but Jesus knows this has happened. He turns, and when he discovers who it was, instead of judgment and condemnation, he reaches down, and lovingly touches her hand, praising her faith and granting her peace.

One woman received physical healing, but a whole society was challenged to its core. In the attempt to stay pure, society and religion had discriminated and excluded many desperate lives. In that one move, Jesus swept those religious obstacles away and began the healing of a whole society and in turn, the world. Reflecting back to the vision of paradise, the leaves on the trees that line the river of God are there for the healing of the nations.

Wow! For those precious lives, meeting God that day was lifechanging. People are healed in their hundreds of a multitude of physical diseases that had no other treatment in that era. And the stories have contemporary comparisons, showing that this work of God was not only for the history books, it is for today too. Today, testimonies abound of people being healed through encounters with God. We have told some stories, but more are occurring all the time, millions every day are experiencing their lives changed by this awesome God-being. Many stories have not been lived out yet. There are people right now awaiting their healing experience, their moment of transformation. Many are on the cusp right now of discovering God and having an awesome life changing encounter with God.

Anything is possible, but our healing is our own. Just as health, well-being, and faith is different for everyone, so healing and wholeness is different for everyone. For some, it is the dramatic disappearance of our illness, for others, the mental strength to survive, for still others, it may be a peaceful passing on. We are all unique, and our experience of God and whatever that looks like in our lives is unique. But these stories do inspire us to ask God for anything we want. When that baby was born two thousand years ago, the world changed. So did we.

In a sense, who Jesus was and exactly what he did to enable us to be free to encounter God in our lives is immaterial to us; it did not involve us and we didn't have any part in proceedings, it is mere historical fact, even if it is totally remarkable. What it does mean for us is that just as those who met Jesus were transformed, so can we be. And it doesn't matter one bit how we do that.

It doesn't matter what words or titles we use or what understanding we have, we just need God. It doesn't matter if we are alone, or standing among thousands. It doesn't matter if you are a faithful Muslim who calls out to God in desperation to help them, a Sikh who just needs to feel God's presence, a mountain tribe who revere their ancestors or the atheist who needs something life cannot give; whoever we are, God hears us and will answer us. Being united with God is not bought about by religion, or a particular expression of religion, it comes through a heartfelt response to God. There is nothing we should, or should not do, in order for God to accept us with open arms. This is why the reams of rules, beliefs and practices religion has developed over the centuries are like dust in the face of the awesome presence of God.

How do we Know it is God?

It is pretty obvious evil exists in this world, and for some reason God has not blown evil to smithereens yet. We do not know what evil is or how it works, the detail is not there to be found, but its presence is clear. A minister friend of mine was concerned that if we strip away Church and Christianity, we might not be able to recognise the good from the evil, and we might get ourselves entwined with evil by going down the wrong path; the original fears of the early Church and one reason why the Church became so focussed on its rules, beliefs and practices. However, in the same way God communicates with us to tell us if we need to change something in our lives, God also will give us that conviction in our hearts and souls if we are getting involved in something which will propagate evil instead of keeping us close to God. If we stay close to God, however we do that, God will guide us, and protect us from evil. We can easily go down the wrong path even with the full weight of the church trying to guide us. The multitudes of stories currently being told about awful crimes done by those in authority in churches show many unfortunately have.

At one time in my life, I was doing quite a lot in our local church, and an important meeting was due; I was part of a team presenting an idea to the rest of the church. I had a dream the night before, where I was walking on the flat roof of a house, when I realised the rafters were rotten and about to give way. I realised I had to tread very carefully or I would have fallen through the roof. I remembered the dream, but didn't realise its significance until that meeting. The meeting went horribly wrong and people were arguing about the idea, and it all turned nasty. There was one point when I spoke defending the idea, but on reflection not presenting it in the best way. I felt as though the dream had significance, as though it were God telling me to tread carefully in what I said, and yet I stupidly ignored it. The dream was right for me at the time.

Similarly, there is a lovely story in the Bible about God caring for people. "If you had a hundred sheep and lost one, you would leave the ninety-nine in the wilderness and hunt for the lost one until you found it. When you have found it you would wrap it lovingly across your shoulders, and when you got home call in family and friends for a celebration. Those sheep are precious to you and you would feel overjoyed that you had found it. In the same way, there is true joy in Heaven when a person discovers God. For a second God leaves the rest and wraps those huge, loving arms around this person."[89] Each of us is important to God, God cherishes each of us dearly, and wants to give us such incredible experiences of God that these become the best times of our lives, times that we might have only dreamt of or can only crave. They are there for those who want them.

So, what is God like? We simply do not know for sure. But experiencing God is flipping fantastic. God is like anything and everything. God is what we need or want God to be. God is ready to reach out and inject us with powerful love and bring a new incredible dimension to our lives that captivates our hearts and changes us forever. God is indescribable, but also describable, by those who have met God.

But do we want it? We might still say it is not for us, even if it does not have to be religious, and it does not mean spending our precious Sunday mornings in a dull church service. The best way to find out whether you like something or not, whether God really can break into your life and transform it and whether this really is all as good as we say it is, is to experience it for yourself. If God really is made of love, then jump in and experience that love, find out if you like it; and a divorce is available if you don't. Don't rely on second hand information. Oysters might well be delicious, but you won't know until you try them.

The best way to truly find out what God is like is to find out for yourself.

Chapter Seven
The Bible…

In the dusty upstairs room of a house in the town of Hippo Regius in 393AD, a group of bishops sit discussing something around an old table. The air is musty, they have been sitting there for hours, aware of the importance of what they are doing, and yet they know they are feeling weary. The sound of the cattle munching the dry grass drifts in through the window, chickens clucking in the distance; they will soon have to be gathered up for the night as the sun is starting to set. They have prayed much about their task, and yet this is not simply a matter of prayer; much thought and consideration has to go into this. What they are doing will direct the course of the Church, Christian belief, and in fact the world, for over a thousand years.

Hippo Regius is now Algeria in northern Africa, and what those bishops were discussing was which books were worthy of inclusion in the Bible, and which were not.

The Bible can be an Incredible Source of Strength

For those who find it helpful, the Bible is an incredible source of strength. When faced with sickness, disease and the troubles of this life, many have gained comfort from the pages of the Bible. It can be a source of great strength and encouragement that can make the difference between coping with suffering and feeling overwhelmed. Bible verses such as Psalm 23: "When on my journey through life I find myself close to death, I do not need to be afraid because you are with me" and the concept of a glorious life that we will enter into once our physical body has ended its journey in this world, bring much comfort to those coming towards the end of their lives. The vision of paradise that we find in the Bible means the doors of death are no longer doors of suffering and fear, but the way through to a wonderful new life. Fear of death is washed away and replaced with a reassuring hope and peace.

Or those struggling with anxiety or mental ill-health might gain comfort from hearing Philippians 4:6-7: "There is nothing you need to worry about, instead, pray about everything. Tell God what you need. You will then experience God's inexplicable and comforting peace which will protect your hearts and minds…"

Countless numbers of people have found themselves closer to the heart of God, able to discover for themselves a little more of God through the Bible. Millions find guidance, comfort and courage through reading its words. In fact, for all of us, knowing that we can take our concerns to God and be relieved of the anxieties they bring can be a great comfort. The Bible can be a great help to us.

It was 40 degrees centigrade, and a hot wind was blowing over the sand. The mountains of Jordan stood majestically on the opposite side of the water; on this side the soft golden Egyptian sand was lapped by the deliciously cool Red Sea. After a morning of snorkelling, we were exhausted but happy. The colours of the fish had shone as the sunlight penetrated the water, colours that you might imagine only exist in aquariums until you find yourself swimming among them. We were in a lovely hotel with all our needs met at a moment's notice.

But I was not at peace. I was at a turning point in my life with a key decision to make and I simply didn't know what to do. That feeling of nervous butterflies in my tummy had affected our holiday, and left me unable to relax. I turned to my Bible, blindly hoping for a miracle. As I parted those slightly worn pages, pages that had been turned many times before in the hope of discovering something more of God inside, they fell open on the verse "From today and beyond I will bless you".[90] Those words went straight to my soul, as though they were put there just for me, and their effect was instant. The worry disappeared in that precious moment, and with a new confidence I lay back on my sunbed, finally able to relax. I knew I didn't need to worry any more. Somehow, I knew that whatever decision I made, all would be well.

The examples of how the pages of the Bible can help us in our lives are endless. Some feel that God speaks directly to us through it, for others it is just simply comforting to read those words. In our many complicated situations, if there is little physically that can be done to relieve our suffering, if the healthcare systems cannot offer solutions or there is no route left by which help can be sought, we can be left feeling alone, vulnerable and helpless. To turn to the Bible and find stories of comfort, help and rescue, to read the miraculous ways that people have experienced this God-being over the centuries can bring great comfort and relief, and inspire our own journey with God. We need this in our lives.

Yet beliefs about what the Bible is vary massively. Some people believe the Bible is the word of God, penned by God's own hand and totally without error; others believe it is the words of people who were instructed by God to write down what God was saying, that God inspired their writing. Some say it is a normal text that God can speak through, others, that it is one of a number of inspired texts; that just as it was inspired, other texts can be too. Some argue that only the events it describes were inspired by God, not the surrounding text. For most Christians, there is no consensus on what is a hugely influential book that millions of people worldwide use to direct their lives.

As much as it is a great help, it is also often used to judge, condemn, and to exclude people from Church and from knowing God. I've seen people riddled with guilt because their Church upbringing has taught them they are sinners. I've seen people removed from churches because of a lifestyle choice when they wanted to stay. I've heard it preached from the pulpits that you are not welcome in church and you cannot be a Christian if you are part of the LGBTQ+ community. If you are allowed in you may not deemed good enough to be involved in certain leadership roles. People are reprimanded the world over on a daily basis for not conforming to so-called Christian or religious standards.

One lovely lady who was separated from her husband had fallen in love and was living with her new partner. She had many friends in the church and attending services was a key part of her life. Her situation was openly discussed in a church meeting and because of her relationship she was asked to leave the church. She lost many friends and her chosen way of expressing her faith.

The Crusades of the eleventh to thirteenth centuries were inspired by Bible texts that people interpreted to mean they should get to Jerusalem as fast as possible and kill the inhabitants. Slavery was justified for centuries partly based on how the Bible was interpreted. Today, some are excluded from Church and potentially from knowing God and are even persecuted because of their lifestyle choices.

All because of the way many people interpret the Bible.

Ask many Christians what the Bible is and you will get a standard answer: 'It is the word of God!' Ask them exactly what that means and they will stutter a little before stumbling to make up some answer to cover up the fact that they really understand very little about this book that they base their faith and entire belief system on.

This creates a problem. Over the last two thousand years the Bible has gained the status of being the very words of God, a guide for everything from what we should do with our lives to who is worthy enough to be members of our churches. It has influenced governments and law courts for centuries; in some contexts, its words have created political turmoil, helped to cause wars, and been the foundation of Church and societal practice and belief. Much of what Christians believe today is taken from its pages; and yet in a dichotomy that is quite clear but that Christians are not willing to admit, there is great contention about what it means and how to interpret it. Over many important issues intelligent, educated, committed Christians, filled with the Spirit and aware of methods of interpreting the Bible, will come to completely different conclusions about what it is saying. This book which is the foundation of the Christian faith is actually hard to understand and very easy to misinterpret. This causes a problem for God, as often the Bible is used to portray aspects of God's character and actions that not be true, it is often our own interpretation of its words. We put words and laws in God's mouth, and when there are so many differing views, it is likely not all of them are right.

This stems from one huge misunderstanding about what the Bible is. Over the last few hundred years the Bible gradually became known as the "Word of God", and this phrase has led to misunderstandings. Many seem to believe the Bible was penned by God's own hand, or dictated to a scribe who wrote down exactly what God said. And therefore, what we have is literally the words of God.

Millions of Christians are led to interpret the Bible literally, or, "what it says is what it means." You will often hear the phrase, 'This is what God is saying…' as a verse is plucked from this book and applied to life today. Because it is proclaimed to be the word of God, we are, of course, told to obey it, although we tend to find that Christians who use this method to understand the Bible do not treat every verse the same; they pick and choose which verses to take literally.

There are many reasons why this is not a reliable way of understanding it. These current popular beliefs that are taught in churches worldwide every week, mean God is disguised in a fog of lies based on errant interpretations of the Bible. Effectively, misusing the Bible perpetrates wrong impressions of God among people, and puts many off discovering God.

The problem is the Bible is a hugely complicated set of ancient texts and it needs interpreting to properly understand it. People are also complicated; if we read a Bible verse, what we think it means will be influenced by the whole wealth of beliefs we hold and the experiences we have had. We do this with everything; our previous beliefs and knowledge, assumptions and experiences will all add to our understanding of what we read and what we believe on a subject. There is no unbiased viewpoint; this is why people come to such different conclusions on a subject, and on the meaning of a Bible verse. Interpreting the meaning of a passage is complex, with many variables and considerations, and yet we tend to believe that understanding the Bible is easy and simple — what it says is what it means — yet what it means is different for everyone.

It is really common to find people who wish to "prove" something they believe by finding a Bible verse that supports their view. Even preachers do it, picking and choosing Bible verses to fit what they are saying. Verses are often taken out of context with not a thought to the different methods of interpreting, or the variety of meanings there may be. Many just use it to give weight to what they are saying. People often proclaim that what they are saying is also what God is saying because they can find a verse that agrees. Therefore, it has to be true. Yet this is soon to be proved mere manipulation.

The Bible remains an incredible source of strength to many and stories abound of God regularly speaking to people through its words. The belief that the writers of the Bible were writing under the inspiration of God may well be true. But herein lies another problem; the original text may well have been inspired by God, but every time we read it and understand it, and teach it or preach it, we are adding our own interpretation, which may *not* be inspired. No one reads the Bible without interpreting it; the preacher does not preach without interpreting it. So, the text may be inspired by God, but the interpretation may not. Sometimes a sermon or someone speaking about the Bible can be spot on, completely correct, relevant, and helpful to people's lives, but often what is taught and preached is merely the opinion of the preacher.

This issue is seen no more starkly than in churches where they bring poisonous snakes to their services, an action based on a Bible verse (Mark 16:18) that states, "Miraculous signs will accompany believers… they will be able to handle snakes with safety, and even drinking poison will not hurt them." So far, several worshippers and some pastors have died after being bitten by these snakes in church.[91] Perhaps it's not the Bible that is dangerous, but those who read it.

Shaky Foundations

There are several common beliefs about the Bible today that can easily be misconstrued, and lead to misuse of the Bible text:

- The Bible is the word of God, given by God to us. Its words, are God's words.
- This must therefore mean it is without error, because it is said God cannot make mistakes.
- God does not change, so what was said thousands of years ago still applies today.
- Anyone can read it, and see clearly what it means.

- What it says is what it means, or the "plain meaning". There is no need to apply complicated methods of interpretation — all you need to do is read the words and the meaning is in those words.
- Because it is the word of God it must be obeyed.

Combine all these common beliefs and you have a text that you can read words of, wholeheartedly believe those words are God's words, they cannot be wrong, your understanding of them is correct and is what God is saying, and it must be obeyed. This belief is prevalent today, and is the overriding way that many Christians will read and understand the Bible.

It may be obvious to some, but this is a truly powerful and dangerous way to read and use a text. We will examine now some evidence that challenges these views, and explore how and why we might want to use the Bible with a little more caution. There are several reasons to doubt the truth of these common beliefs about the Bible; and reveal that we are often misusing it:

- How the texts evolved from being a collection of writings useful for teaching about God to becoming known as the "Word of God".
- How the Church has dealt with the text, including changing the list of books included and altering what the Bible says to fit its own beliefs.
- Cultural influences in the text which may be more significant than many believe; revealing the influence people have had on the Bible text.
- Despite good scholarship giving us reliable Bible texts, we do not have the words as originally written. There are multitudes of translations and many versions of the Bible within those translations. They are all different, but they are still called the Word of God.
- There are many ways of interpretating the Bible to gain a reliable understanding and meaning. It is a diverse and complicated set of texts, read by diverse and complicated people. Issues of interpretation are vast and we offer a mere summary, but we conclude that we simply cannot say, 'What it says is what it means.'

These considerations reveal we are sometimes in error when we use the Bible. When for personal use this may not matter too much. When on that Egyptian beach, if I felt God said I would be blessed but I was wrong, there will be no great consequences. But when we use that text to consider whether the life preferences and actions of others may be incompatible with knowing God or being part of Church life, or for labelling people as sinners, pouring guilt and condemnation on them that may affect their well-being, or worse, some of the awful atrocities that have been committed in the name of God, it is much more serious. Yet stories abound of these things happening regularly based on someone's understanding of the Bible text — an understanding that may well be wrong.

There are reams of books and theories on the subject of how to understand the Bible, written by excellent and trustworthy scholars and evidence comes from all angles; theological, historical, philosophical, emotional and more. We cannot hope to include it all here, but we will explore and summarise some of this evidence to build the case that many are using this book wrongly, and that this is negatively affecting the lives and faith of multitudes of people, and perpetuating misunderstandings about God. Those who wish to can go into much greater depth; the aim here is to highlight the issues and suggest workable solutions so we can ensure we are using it correctly, and to enable us all to find God through its pages.

One of the issues is that modern Biblical scholarship has moved on so much and developed techniques that challenge long-held views. So, while many retain their traditional opinions, the facts are being disputed at a higher level. But again, much of that information is not filtering down to the those who use the Bible regularly, and even if it were, emotions run so high on this subject that many would not allow their beliefs to be challenged even in the face of evidence.

The beliefs about the nature of the Bible is an emotional and passionate topic for many. The task of this book is not to cause offence, anything that is said should only be right. Of course, if, as some believe, the Bible is the very words of God, true in everything it says, then it will stand up to scrutiny. If God has written those words, then God will not let them be silenced. But if the many questions and concerns over the nature of the Bible and how much exactly God did have to do with it have some basis, then we should be seriously asking those questions. Questions over the nature of the Bible, how we should understand it and what influence it should have over our lives are not asked so that the Bible or God is brought into doubt and disregarded, or to offend those with whom we might differ in our beliefs. They are asked so we may knock down the barriers to understanding it properly, free the Bible to be what it was meant to be, and free us all to experience God and faith in ways that are right for us, all obstacles removed.

The desire of many is simply to know God, to understand more about this *something,* this God-being that many believe exists. And if the Bible can offer us a glimpse of this God and help us discover God through its pages, then let that be our purpose for exploring it. The hope is that we can all explore God, faith and our own selves in a deeper way, and find relief in the complicated lives many of us find ourselves in. But first we look at what the Bible is, and how we might understand it.

Journey from Useful Writings, to Scripture, and on to the Word of God

Beliefs about what the Bible is, how much God had to do with it and what influence it should have over our lives have changed at the hands of people over the last several thousand years. What began as a scattering of writings loosely circulating in society and regarded as useful for teaching people about God, evolved to become "scripture", and went on to become known as the Word of God. This journey from being a few useful texts to becoming the Word of God was not as smooth as many modern Christians would hope or believe. It also offers some insight into how we should be using the Bible today.

As the Church was in its embryonic state, it was a chaotic blend of people trying to determine what this new faith should look like. There was no guide on how to do things and on key issues like who Jesus was, how one becomes a Christian, or how Christians should behave; people were uncertain.

Over time, letters were written to help guide people in the fledgling churches, and biographies of Jesus' life soon followed. There may have been up to twenty of these biographies written (Luke 1:1–4 says *many* had written an account of the events surrounding Jesus). The authors of many could not be verified but four began to be treated with more reverence and for ease these were attributed to Matthew, Mark, Luke and John. The authors of some of the other books of the New Testament remain unknown. Early Christians may have valued the stories and sayings of Jesus more than the wider structure of the biography or "Gospel". It was the same with stories of Jesus captured in Gospels that did not make it to the Bible, such as the Gospel of Thomas.[92]

Communities would have used whichever texts they felt were right for them, or were available to them at the time, as texts were often difficult to get hold of. Some churches or religious communities may have had either no texts to consult at all, or if they were lucky, they may have had sections of books or letters of the now Old and New Testaments. Many of those Old Testament texts were by now established as scripture but users may not have been aware they had been heavily edited over the centuries, with books compiled from scraps of texts and verbal stories.

When they did obtain sections of texts, they revered some more than others, such as the first five books of the now Old Testament, Psalms and Isaiah. What was given priority was slightly random; if Jesus or Paul mentioned an Old Testament text it soared in importance, despite its status beforehand. There was a chaotic scramble to find whatever would help them understand God, this new faith and what part they had to play in what was happening. The Bible that we have now did not exist in the early church, and any two church communities may have very different core beliefs—although in a sense this did not matter to them; what was important was their relationship to God, experiencing God and helping others discover God for themselves.

Those who wrote the New Testament books and who used them to teach did not view them as scripture at first, and they certainly did not intend them to be seen as the very words of God; that idea developed later. They knew *they* had written them, albeit perhaps inspired by God to do so.[93] The texts that many now refer to as the Word of God began as a collection of useful texts written by characters who wanted to share their experiences of God, those who had seen Jesus in action, met him, worked with him. As they knew they were dying out, those who had seen Jesus wanted others to know what had happened. Gradually, the writings grew in importance and were used to establish Church belief and practice, but access was only for the elite; most people could not read, and copies were handwritten and rare.

The big change came in the sixteenth century. A view that started innocently enough with Luther was quickly taken out of proportion. The Church had asserted that it held the authority on all matters of faith and conduct, but Luther truly believed this same Church was corrupt. Authority must lie elsewhere; and Luther felt the Bible had to be it. He taught that people were saved by faith alone, not by paying money into the church coffers. He also said that the Bible was able to be understood by anyone, not just Church ministers. Reasonable enough, but Luther never intended this to be taken to an extreme as he knew that those scriptures needed careful interpretation. But others ran with the momentum, the idea escalated, and the powerful notion of *Sola Scriptura,* by scripture alone, was born.[94] The Bible was given authority instead of the Church. This belief became one of the central tenets of the Protestant branches of Christianity that sprang from the Reformation.

By the seventeenth and eighteenth centuries beliefs had radically changed. Fiery preachers began to bulldoze concerns over proper interpretation, and began preaching that the Bible was literally uttered by God. This reached a peak in 1861 with a book by John Burgon in which he makes this passionate proclamation:

"The Bible is none other than the voice of him that sitteth upon the throne! Every book of it, every chapter of it, every verse of it, every word of it, every syllable of it, (where are we to stop?) every letter of it, is the direct utterance of the Most High!"[95]

It wasn't long before preachers took this view to extremes for two reasons. In the New Testament there are several references to "the Word of God". The meaning of this phrase is often uncertain but it became a label for the texts that we now call the Bible. One particular verse contributed to this phenomenon. 2 Timothy 3:16 says, "All of Scripture is God-breathed". In the original Greek this meant "*inspired* by God", but translations of the Bible that stated scripture was God-breathed rather than the more accurate "inspired",[96] led some to believe that God had indeed directly spoken the words that were embodied in that collection of texts those bishops decided upon in Hippo Regius that day. "All of scripture is God-breathed" does not mean our 21st Century Bible text is God-breathed—except in the minds of those people who have made it so.

The concept of inspiration is complex. The common belief is that the Bible text was inspired by God, yet confusion sets in when we refer to it as the Word of God, suggesting more than mere inspiration. Did God stir the authors to write in their own words what they felt God was saying, or did God literally dictate the words to them? If God had written every word, some Bible books seemed to contradict each other and there are obvious errors. There are also parts clearly written by various characters, who put their names against their work. And of course, there are the many different versions of the Bible in many different languages. All different, and yet all the Word of God. Which one do you believe?

Beliefs on what the Bible is have evolved, and have been impacted by people who have simply not been aware of the journey the Bible has been on, or the complications over using it. Some unscrupulous people have at times used the concept of the Bible as the Word of God to assert their own views, manipulating it and faith in the process. There is a key difference here between the Bible itself, and what the Bible has been made to be in the hands of people over the decades. The Bible has great value for many, but some have taken it to extremes and stretched it beyond what it is able to do. The status of the Word of God has been manipulated, launching it, and faith into a cascade of popular beliefs that have no foundation.

Someone now could be handed a book which they are told is the very words of God with often little attempt made to emphasise the importance of properly understanding it. Anyone can pluck a section out of the Bible and proclaim it to be the words of God — of course then it has to be correct, if God said it. Powerful preachers regularly teach that "what it says is what it means"—the words on the page mean what we personally understand them to mean, no interpretation needed. And so we end up in all sorts of problems. It is no wonder innocent people are led into misinterpreting and misusing this text.

If a verse says that "No woman should teach or have authority over a man, she should stay silent" (1 Timothy 2:12), then as the Word of God it must be true, and must be obeyed. Proper interpretive methods would take this verse with great caution and appreciate the cultural aspects of it. Yet thousands of crimes are committed against women every year across the world. Misusing the Bible contributes to this and other crimes.

Other verses are treated the same. Taken literally and applied to Church doctrine and practice and by multitudes of Christians in their everyday lives, they can result in the exclusion and judgment of many who are deemed to have a lifestyle that a verse in the Bible might be seen to condemn. Hate crimes against LGBTQ+ people remain rife. The causes are complex but in part, stem from misuse of the Bible. Often people determine what is right or wrong from the Bible, yet for many reasons the Bible text is unable to fulfil that purpose. Many will have suffered at the hands of those who use the Bible in this way, and still do, but it is not the Bible that is the problem, it is those who misuse it, and lead others to misuse it. Such corruption builds barriers between people and God — and worse, gives an impression of God that is incorrect.

Modern Bible interpretation and the study of the scriptures has advanced hugely in recent years and scholars can now be more confident in ascertaining proper use of the Bible, although in many cases disputes continue over meaning. Biblical interpretation is layered with complication and scholars have for centuries argued over meanings, but the academic world would generally assert that the text was *not* literally scribed by the hand of God, or spoken word for word to an Earthly scribe. It is likely God prompted authors and editors to write and inspired their words and concepts, and the human elements are well-documented. But the results from research often do not reach the multitudes who do not have access to this knowledge. This includes some minsters and preachers, who can inadvertently propagate wrong or misleading information. The Bible became the Word of God at the hands of people.

Was it Scripture or was it Not?
A Changing List of Bible Books

The contents of the Bible have been on a tumultuous journey since those early days of the church. As time crept by and in response to various characters who taught things the Church felt was not right—and to enhance political stability—it was felt necessary to firm up a list of books seen as reliable for teaching. By the first century BCE, a list of Old Testament books had been generally accepted, and the bishops sitting in that dusty room in Hippo in 393 AD finally decided on a list that should be included in a compilation they decided to call *The Bible*. The name came from the Greek work for book, *biblíon*.[97] The books they included are different to those in the Bible today; since then, books have been inserted or excluded at various times for many reasons.[98]

While some books were in doubt but got into the Bible, other books were viewed with more suspicion; they now appear in some versions of the Bible and not in others; and are called the Apocrypha or, hidden books. The books of Tobit and Judith, a few additions to the book of Esther, the Wisdom of Solomon, the Wisdom of Jesus, a letter of Jeremiah, additions to Daniel and the books of Maccabees all nearly made it to the Bible. Some Christians accepted them as scripture, but arguments over their status have raged on through the centuries. Augustine, that key Church father who wrote much Church doctrine, decided they were indeed scripture and wanted them included in the Bible. In the fifth century they were called into question again, and in the Reformation they were excluded from most versions of the Bible. They bounced in and out of the Bible in quite a comical way. This may have been because they contain information that did not concur with Christian belief of the time.[99]

The authors of some New Testament books used these extra books and so they must have been felt to have some importance. The New Testament book of Jude quotes from 1 Enoch, a book obviously circulating in the early Church, but which did not make it to the Bible. Jude also appears to quote from a text called *The assumption of Moses*, in a curious comment where the archangel Michael and the devil are arguing over what to do with the body of Moses. These two texts are used by a book that *did* make it to the New Testament, but they themselves did not.[100] Other key characters have questioned whether certain books should be in or out of the Bible depending on belief of the time. Luther particularly disliked the book of James and wanted it removed from the Bible as he felt it contradicted his core beliefs.

The Bible that those weary bishops in Hippo Regius decided upon is not the same as the Bible that we now have; the contents of the Bible have changed over the years at the hands of those who felt they should mould it to be what they felt was correct. It would be good to know how God feels about a collection of books that has been so revered as the Word of God, and yet has fluctuated and changed so much at the hands of people.

As faithful people today cherish every word as the words of God, I wonder if they are aware of the tumultuous journey this collection of texts has been on, how it has been shaped by people, and not always for the right reasons?

Altering of Scripture to Fit Beliefs

The Church has been a little naughty by occasionally altering the Bible text. As the church grew and developed its own doctrines and beliefs, what was in the Bible was sometimes altered so that it mirrored what the church had grown to believe.

Many central aspects of the faith are not found easily within the pages of the Bible, such as Church leadership, the Trinity and who exactly Jesus was. The Bible just did not answer some of these huge questions, just as it does not now for many current issues. In order to prove what it thought to be true, the Church had to force the text to say what it believed. Many translations of the Bible were made, some from the Latin, some from the Greek, and others from the Hebrew. When Luther translated it in the Reformation from the original Hebrew, the Catholic Church did not agree with some of the terms he used so they re-translated it, ensuring that the terms used would agree with some of their long-held traditions. The word "repentance" in older versions of the Bible was originally translated "penance", and from this a cascade of beliefs and practices stem, linked to the idea of paying for your so-called sins. Luther realised repentance was a closer fit to the original,[101] with huge implications for Church belief and practice. By changing it to repentance, people were no longer compelled to pay the church to delete their sins. A sixteenth century Bible translator, William Tyndale, was arrested and charged with heresy after his translations of the Bible concurred with much of Luther's and the growing Protestant movement's beliefs. He firmly believed that faith alone, not adhering to the multitude of church beliefs and practices, was all that was needed to be close to God. He preached and wrote and did all he could to spread this message but he paid a high price for it. He was hanged and burned at the stake.[102]

Outrageously, in 2011 the New International Version of the Bible, one of the most popular versions worldwide today, *changed* several Bible verses to make them clearer on their condemnation of homosexuality. Several words were altered in an attempt to clear up arguments on their meaning, including changing the word "pervert" to "those practising homosexuality" in 1 Timothy 1:10.[103] It seems if you truly believe something, you can alter the Bible to fit those beliefs, whilst still maintaining the stance that it is the Word of God, correct in every way.

Tindal (1657-1733), another Bible translator, highlights the irony: "It's an odd jumble, to prove the truth of a book by truth of the doctrines it contains, and at the same time conclude those doctrines to be true, because they are contained in that book."[104] Reasons of belief and practice are not the only reason the text was altered.

The original authors and editors of the Bible thousands of years ago were part of a culture very different from our own and many cultural factors have inevitably crept into the text. Part of the process of establishing what the text means is finding these cultural deposits; which are perhaps not what God would wish to say but which reveal the human elements, and form much of the Bible text. Some of these cultural features have crept into Church doctrine and belief, such as the status and role of women. One case is found in Romans 16:7, concerning a person called *Junia,* who is labelled a significant church leader. *Junia* was a feminine name, but it is believed that at some point in the history of the Church the name was changed to a masculine form because it was thought impossible that a woman could be called a leader. For centuries it was thought this name was masculine until early texts were analysed, and it was discovered this key Church leader was in fact a woman.[105]

Because of their presence in the Bible some cultural features became doctrine and were deeply entwined with Christianity and western culture. They are not essential for faith but Christianity adopted them.

It is doubtful that the people who made these decisions did so out of spite; it was a tumultuous time for the early Church. In these times of persecution, political upheaval and war they were desperately trying to establish Christian belief and practice, and determine right from wrong. The Church felt it had two objectives: to defend the faith, and to instruct believers. But there was the political influence after the state and Church merged under Constantine; dispute in the Church threatened state stability. The Church had to retain its authority and the Bible was their best asset. The teaching of the Church and the teaching of the Bible had to agree.

One crisis was over who Jesus was. Was He man or God, or both? This man had changed the world and faith, and so the question was important. The existence of Jesus and mention of the Holy Spirit led to the key Christian belief of the Trinity. Yet early versions of the book of 1 John were discovered to not contain verse 5:7, "There are three in Heaven, the Father, the Word, and the Spirit. These three are one". This verse appears in the later translations, but its absence in the earlier texts probably means it was added by the early Church to give credence to the idea of the trinity and to counter heresies about the nature of Jesus. The Trinity otherwise only has one clear reference in the New Testament, and yet this became a key doctrine in the Christian faith.[106] These changes may indeed be minor but they highlight the challenge of disentangling the influence of God in the Bible from the influence of people, and many have not been successful in this.

Amalgamation of Cultures

Some of what we find in the Bible is adopted from the culture it was written in. The people whose stories are told in the Old Testament lived in areas they shared with other people groups and that land was on a busy trading route. There would have been people from differing nations and cultures living together and sharing knowledge, telling stories to their hard-working agricultural communities and to travellers as they passed the evening sitting around their campfires after their evening meal. The early part of the Old Testament stems back to a time when writing was uncommon and only for the elite, and this campfire storytelling would have been their way of communicating traditional stories and beliefs.[107] It was a world of mythology, philosophy and religion, a world of characters such as Socrates, Plato and Aristotle, and of people trying to understand life, death, suffering and the natural world. It was a world where the gods had to be appeased or they would be offended; you had to do all you could to please them, even sacrificing your own children.

Some of these stories, concepts and myths from ancient times crept into the Biblical text as those cultures and their beliefs naturally became entwined. The true extent of these cultural insertions in the Bible text is the subject of much heated debate. It is possible the strange verse in Genesis 6:1–4, "When people began to multiply on the Earth and daughters were born to them, the sons of God thought they were beautiful, and married whoever they chose… The Nephilim were on the Earth at that time, when the sons of God had children with the daughters of humans. These were the heroes of old, warriors of renown", was based in this mythological world.

In a world where little was written down, images were important. Biblical images such as cherubim and seraphim reflect the iconography important to that ancient world, and similar images appear in the carvings that remain from cultures that surrounded those who wrote the Old Testament. Often captured in images and statues of human or animal-like figures with wings, sometimes with horns, they were seen to protect people. The ancient seventh century BCE King Esarhaddon placed figures representing lions and other creatures with human features and wings made of gold to guard his temples. Nabonidus, a Chaldean king in the sixth century BCE did the same; he placed bulls made of silver and fierce looking god-figures with human features called *Lahmu* to protect them from their enemies.[108]

In the British Museum stand two examples, grand figures of winged lions with human heads, 3.5 metres tall that once guarded and protected the entrance to the throne room of the palace of Ashurnasirpal in Nimrud, around 800BCE.[109] They clearly didn't protect quite well enough, as they were found in the ruins in a nineteenth century archaeological dig in Iraq.

There is not a great difference between these texts and symbols, and the Old Testament descriptions of the temple; in 1 Kings 6 and 7 Solomon places two cherubim covered with gold in his inner sanctuary, their 30 foot wing span no doubt an awesome sight. He also decorated the temple with carved lions, oxen and more cherubim. Our perception of angels and demons may originate with these images originating from cultures contemporary with the people of the Bible.

As cultures overlapped and ideas and worldviews were shared, it is understandable that the writers of the Bible text took some of these ancient concepts and myths and moulded them into what they were writing. To them, they were a tangible part of their life, notions and beliefs that were relevant to their culture and things they wholeheartedly believed were true. Some concepts that have become embedded in Christianity through their presence in the Bible are not unique to the Bible or Christianity, and we cannot be sure *God* intended to put those images there in the text; it is possible they are mere human influence, although this is not evidence that they are fictional.

I had an odd experience one night while lying in bed. I had been involved heavily in a church service in which people had truly been able to meet God; people felt incredibly touched by God, some felt they had been healed of deep inner hurts, some had felt real peace for the first time, others felt their mood lifted and were inspired. God had been moving and it had been good. That night, I awoke to the feeling of something entering the room. I had earplugs in, and I tried to lift my hands to take them out, but suddenly there was a heavy weight lying on me that prevented me from moving. I somehow knew I had to shout for God's help, but I could not speak. I remained there for what felt like a long time before I was finally able to shout, 'Jesus!' As I did I felt this thing move off me, onto the floor, and disappear. I lay there, partly in shock but partly excited as I felt as though I had encountered God rescuing me from what I can only presume was a negative force. I don't believe we can be certain of the nature or activity of angels and demons, but that night I had an experience of something dark, something not good.

As I called out to God, apart from scaring my husband witless, it disappeared.

Other common ancient beliefs that may have been borrowed by Biblical authors include the ideas of a structured universe with three tiers; the heavens where the gods lived, the Earth, and the watery depths of the underworld. The sky was believed to be a solid structure, and held back vast waters above it. All have roots in ancient mythological language and all appear also in Biblical texts. Planet Earth was thought to be flat and resting either on pillars or floating on the seas, an idea reflected in the book of Job 9:6: "God shakes the Earth and it trembles on its foundations." Isaiah mentions the four "corners" of the Earth. In Genesis 1, a dome is created between the waters of the heavens and the waters of the Earth and this dome is called sky. In Job, God walks on the "vault" of Heaven, and there are many references to the "windows" of Heaven, suggesting a solid structure with access holes. Even the angels appear to come through a portal when they appear to the shepherds after Jesus' birth.[110] It was modern explorers who began to reveal that these things may not be true.

God is described in the Old Testament as a king surrounded by a celestial court, or an entourage of angels and beings, for instance in Deuteronomy 32:8, "God distributed the human race, according to the numbers in the heavenly court." This concept is also found in Ancient Near East writings, also called the "Divine assembly".[111]

The presence of something in the Bible is not proof of its existence, although there may be elements of truth. Ascertaining this is part of the process of interpretation, but there are some things we simply will never know for sure.

Praise and Worship

The same applies to praise language. Worship is something the ancient people of the Bible were called to do several times a year at certain festivals, and only to their God; and no others.

However, praise and worship are not unique to the Bible or to Christianity; in texts thousands of years older than the Bible other gods were praised too, and the language is very similar to the Bible praise language. Enlil was the god of the elements, and praises to him reflect the creation and flood stories found in Genesis. He is said to have separated the earth from the sky, and then to have broken the hard ground, from which sprang people. Enlil is one of the gods who becomes angry with mankind because they were making too much noise, and sends a destructive flood to wipe them out. His name means "lord wind" in the ancient Sumerian language, he is described as a mighty king, the greatest in the universe. The hymn to Enlil has been found on clay tablets dating from the third century BCE and the discourse is incredibly similar to praise language found in the Bible, such as Psalm 104.[112]

The ancient people of the Bible were not the first to believe in and worship one God either. The Egyptian Pharaoh Akhenaten in the fourteenth century BCE decided there was only one god, and that was the sun god, Aten.[113] The hymn to Aten is also incredibly similar to Biblical praise language. In these two ancient texts which are much older than the Bible text, we could be reading a Biblical psalm praising the God of the Bible, revealing the amalgamation of cultures, and how local language and concepts have crept into the Biblical text. The human element of the Bible text is greater than many might imagine, but this need not undermine faith. It does mean that where we currently use the bible to define genuine faith and practices such as worship, we perhaps ought to be more cautious.

The crossover of cultures is evident but of course does not mean we should not praise God. Many are blessed by standing among thousands lifting our voices to God, or singing alone and meeting God through our worship. To leave behind a challenging life situation we may have been trapped in and then stand and sing, "Long my imprisoned spirit lay, fast bound in sin and nature's night, my eye diffused a quickening ray, I woke the dungeon flamed with light. My chains fell off, my heart was free, I rose, went forth and followed thee",[114] is incredibly inspiring and can bring great freedom.

Or to find yourself standing amongst thousands of others singing in unity about how God has helped us, rescued us, and can rescue us again. Let more of us experience that freedom! It warms our hearts and rouses our spirits, giving us the perseverance to continue the complicated journeys we find ourselves undertaking. When we feel overwhelmed by the storms of life these songs can give us strength, hope, perseverance and an energy not found elsewhere.

But singing is not for everyone. Some really are not at ease singing or attending services with others. And we don't have to. Praise language is not unique to Christianity, and there is a theme running through the Bible that suggests singing songs is not the worship God wants; the kind of worship God wants is for us to be compassionate to others and treat people fairly. Yet churches everywhere will regularly proclaim that they worship God by singing, and some claim that this is an essential expression of a genuine faith.

Worship can be good, but it is not necessary. It might be that as we discover our own faith preferences we might occasionally listen to a hymn or song, but when and how often we do that is up to us. God does not prescribe a regular dose of worship to legitimise our faith or give us entry to God's presence. Frankly, some modern Christian sings leave one baffled, rather than able to worship. During a run one sunny afternoon my headphones suddenly blasted out, "Boom Boom Boom, get ready, there's a ghost in the room!"[115] This apparent worship song left me perplexed, once I'd stopped laughing.

Two other major Biblical stories reveal this amalgamation with other ancient societies and their beliefs.

Ancient tales of Creation and a Flood

Some stories from the Old Testament appear in cultures thousands of years before the Bible eras. Archaeological and documentary evidence has shown that the nations of the Ancient Near East that existed well before the ancient people of the Old Testament had their own versions of the story of Noah's ark and of the creation of the world and of its people. These stories are the oldest known stories to exist; recorded on clay tablets now four thousand years old and written in Akkadian, the common language of the ancient Mesopotamian people.[116] Those ancient trading routes ensured these stories were carried far and wide; and many versions have been found across the world where details have been altered to ensure they are relevant in their context. The stories were popular and would have been told with dramatic detail and acted out at festivals, or to entertain the elite.

Atrahasis (meaning extra wise), was a character who built an ark to rescue mankind from a flood. The similar epic of *Gilgamesh* also contains the flood story and the character here is called Utnapishtim, meaning "he found life". Local floods were common in ancient Mesopotamia (modern day Middle East), but modern archaeological and geological evidence has shown there was no worldwide flood; any flood that may have inspired these tales would have been only local.[117] One theory is that the tale of a worldwide flood was told in order to explain the presence of aquatic fossils in rocks well above sea level.[118]

The stories of the creation of the world and mankind also appear in these texts. In Atrahasis, the goddess Mami and the god Ea create people out of clay, so that they could work for the gods. There are several versions of the text, including the *Seven Tablets of Creation*, or *Enuma Elish*. In *Enuma Elish* there is a chaotic mass of water which is divided into sweet water, the god Apsu, and bitter water, the goddess Tiamat. They give birth to other gods, and there follows a dramatic tale of fighting and arguing over the universe, and several gods are killed. With their remains, the victorious gods create man to help bring order to the chaos.[119]

The creation and flood stories in the Bible clearly contain strong echoes of these ancient tales, and the current thought is that the people of the Bible re-crafted these stories to make them relevant to their own culture. Augustine, that great thinker of the early Church and to whom we owe much Church belief and practice, thought the creation account in Genesis a "naïve myth".[120]

For some it may negatively impact their faith to think that the Genesis account of creation is not literally true, that God did not create the world exactly as the Bible says God did. But their faith can remain secure. It may still be that God made the world and all in it, setting time in motion. We just do not know — theories of creation and evolution can harmonize with a God-being. What we are saying is that it probably did not happen in the way Genesis says it did. The evidence is conclusive; the accounts of creation and the flood existed long before the people of the Bible existed and many versions have been found, indicating that the authors and editors of Genesis moulded them from pre-existing tales. This may be true of other elements in the Bible.

The similarities between the Biblical text and the writings, images and concepts from the Ancient Near East are many, and hint that the human elements in the Bible text may be far more significant than many would wish to believe. Like an emulsion, it is hard to find and separate those cultural deposits. There is yet more evidence to consider, however.

The Problem of Translation

It is often impossible to translate a text word for word and convey the exact meaning as those words and concepts may not exist in the new language and culture, which means the translator needs to inject their own interpretation into the text. It's difficult enough, but the events surrounding the translation of the Bible are also quite comical.

Scholars had translated the Hebrew scriptures (much of what is now the Old Testament) into Greek in the second or third century BCE, and subsequent Christians who spoke mostly Greek used this translation. People believed the scriptures had been inspired by God, but could not decide when the divine inspiration occurred — was it to the original writers and editors, or did it occur when the text was translated into Greek? For some bizarre reason it was decided that the new Greek version must have been inspired by God, but not the original text. However, the texts had not been translated very well. These poorly translated Greek scriptures were used for teaching until the fourth century AD when many people were now speaking Latin, so a scholar named Jerome translated the texts into Latin, but was criticised as he used the traditional Hebrew text, not the Greek, and therefore, it was believed, not the one inspired by God.[121] The Church, who had the final authority on matters of faith and conduct, was using a dodgy text of scripture as their main source of information. You couldn't make this up.

Translation issues creep into the work of Jesus too. Some tend to treat the words in the New Testament biographies as Jesus' own words because that is how it is presented, but in fact Jesus probably spoke Aramaic, and yet the writers of the gospels would have written in Greek. This means that everything that Jesus said has been translated by the original author and then re-translated into modern languages. We do not have access to Jesus' original words and we can only get the *gist* of what Jesus said and meant. Similar problems occur in the other New Testament writings.[122] One has to hope that God inspired the translating as much as God may have inspired the original author. The same applies to Old Testament texts that were heavily edited, the original documents being lost forever—let's hope the editor was as inspired as the author.

In many Bible texts what the original author wrote has been edited and then translated many times, then different versions created within languages with minor differences in wording. Although modern Bible interpretation tends to base itself in good scholarship, the result is multitudes of versions of the Bible, all slightly different, and all claiming to be the word of God. It is a confusing picture that gets more out of focus all the time, and highlights that we must be cautious in how much weight we give to the Bible text.

Inconsistencies in the Text

There are also many inconsistencies in the Bible that are undeniable, but they are explicable when we consider the complicated journey the Bible has been on over the last few thousand years (see appendix 1). Origen was a Biblical scholar in the very early days of the Church and is another key character in the development of Church doctrine. He said, "On the basis of numerous other passages also, if someone should examine the Gospels carefully to check the disagreement so far as the historical sense is concerned… he would grow dizzy."[123] However, for Origen and many others, these inconsistencies are not significant because at that time the Bible was certainly valuable for understanding more about God, but was not seen as the literal word of God as it often is today. Those early scholars felt that if one could understand the gist of the passage, that was all we needed.

Uncovering the Meaning

Different types of writing need different ways of reading them. If you read a newspaper or a leaflet advertising something you would understand its meaning to be very different from that of an academic textbook. Law is treated differently to a history book, and a novel differently again. We naturally treat texts differently according to their type of writing. The Bible contains various types of writing; stories, ancient laws, prophecy, and descriptions of revelations or experiences of God, and these all need to be read and understood differently.

There are three main options for interpreting the Bible. Some believe that what the author meant to portray really matters, otherwise you can twist the text and make it say something it was not intended to say. The challenge is that we may not be able to ascertain the original meaning because we do not have the author with us to ask what they meant and we do not have comprehensive knowledge of their language, culture or worldview.

Another way of interpreting is analysing the text for grammar, speech nuances and words. But words and concepts change meaning over time, so this may also not be possible in some cases. Readers of the Bible today often take an ancient word and inadvertently apply a contemporary meaning to it, thereby changing what the verse means.

Another method is for the reader to interpret as they read and this is most popular today. We inject meaning to the text as we read, and hope that God will speak to us through it. Most of us do this to some extent, and there is no harm in using the Bible in this way, as a source of strength and method by which God can speak to us. The danger is in misinterpreting, and then doing something with that information afterwards, because it is extremely easy to inject our own meaning and then believe truly that this is what God is saying. In fact, it is often what *we* are saying, as we use the Bible to justify our own views. We can so easily make the Bible say what we want it to say.

Then there is the possibility of hidden meanings, or allegory, a popular idea among early Church fathers. If a text appeared too difficult to understand or didn't make sense, it was thought allegory, or the deeper meaning must be the explanation.[124]

Take the notion of lambs. Jesus is described in John 1:36 as the Lamb of God, quite an odd thought, until you explore Old Testament sacrifice. The people of the Old Testament had to sacrifice lambs to pay for their sins and appease God. The idea of Jesus representing a lamb was that he then was the top-dog sacrifice and he, representing a lamb, meant we do not need to make sacrifices any more to make us right with God. 1 Peter 1:17–19 also uses this analogy of Jesus as a lamb making us right with God. This analogy is perfect for the context, as in that culture they would have fully understood the meaning; not so much today, of course. Another analogy is in Matthew 13:3–9, where seed is sown representing the moment someone considers God. That seed grows and becomes faith.

Analogy can be useful for helping us grasp something of God. What is indescribable and what we simply cannot fully comprehend, we can perceive to some extent. But analogy is fraught with difficulty and it has been exploited in the past. People could make the Bible say anything they like and call it God's word (if it agreed with Church teaching); a problem that was ignored, and is still ignored today.

Misuse Causes Problems for God

The Bible certainly has been on a complicated journey. Beliefs have been fuelled by passion for God and one's own opinions, and these views can be highly emotive. It is not just a text; it is a whole belief system and it matters deeply to many people. Bizarrely, this text that can be a source of strength and help to so many, can also be used to judge, persecute or exclude others. Snakes in church is not the biggest problem; people use it to manipulate the behaviour of others, limiting access to God and defining the faith of thousands.

It is becoming clear that the current way many of us use the Bible can lead to misunderstandings. It is surely right to question beliefs that reliable evidence shows may not be accurate, but this does not mean we should discard it; it still has a valuable place. Unfortunately, the essential process of interpreting often does not happen; people instead continue to take a random verse and declare, 'This is what God is saying…' equating what the bible says with what God is saying, when actually it is *their interpretation of what the Bible is saying*. Often what we say about God, faith and what this all might mean for our lives is merely our own opinion, loaded with those preconceptions we all carry. This has the potential to spread lies about God and prevent people from encountering God and discovering their own spiritual preferences. This misuse of the

Bible obscures God, as we put words in the mouth of God, and condemn others by doing so.

For some though, the Bible remains the literal Word of God, spoken or dictated by God to people who wrote down what God said. Not even certain evidence based on modern scholarship will shake their belief that the Bible is the Word of God. Even Christians who do not hold such an extreme view often read the Bible with this view in mind. This is the paradox; if you ask many Christians what their beliefs on the Bible are they will probably say it is the Word of God, without thinking through what that means or implies. When the Bible is used for preaching and teaching, we treat it as if it is the words of God, assuming that what is written is what God would want to say to us without considering the complexities of interpretation.

It is convenient to have a text that we can apportion blame to, rather than take responsibility for our own actions and beliefs. Much like the constitution of a club or society can take the blame for actions, leaving the managers of the club relieved of criticism. We can justify discrimination because of what we think the Bible says.

But ignoring the issues only leads to misrepresenting God and faith. Many have not grasped the necessity of properly interpreting this complicated yet hugely influential book. Ignoring evidence that goes against beliefs we might hold because we want to defend those beliefs rather than challenge them, undermines faith, causes conflict and worse still, continues to uphold incorrect belief. It deeply impacts the delicate lives of those who have been affected by misinterpretation, including those who have been excluded from church life and from encountering God because of perpetual and widespread misuse of the Bible. It also denies much of the valuable work done by Bible scholars. Those who do so must stop putting words in God's mouth, telling people what is right or wrong and how to live, and only accepting people once they adhere to what *they* believe the Bible says.

It is hard to challenge strongly held beliefs, particularly if they are what the community you are part of believes, and particularly if we are taught those beliefs by influential people. Many have been convinced by hearing powerful preachers on flashy stages energetically shouting, 'This is the Word of God!' and 'This is what God is saying!' Yet the evidence shows the Bible is the words of people, albeit inspired by God, and those words have been translated many times so that what we have today are *translations* of the words-of-men-inspired-by-God. And the Church, along with multitudes of individual Christians, has created doctrines and core beliefs from these many-times translated words-of-men-inspired-by-God that often go beyond what the text can say. And so the whole weight of Christianity with all its beliefs, structures and practices, teeters on very fragile edge; a Bible that may prove not to be as clear to understand as we may have thought; and yet is the foundation of much of what Christians believe. The impact this misuse of the Bible has had during the last two thousand years is huge. It can deeply and adversely affect many people's lives. Such conflicting views and misuse of the text create real problems for God, and for those who wish to know God.

Shaky foundations indeed.

So What?

So, what can we do? Views about the Bible vary so widely and it is likely that Christians will never agree. The Bible is hugely influential in the lives of millions of people and will even today create conflict and tension; enthusiastic preachers will speak for hours from the Bible but their views will not agree with other, equally enthusiastic preachers. Who can know what is right or wrong when such influential and educated people, those who appear to have the credentials to understand it, come to such different views? Everyone believes their view is correct, and yet they all differ; an impossible situation, and one that makes it difficult for people to find God.

And so we risk disguising God in a fog of misinterpretation and lies.

In the face of such contrasting views on the meaning of the Bible and what we should believe, what do we do? The Bible needs interpreting, and yet interpretation is complicated and inevitably comes with extremely powerful, emotive views. Most people do not have the time or the energy to bother, and will just passively listen to that preacher and believe what they say; or reject faith and the idea of God altogether.

I had a discussion recently with a friend who is a preacher and temporary minister who is devoted to his belief that the Bible is the Word of God and is to be interpreted literally word for word, and that we must do all it says. Based on his understanding of scripture, he regularly preaches and teaches, among other absolutes, that gay people should not be allowed into church. I mentioned to him that there are various study courses that might be of value to him to help him understand the Bible and how to use it in a reliable way, and to ensure that what he teaches is correct. He replied saying he does not want his beliefs about the Bible and Christian teaching to be challenged by studying. It is a difficult thing, when people are so fixed in their beliefs that they are not willing to explore evidence that may challenge those beliefs, particularly when the person may be preaching inaccurate information publicly. Hence we must all be careful with what we are taught in church settings. Giving someone a suit, a microphone and a stage does not make them right.

Christians have for too long misinterpreted this text, the majority believing you can take it at face value, and do what you think it says, holding a belief because you can find one Bible verse that agrees with you. We have not asked the difficult questions or admitted that there are concerns with our use of the Bible. And yet we have used it to make important decisions. We have used texts as laws, based Christian doctrine and belief on it; we have used it to determine truth, when we do not fully understand it and are often misinterpreting it. Something needs to change, because this issue divides Christians, causes conflict and stops people finding God.

I believe we are using it wrongly.

It was never meant to be used as a book of rules on how to live, how to be Church, how to be Christians. It was never meant to be a weapon that we could use to tell others how to live or whether they are good enough, or that they might go to hell because of their lifestyle choices. It can't be that, because that's not why it was written. The authors of the various books never wrote it as book of laws that people should follow for all time, for us to determine how to conduct life as a Christian, and what to do if a person does not act as we believe they should.

The Bible is there to show us what *God* is like, not what *we* are meant to be like. That statement needs a brief explanation: we should use the Bible (if we wish to) to know and encounter God, not to find rules for living. The desire of many is to have a fulfilling relationship with God and experience God for ourselves in way meaningful to us personally, to experience God's refreshing touch in our lives, bringing new life and hope, healing that deepest part of our souls, not to have another set of rules to follow or to feel judged. Let's use the Bible to find God, and stop using it as a rule book to make others feel guilty for their lifestyle choices.

Many in churches will have the impression that we need to cleanse the Church of so called sin, and we each need to be as good as possible, because God will not tolerate sin. But defining sin is too difficult, especially when using an ancient complicated text that takes great skill to fully interpret. Many things labelled sinful by Christians today are simply cultural preference or found in the ancient Old Testament law. They may be wrong in the opinions of some people, but we should not put our own cultural beliefs in the way of people finding God.

Thankfully, the Bible can be rescued from its Church-shaped quagmire of condemnation. It is possible to pull it out of the pit of despair and to find God again through its words.

Not Law but Love

Even the Bible itself suggests that we do not need books of laws in order to know God. Jeremiah writes that God says a new time is coming: "It will not be like the old times… I will engrave my law within them, deep inside their hearts, and its guiding principle is love. They will not need to teach one another… for they shall all know me."[125] The time Jeremiah refers to is likely to be the moment Jesus appeared and changed everything.

Around 740 BCE, a chap called Isaiah began saying that God was giving him messages to pass on to the religious people of the day. What he writes is truly condemning and reveals God's view that religion is meaningless, it's people that matter. God releases a tirade through Isaiah, a damning indictment against the religious of his day.[126] In their feverish efforts to follow their religious laws they excluded God.

Tradition reports that Isaiah was sawn in half some years later as he had clearly made some enemies, but his words remain to challenge the pious. What was written about Jesus continues the thought that God would live within us, guiding us as to right and wrong, thus there is no need for a book of laws on how to live (including the Ten Commandments, they were not treated any differently). When our soul connects with the heart of God, that injection of love and power guides us for the rest of our lives. The Spirit of God that dwells in our hearts guides us. Whilst there may be much contention and debate about the meaning of many Bible verses, those who have heard God speak know God's words are crystal clear. So, we do not need to tell each other what is right or wrong because God will do that. So let's stop, and accept each other and our preferred ways of living.

We have not shown people God, we have shown people Church and religion. And God seemed to suggest to Isaiah over three thousand years ago that God doesn't like religion. Two concepts sweep away centuries of argument about how to discover God and what that discovery should look like; love God, and love everyone else. They indeed are found in the Bible, but also in the hearts of all those who have encountered God. We are not meant to teach others right and wrong from the Bible because God will do that for each of us.

We are using it wrongly.

A Glimpse of God

The Bible can give us a glimpse of God, inspire our discovery of God, and show how God can help us in our lives — if God did it to others God can do it to us. The Bible has a few places where it says God told the people to write down what they had witnessed in order to remember what God has done — and therefore can do again — suggesting that is a large part of its purpose.[127] People from cultures the world over gain much benefit from reading the words of the Bible, and finding strength and experiencing God through it. The Bible is bursting with stories of how people encountered God, of incredible events, the ways God led them in times of trouble and saving them when their lives were in danger. There are countless stories of God blessing, leading, saving, speaking to people, giving people dreams that lead to lifechanging decisions, of lives touched by the power of God and transformed, visions of God and of Heaven so incredible they were hard to write down. It is a sketch of some of the moments when God reached in and touched the hearts and lives of people, and of how to connect with this awesome God so that everyone can experience the same.

People have seen God; Moses saw God's face, so awesome he had to hide and not see God's full glory or the experience would have been so overwhelming he thought it would kill him. Isaiah saw God and said God was so awesome that only a part of God's robe would have filled what was then the massive temple in Jerusalem. Ezekiel saw awesome visions and had dreams of God. Paul, who was racing along on a horse, was stopped in his tracks by a bright light and a voice from Heaven, God calling his name and giving him his life's mission. People tell stories of incredible experiences that show us a glimpse of God and reveal what knowing God can be like.

We do not need the Bible to know God, none of those people had the Bible when they had their incredible experiences of God. Neither God's existence nor ours is dependent on the Bible. Our faith isn't either. God is there and we can meet with God even if the Bible were never to have existed, but if we wish to read it, it may help us in our search for God. God can speak to us through the Bible, but God is not restricted to speaking that way. The Bible as it is today didn't even exist in the very early Church, but people had wonderful times with God and the Church grew exponentially, spreading across the entire world. Today, it can be more a source of conflict and disagreement than of finding a fulfilling relationship with this God-being, but this is only because we are using it wrongly.

The Bible is there to show us what *God* is like, not what *we* are meant to be like.

Some believe wholeheartedly that the Bible was dictated by God to an Earthly scribe, or was penned by God's divine hand. Many have come to believe it is the very words of God. But our brief exploration of the history of the Bible and the complications of understanding it deeply challenge these commonly held views. The Bible is a compilation of ancient texts that people wrote in response to what God did and said. As much as it is full of wonderful stories of what God was doing, it is also full of cultural deposits; the words of the people who wrote and edited it, even if they were indeed inspired by God. It takes great skill and knowledge to disentangle what God would say from what people said.

This information need not shake our faith. We just need to be a bit more cautious in how we use it. We should all question whether our beliefs are based on fact or religious fiction, and stop using the Bible to justify our own beliefs or obtain our beliefs from it, unless we can be sure we have the skill to interpret it. It would also reduce confusion and misuse if we stop calling the Bible the "Word of God", when it is clear there is a large element of human design. It is God we need, not a book.

People have been condemned and excluded, when they should have been loved and welcomed. Decisions have been made about what is right or wrong when only God should do that. Rules have been made and access to God denied to some. Instead of discovering together this amazing God and all that means for our lives, we created a religion and pointed to a book of rules we made. And the fog disguising God gets thicker. It is time to change this.

God stands hidden behind a wall of rules and judgments that the Church and Christianity have erected over the last two thousand years because of how we have used the Bible. We don't want to chuck the baby out with the bathwater; I continue to use Bible texts and stories in this book to explore who God is and how we might know God. We won't ditch the Bible, just the tendency to misuse it and in so doing causing damage to people's lives and creating a wrong impression of who God is and how we might discover God.

Let's start using the Bible for what it was meant for, and what we need it for; for knowing God, and God knowing us. This might dramatically change what our churches look like, and many of the things churches do and believe. But this may be good; because after all, all we need is God.

Those key common beliefs about the Bible that are rife in our churches today, that the Bible is the word of God, its words are God's words, it is without error, anyone can easily understand it and as the Word of God it must be obeyed… crumble before our eyes. Yet in the ashes lie the treasure that is contained within its words; a vision of an incredible God, awesome and powerful, able to do much more than we can even imagine. A God that loves us all with a feverish intensity, and who would do anything for us. A God that one day we will see, face to face.

Chapter Eight
Who's In and Who's Out? And How Do You Get There?

I lay there on the hard hospital trolley in deep shock. How had this happened? I had been loving my life, living on a beautiful island enjoying the sun and the sea and living in blissful happiness. Suddenly I was here in this cold clinical room with doctors and nurses rushing around jabbing needles into me. Yet nothing they did could relieve that pain. Nothing could take away that deep agony that seemed to penetrate to the very heart of my being. I felt intensely cold and I could not move. I focussed on breathing and keeping my eyes open, knowing I could not let them close. Yet I could feel myself slipping away. The memories of the events began to fade, as if a cloud were forming in my mind.

I hadn't been lying on that hospital trolley for very long when I felt myself begin to lose the battle to keep my eyes open. I watched the doctors and nurses rushing around and I desperately wanted them to help me. But at the same time I knew I was fading. I knew there was nothing more I could do. I did not feel fear any more, I couldn't really feel anything at all. I gave a deep, resigning sigh, and I felt my eyes slowly close.

I suddenly found myself standing in a cold, dark room. I wondered why the doctor had turned the lights out, and tried to feel my way around. I felt dazed and confused, and shuddered with the cold, but I was grateful I was alive. I cried out to God; I knew I had prayed in that ambulance and so why was I here?

As I prayed, suddenly, a brilliant light shone around me and lifted me up into a tunnel. The light got brighter and brighter, and brought a welcome sense of love, peace and joy. I looked at my body and it was transparent, yet also filled with the light that was darting around me.

I was drawn deeper into the tunnel at an incredible speed and found myself focusing on the source of the light, which was emanating from the very end of the tunnel. The light was more brilliant than the sun, more radiant than the brightest diamond, as if it was the centre of the universe, the source of all light and power. Yet you could look right into it. I didn't want to look behind me as I had found the darkness too scary. I wanted to stay in the light.

As I travelled through the tunnel waves of light shot into me. Each wave seemed to permeate my very being, as if it were reaching into the deepest parts of me. The waves of light each bought love, power, warmth and comfort. The light seemed alive, vibrant and totally captivating. It seemed to be healing me, making me whole again. There was total peace and joy, this was not something to fear, this was incredible. It was the most awesome experience of my life.

I came to the end of the tunnel and found myself standing upright before the source of this light and power. It was an incredible sight. There was a scene of indescribable brilliance; like a mountain of diamonds sparkling in the brilliant light. Like a city, this place shone with the glory of God, and its brilliance was like that of a million precious stones. The walls were made of diamond, and the city of pure gold, as pure as glass. A brilliant, enchanting light shone from this being across the whole city. There was a river, flowing with crystal clear water through the centre of this stunning place. On each side of the river grew luscious trees; their leaves were used to heal the nations, and to heal the people.

The judgmental God of the Old Testament was nowhere to be found. There was only a vast and eternal presence of love, a being who loved every aspect of myself and was intimately entwined with my evolution. God loved me, and I was all at once humbled and empowered by being loved so much. I was in awe, astounded by what I saw.

I turned suddenly as a deep, penetrating voice spoke to me from the centre of the light. It was as though the light was a being; as I looked, I could see that its head and hair were as white as snow, and its eyes were like an incredible fire. Its feet were shining like polished bronze, and its voice resounded like thunder, or like huge waves crashing onto the shore. Its face was bright like the sun.

When I saw this being, I fell at its feet, overcome by the sight. But it laid its hand on me and said, 'There is no need to be afraid! I am the living one. I went through physical death, but look, now I am alive forever! Death means nothing to me, and I open the doors of eternal paradise for those who wish to come. God will gently wipe every tear from their eyes, and there will be no more death, sadness, pain or suffering. All these things are gone forever. And everyone is welcome.'[128]

Many are lucky enough to have experiences of God during their lifetime, experiences which give them a new perspective on this spiritual realm. Others are desperate to witness these things, craving an experience of God. Still others are ambivalent, not sure of what they really believe, perhaps having a hunch there might be something in it all but not wanting to commit to any religious ideology. Many people express a belief in *something*, they are just not sure what. If the existence of God and this spiritual realm were all proved true beyond doubt, most of us would probably reach out and grab it with all we have got.

The stories of people's experiences, whether from the Bible or from contemporary life, amount to some evidence of a being that is in existence that we are calling God, although it does not matter what you call it. With this evidence assembled from real experiences and the millions of other experiences that could be documented, we have an overwhelming number and variety of accounts of people encountering *something*. And there are multitudes more encounters and stories. We have recorded only a snapshot and the Bible also records only a tiny number of events, when people have been experiencing this God-being for thousands of years before and after the Bible was compiled. There are so many cases of supernatural experiences such as voices, dreams, visions or feelings, stories of indescribable encounters as if God reaches out and touches the heart and soul of those who are seeking God, or stories of diseases being healed or even people being raised from the dead. The many accounts from cultures across the world encompassing many millions of people mean it is hard to dismiss this evidence and say there is no God.

There are, of course, many stories of people having had near-death experiences, where they have seen a figure or a light, and these experiences have often prompted faith once the person recovers. But some doctors would rightly claim that the brain can produce such experiences at times of great stress; such experiences alone are not evidence for the existence of God or an afterlife. Some stories of healing can be dubious too, lacking conclusive proof of a miracle. But they are not alone; the evidence of a multitude of experiences that are many and varied is overwhelming.

We don't fully understand these events or the being behind them, but for those who have these encounters, they are blown away; forever changed, never to be the same again. It is also good; the experiences we have recorded are all positive and helpful for those who experience them. Where there has been dispute and evil acts performed, this is often done by people, either using religion as an excuse or just with some warped sense of what it means to know God and express faith.

This God-being that we have some evidence of the existence for must exist in some place other than the physical Earth, unless God really is Santa Claus, and lives in a hut at the North Pole. As far as I'm aware those who have visited Santa Claus have only come away with a plastic toy, not eternal life.

Just as there is some evidence for the existence of a God-being, there is also some evidence for an existence after death. It is difficult to obtain fact from the Bible on the subject of life after death as some features and terms are expressions of the culture of the ancient world, or of the visions and experiences people have, which can be so awesome and mind-blowing that people may not fully or comprehensively describe them, certainly not well enough to ascertain fact from them. There are also the complications over interpreting the Bible text to gain information. We simply cannot be certain over details, but we can get an idea.

It is possible that the concept of eternal damnation in hell was introduced as ancient societies wanted to get people to conform to religious laws; the threat of hell would create compliance. Its mention in the Bible is not confirmation of its existence, the route by which we get there, or whether we stay forever, but just as some report having seen a glimpse of Heaven, some also say they have seen a much darker place. The Bible is just not clear enough on the subject of Heaven and hell; but that is not what the Bible is there for, the Bible exists to help us connect with God, not give us a description of the set-up of the universe.

So, if God exists, God exists somewhere. It makes sense that there is something in the theory that humans can also exist after death in that same place, in that perfect world where we will no longer be separated from God, but will once again walk and talk with God in the cool of the day, standing with God face to face. We will see God as God truly is; and God will see us as we truly are, with the heavy burdens that we carry through life stripped away, much like the dramatic finale of *The Chronicles of Narnia*. So how do we get there?

A Confusing Journey to God

Over the last two thousand years Christianity has developed the belief that we need to do a number of things to be declared a Christian, be "saved" and receive a place in this cosmic paradise. However, I do not believe it is so clear cut.

The problem with Christians is we don't know what they are!

The journey to finding God has become a quagmire of confusion. There are several different theories about what salvation is and how you obtain it, and there is no consensus. Oddly, Christianity has always argued about what it means to be a Christian. You would expect, with something apparently so important, that it would be clear, but it isn't; over the years Christianity has changed what it says we must do to be "saved" and be counted in.

For the first 1500 years of Christianity, we simply had to be members of churches and perform the religious tasks set, such as sacraments like being baptised, taking communion, attending services and confession, and giving money to the Church. This is still the case in many churches. Today, some call themselves Christian because they were baptised in a church as a child, or because they live in a so-called "Christian country"; others, because they attend church regularly and conform to the beliefs and practices of their particular Christian community. In some there are strict dress and behaviour codes to adhere to, while others have minimal demands. Other religions have their own requirements.

Even if you choose to be baptised, churches do that differently too. Some baptise babies, some only adults. Some have full immersion into water, some a mere sprinkle. Many believe it is merely a symbol of what has happened already, an outward expression of an inner reality, such as when two people fall in love and start a relationship, the wedding is simply an outward expression of what has already happened. Yet others firmly believe that the act of baptism actually confers salvation.

Additionally, in many churches it is argued that you need to attend regularly or you are at risk of withering as a Christian and losing your salvation. Confession of sin is different too; in some you need to confess to a priest, in others you can sit quietly and ponder your own depravity. The practice of taking communion also varies. Some churches believe the bread and wine miraculously and literally changes into the body and blood of Jesus; in others it remains as bread and wine, acting as a mere symbol.

In the last few decades modern Christianity generally has taught that there are a series of steps to becoming a Christian: repent of your sins, ask for forgiveness, ask Jesus into your life, be baptised, and there is some expectation that a person should attend church and show some evidence of growing in their faith. And so we learn how to become a Christian according to that particular church's way of doing Christianity.

It is a confusing picture! How do we navigate this melee of perplexing doctrines and ideas? How does the average person know what is right or wrong? If you want to know how to connect with God you may be told different things in different places. Surely they cannot all be correct? And do we need to learn how to become a Christian if all we want is God?

So, there are hurdles to jump in order to be verified by the church as a Christian and be reassured you will reach that cosmic paradise; but the hurdles change from church to church, dropping the first hint that they may not be necessary. These things are what two thousand years of Church history has said, not necessarily what *God* has said.

Many people who reject Christianity and Church are more Christian than many Christians. I've seen many loving, caring people who prefer to reject Church, who display in huge volumes more Christian traits than many faithful churchgoers. The term Christian was a convenient name given to those who were swept up in that incredible move of God that started after Jesus came. Since then, this has evolved to be those within the Church, accepted because they conform to the perceived image of a Christian, and because they successfully negotiate those hurdles; the things deemed necessary for the Church to declare that a person is "saved".

We will examine some of these hurdles briefly to see if they are necessary.

The Problem with Sin

The problem with sin is that we don't know what it is!

Christians, and those wishing to become Christian, are told to confess their sins and ask for forgiveness. When attending the service at the Church in the Wilderness I was struck by how it focussed so heavily on what an awful sinner I was and how I could barely match up to God's requirements. The problem is that many people are good people who generally have not done anything wrong. People find themselves scrabbling around in their minds trying to think of something and dredge up what they think must be sin when asked to confess or repent. Or taking it to the other extreme and worrying over every tiny thing we think we may have done wrong, believing we have jeopardised our faith. The problem is we do not have a robust definition of sin, and many Christians do not fully understand sin.

The Christian concept of sin originates with that story in Genesis with Adam and Eve and a Granny Smith, where God throws the couple out of paradise, apparently fracturing the close relationship between God and people. How exactly this worked and what the beginnings of life were like are unknown; as we have said, the evidence shows this story is unlikely to be factually true and was probably moulded from ancient pre-existing tales. It acts instead as a way of describing the apparent distance between people and God in terms we all understand.

There are clues that the story of Adam and Eve is the result of a scholar's fertile imagination; after all, eating an apple is not the worst thing that has happened in the history of mankind. It acts like the parables in the New Testament; it probably did not actually happen that way but the story contains clues to suggest that our natural connection with God is not ideal, and at some point in our lives we discover and connect with God, gaining an element of closeness to God.

The story itself also doesn't matter too much, the existence of the Bible and all it contains does not change facts; we don't need to read this information to know that we don't have that closeness to God that many of us crave. If the Bible didn't exist, life would still be the same (minus a few arguments).

The Christian belief is that something fundamental changed at some point in the relationship between people and God that required repairing, although I am not convinced that anyone can be certain what the relationship between God and people used to be, and if it has indeed changed. It is taught that the key to the repair and therefore to salvation are the various religious tasks set by the church.

However it all came about, some have called the apparent separation from God "original sin" and Christians today will often label this distance between us and God as sin; which is slightly confusing because it is easy to think of it as things we do wrong when in fact original sin — us being distant from God, was nothing to do with us; we didn't actually have any part in it because we weren't there.

It is taught in Christianity that in order to repair this separation from God and remove forever this taint of original sin, we should leap through these prescribed hoops: repent, be baptised, take communion and attend church. But without a robust understanding of what sin is it can be confusing; both to those who wish to connect with God and those who wish to help them; the things we might get wrong in life are different from this apparent distance with God which seems integral to our being, and yet we have confusingly called them both sin. The so called sin that is attributed to Adam and Eve's vegan diet is different from the things that we might do in our lives that might be considered wrong.

Certainly, if there are specific things we are doing that are breaking laws they must of course be put right according to the legal system and we might feel the need to apologise. But this is different from any inherent separation from God.

Original sin can be a useful way of understanding the relationship between people and God but it is only an analogy. We do not fully understand the relationship between people and God, the causes of any fracture, or the solution. A repair is also not created by desperately trying to dredge up something to say when you're asked to confess. If repair is needed, repeating a prescribed set of words or performing actions we may not understand the meaning of anyway is unlikely to be effective. The term "sin" to describe our distance from God and the absence of that close intimacy we might desire to have with God causes confusion. The route to "salvation" may be simpler than we think.

It is hard to define what is right or wrong. Some things are obvious: stealing, murder, abuse, breaking the laws of the country you are in. Other things such as swearing, drinking alcohol, sexual preference or religious observances can be cultural or religious taboos, seen as wrong by some people but only because the culture you are part of would dictate that they are wrong, or because of our own personal prejudices. I remember once telling my mother-in-law that I had gone for a run one Sunday morning instead of going to church. All hell broke loose! She was horrified and said how wrong it was not to attend church, but only because that is what she was taught and she never questioned why. Yet when you examine the roots of some of the many religious rules and demands, they crumble.

Christians have often condemned tattooing, because there is a verse in the Old Testament that says people should not cut or tattoo their flesh. In fact, this law was specifically for the ancient people of the Bible because the cultures around them would cut their flesh and tattoo their skin with the names of their gods as an allegiance to those gods. Today, it is just personal artistic expression, but Church culture has continued to condemn it. People with tattoos therefore tend to feel judged in Church. Interestingly many of us do not condemn other things that the same Old Testament verses speak of, such as not cutting the hair on the sides of your head or trimming your beard, avoiding wearing clothes with different types of fabric, not coming to church if you have damaged testicles, and the more extreme, like stoning your daughter to death if she was found not be a virgin. The problem is we get many of our ideas about what is right or wrong from the Bible, and yet the Bible simply cannot reliably give us that information. Much of what is said to be sinful is actually cultural preference or the beliefs of the Biblical authors — the human element of the Bible. If we simply use the Bible to discover and experience God and do not stretch it beyond its capacity then we do not get into these problems.

Whatever the facts around the theory of original sin, the reality is that we do not have that close relationship with God that many of us crave, walking beside God when we want to chat about life or having a coffee with God when we fancy it. What we can do to be close to God will be explored in due course; but our stories reveal precious glimpses of what it can be like. Perhaps no words and no performances are needed when we have experienced the wonders of God touching our heart, soul and lives.

If God feels there are things we are doing that we need to change, God will tell us. The fact that God does this — and it should *only* be God who does it — means it is not the job of other Christians to point out things to us that they may consider right or wrong. The Church and the Christians in it have for too long been known for judging and attempting to make us comply with rules that turn out to be man-made, not designed by God. What people tend to do is disapprove of something, find a bible verse that backs up our opinion, and use it to convict the supposed offender. It would be much better to help that person discover God, and leave it to God to convict, if conviction is needed. Picking and choosing Bible verses in order to say what is right or wrong for those trying to find and know God simply causes confusion, propagates lies about God and about us, and puts barriers in the way of people truly knowing God for themselves.

This is why how we use the Bible is actually really important and improper use can have truly negative consequences. At best this creates unnecessary guilt and feelings of unworthiness instead of helping us connect with God; at worst it stops people finding God. I am aware of several people who had a strict church upbringing and have been left guilt ridden, convinced they are terrible sinners because that was drummed into them as a child. Millions of others feel the same. The stress that this guilt adds to people's lives is unnecessarily destructive. We simply do not know what sin is, and it is highly likely God isn't as bothered about right or wrong as many religious people are.

Being free of so called sin and right with God leads onto another Christian concept; holiness. But can we be holy?

Holiness

The problem with holiness is we don't know what it is!

There are several popular Christian worship songs talking about Christians being holy and set apart for God. I was listening to one recently and although having been captivated by it many times, I suddenly realised I did not know what holiness is, even though I had been singing about it for thirty years.

Christians would say it is the idea of being free from sin, choosing to be righteous and being ready therefore to do God's will. But as we have examined, we do not really know what sin is. The idea that you could feel holy because you are resisting the urge to do certain things that might not be wrong anyway is questionable. Holiness is a remnant from the Old Testament, where the ancient people of the Bible record that they were told by God to be holy and set apart, to be different from other people by loving just their one God, and caring for everyone in their society; showing love to everyone regardless of status or lifestyle. Some Bible books record in a historical sense that they did not manage to do this; they instead believed holiness was adhering to religious laws. Sounds familiar.

Those early Church controversies also resulted in some people teaching that we all had to be perfect, although many others realised this just was not possible. There was an argument going on between Augustine who said we all have a natural tendency to sin, and a chap called Pelagius who thought we must all aim for perfection.[129] It seems people have never been completely clear on what it takes to know God, and how we should act once we do. No wonder many of us are confused! Some Christians like to retain this sense of being set apart, being different, being the perfect Christian, with an element of being better than others, probably stemming from their reading of the Bible. In fact, holiness, or a "faithful Christian", in many Christian circles largely encompasses that typical image, of the white, western middle class, married, heterosexual person with children who works hard, dresses smartly and faithfully adheres to Church teaching. Our churches are full of them! Christianity has created a vision of holiness based on this image; the model Christian. Anyone who does not conform to this ideal is probably discussed in many church meetings about whether they should be allowed in or not. We have created a culture which condemns any deviation from this holiness image and in the process labelling personal differences as wrong or sinful.

We are all the same, and we all connect to God in the same way. There is no perfect image to try to achieve in order to connect with God and we don't need to perform a physical act in order for our hearts and souls to connect with the heart of God. The concept of having to adhere to the image of the perfect Christian in order to be verified as being "saved" creates obstacles to knowing God. Often, what God wants and what churches demand are often two very different things. Holiness is a man-made concept that in reality simply does not exist.

What on Earth is Salvation?

The problem with salvation is we don't know what it is!

Salvation is a term that we also do not fully understand, and which carries with it many connotations, some unhelpful. Many may recollect images of excitable preachers on stage compelling us to repent and be saved to avoid the fiery depths of hell, and yet the theory of a possible afterlife, what it is like and how we get there, whether hell exists or what exactly salvation means, are hotly debated and there is no consensus among scholars.

The ideas around the term salvation stem from the notion that there is a moment in time in which we fix that separation from God and gain our ticket to Heaven. We have already outlined the confusion that surrounds the notion of salvation and how to achieve it. Traditionally Christianity has this list of necessary requirements such as repentance, prayer and baptism, communion and attending church, but there is simply no consensus on this. And yet it is hugely important to many people.

But it does appear that this natural distance from God that we all face requires some correcting, a catalyst, a point at which, somehow, we connect to the heart of God and achieve that closeness to God. Like a spark, an awakening of our souls to God, almost like plugging in a new phone for the first time; the power has always been there and the phone is waiting to connect — and there is a moment when the phone is plugged in and comes to life. We suddenly realise there is this *something*, this God-being in existence and we respond. It is the moment we realise it's all true, there really is this God-being in existence that can transform our hearts and lives and open our eyes to all the wonders of God. It is the moment our hearts connect with the heart of God, and our minds and bodies experience being injected with God.

Many experts who study existential distress (end of life distress that we examined with the fear of death) feel that humans may well have a spirit or soul that is connected to the very heart of our being; it is integral to who we are. It is possible that this is the real us; the body is a mere shell that houses us until we are released and free to fly. Models of wellbeing often describe this spiritual part of our being and the nurturing it requires. It is as important to look after this as it is the physical body, as all areas of wellbeing impact our physical and mental health. But our spiritual self is not dependant on our physical self for life, as shown in the stories where people continue living after their physical body has died. This leads on to suggest that we have an existence after death, and there is a place to have that existence.

It also means that our spiritual self, in order to reach its full potential on death, *requires* this connection to God. It means our spirit or soul is intimately entwined with God's being, and is dependent on that connection for life. We need God. But our spirit or soul achieving this connection with God is not dependant on any physical thing we do. Physical religious activities *can* produce this effect, but the spiritual is not dependant on the physical. This is why no church or religious activity is necessary for discovering God and all the wonders therein. Our soul or spirit can connect with God in a multitude of ways and this will be different for everyone, but always just right for us. Something will spark our connection with this God-being; there will be a point in time when it all clicks, when we connect to the heart of God. This is the heart of salvation.

As we continue, I will use the word salvation to describe the phenomenon of that moment of connection with God; it is a term we are familiar with and out of convenience we ought to call it something. We want to retain the idea of that moment of connection with God whilst questioning the religious hurdles we are told to jump to reach it.

The Concept of an Outward Action Creating an Inner Reality — The "Sacraments"

It was a hot, dry day in a remote, mountainous region of Jordan. The ground was dusty and dry after an extremely hot summer. Temperatures had reached into the forties for weeks, and people and animals alike began to tire of the heat. But this did not prevent hundreds of people coming for what they felt was a profound moment for them, a moment to treasure; an event they had been waiting for with great expectation. They were here to be baptised.

The River Jordan was lower than usual due to the drought, but the priest said this made it more genuine; it represented the conditions of over two millennia ago when a man called Jesus was here, apparently on this spot, to do exactly what these pilgrims were doing today. Jesus was also baptised in these waters and many have since done the same, hoping for one thing through their experience; to encounter God for themselves.

As we turned a corner and saw in that moment the place where it is said Jesus was baptised, we felt a sudden intense rush of emotion. We stepped down the dusty path that led to the water, eyes fixed on the spot, becoming more aware of a heightened sense of a presence, some kind of power, something awakening our souls. We were not there to be baptised, merely to see the place where it all apparently started two thousand years ago. We wanted to see what Jesus saw, see what those people witnessed who actually met the man himself. Perhaps even to meet God again, afresh, for ourselves.

People for centuries since that day when Jesus stepped into that water have been doing the same across the world. Not on Jordan's dusty pathways or in that beautiful, gently flowing river, but in their own swimming pools, lakes and churches. People have been led through ceremonies where they have received prayer, been asked to confess sin and repent, and then been gently lowered into the water, afterwards feeling spiritually clean, closer to God. Babies have been prayed over and had water sprinkled on their heads in the belief that this confers on them grace and salvation. These ceremonies are incredibly meaningful to those who undertake them, and can be lifechanging.

But how these ceremonies should be done and what exactly baptism means, and even if it needs to be done at all, is hotly debated. The debate is not helped by the overwhelming range of emotions that accompany the idea of these various ceremonies or sacraments as they are called, within Christianity and religion. There are many who wish to have the spiritual connection with God but do not wish to, or cannot, connect with the groups who perform these ceremonies. Often performing them means also joining the religious community, and for some this is not what they might choose. If they are found *not* to be necessary this releases many more people to experience God without having to perform for the Church in order to do so.

Behind many of the things that Christians and those of other religions do is the belief that performing a certain act, a ritual or rite will create a spiritual reality, or an effect within the person. So, if we pray, say certain words or do certain things, this acts as a key to get us closer to God and be saved. Many are willing to do these things if they believe it will have the desired effect and they will be saved, and enter paradise at their death.

If it is true that we must jump through these prescribed hoops, then we ought to get on and do it. But if this is not true, then we can remove another obstacle to knowing God; the prescribed list of things we are told we should do in order to be close to God and be saved.

The beliefs across the churches about how to achieve salvation vary hugely; and stem from a decision made in northern Italy in the sixteenth century by a group of clergy of high status and including the pope.[130] It was decided that various acts that a person could perform or have done to them would actually confer grace or salvation upon the person. These acts or rituals, these sacraments, it was said, were effective in bringing salvation upon a person, that it was through performing them that God could transmit the desired effect, even if the person did not wish to do them. They were declared the key to salvation. Suddenly, if someone wanted to know God — and everyone did in those days, salvation was the only sure promise in a difficult life — they had to go through these ceremonies, otherwise they were told they could not be certain their faith was genuine. The threat of hell made everyone conform.

This meeting in northern Italy was organised because Martin Luther, the German priest who challenged everything the Church was doing and saying, and transformed faith for millions, had been saying that people could be saved through faith alone, and that many of the things the Church said we should do were in fact not necessary. Yet these performances were so ingrained in church life and tradition that they could not be done away with so easily; the priests at the meeting decided that Luther was wrong, these religious acts were indeed essential to faith and salvation, even if the recipient was not able or willing to agree to performing them.

The idea that we need to perform a series of religious rituals or sacraments to secure our salvation, for that connection with God to be genuine and to result in a ticket to paradise, became entrenched in Christianity. The various Churches have adapted this to their own beliefs, and today we have those variations on the route to salvation, different in every church. For the many vulnerable people who need God in their lives and wish to have proof their faith is secure, they are willing to do whatever they are told.

But are these things truly required by God? Is it the Church that demands these things, or is it God? Do we have to tick a series of religious boxes in order to connect with God, to know God and to experience a life with God after we have died? Do the words of our prayers act like a magic spell (but a spell that changes according to which church you go to)? Do we need to call ourselves Christians in order to know God and be saved? Does the name matter? If it was merely a convenient title then we probably don't.

Speech-Act Theory

One reason for this need for official records to declare faith as genuine is speech-act theory, the idea that words that we say will convey a reality and have a causative effect. For instance, if I have the power to do so and it is done in the right context, then I can say 'You are elected Prime Minister,' or 'I pronounce you man and wife,' or, 'I name this ship the Cutty Sark,' There is more involved than just saying the words — they have to be accompanied by the official ceremony and the right people — but afterwards it can be proclaimed that the act has officially taken place and the deed is done. The act is legitimate, and there is a point of reference if there is ever a question over the status of something; you can say it is true because it happened in the right way and was officially recorded.

On the flip side, I can say these same words without the official ceremony and it will be meaningless, the effect will not be created. This is true then of official customs, but does God need us to perform the official tasks and ceremonies? What is true for official ceremonies for people is not necessarily true for God. Historically, these religious acts were deemed necessary in order to bring stability and structure to the Church, faith and society. Just because people decide something is necessary does not mean God needs this in order to verify the encounter.

Official procedures are needed in order for society to function correctly, but if in an official ceremony the ship is named the Cutty Sark, it has no inherent difference to other ships. That ship is still a ship, sailing the same seas, doing the same thing other ships do. If it didn't have the official status, it would be the same ship. A couple may see themselves as married even if someone has not said those words to them. A person can surely ask God to help them even if they have not got the right certificate. We will soon explore how our spiritual self may not be dependent on any physical act in order to connect with God.

Baptism

One example is baptism. Baptism is something Christians have said for years is necessary for getting right with God, and that if we are to know

God closely and have that glorious existence with God after death, or be saved, then baptism is essential. There are many Bible verses that say "Believe and be baptised!" Hence in many churches you will go to services where there is a tank of water and people are ducked in and prayed for, or where babies are baptised in a font. Millions have gone through this ritual and for many it is a valuable and meaningful time. It is a key aspect of the Christian faith.

The practice of baptism today is commonly thought to signify our cleansing of sin, healing of the fractured relationship with God caused by that apple, and the start of the new life with God. The theory is that when you go down into the water the old You, who was separated from God by that original sin, dies, and a new You comes back out. Many believe the act of baptism is essential to salvation.

When you dig deeper and ask Christians what this practice means, however, you get some hazy answers. I recently asked a theology lecturer and Baptist church minister what baptism is. Clearly fumbling for an answer, he said it has meaning, but it is simply an outward expression to others of what has happened inside a person's heart. So, I asked if it is merely just for show; is it really necessary for making us right with God? He said no, it is only so that others can see evidence of the connection a person has with God; society needs that verification as in speech-act theory. If this is true, then it is not *necessary*, although it can still be beneficial to those who choose to do it.

Christians have argued long and hard about baptism, and what it means remains unclear. A great deal of importance has been placed on this ritual, making it a key part of salvation, yet the confusion that surrounds it does prompt questions over whether we need to do it at all. So, how did baptism become so central to the Christian faith? If it is essential, why is there not one standard way of doing it?

It all began in ancient times. Water that was set aside for ritual cleansing was a feature of ancient civilisations long before Jesus came and the Church began. Entering a pool of water for ritual cleansing would often be accompanied by repenting of sin, and getting the ritual done correctly was important for acceptance into the community. Pools have been found in archaeological digs that show an entrance and exit system that represented this cleansing; a person goes into the water supposedly contaminated by sin, and emerges from the water clean, and acceptable to the community, a common practice long before Christianity.[131] In the Bible Matthew 3:6 and Mark 1:5b describe how people confessed their sins and then John baptised them in the Jordan river, reflecting this ancient ritual.

In the ancient Greek use of the word, baptism did not need to involve water.[132] The original Greek word 'baptizó' had several possible meanings: to dip, dye clothes, immerse, wash or cleanse, or to overwhelm,[133] and also to pickle vegetables.[134]

By the time of John the Baptist this ancient pre-Christian cleansing ritual had become attached to the word baptism. Early Christianity then began to associate this practice with Bible verses that say "Believe and be baptised". Its status as a key to salvation and knowing God in the Church was sealed early on. But what those Bible verses meant originally may not be the same as the current baptism practices of the Church. One day in Jerusalem it is recorded that there were 3000 people baptised; the practicalities of using water to do this in a city where water was scarce hint that it may be worth re-visiting our baptism practices.

Immerse Ourselves in God

The practice of baptism did not begin with Christianity or with Jesus or John the Baptist. In fact, there are suggestions in the Bible that it was to *end* with those key Biblical characters. In the early days of Jesus, it was said that although John baptised in water, Jesus would baptise with the Holy Spirit; Matthew 3:11 says that John baptises with water but Jesus will baptise with the Holy Spirit and with fire". In Acts 1:5 there is a distinction between the baptism with water and the baptism with the Holy Spirit, with the latter surpassing the former. There are hints in the Bible, therefore, that the ancient practice of using water to ritually cleanse someone should be discontinued once Jesus appeared on the scene and Christianity began.

There is a strong suggestion that we are baptised by immersing ourselves in *God*, not by immersing ourselves in water. Some call this "Baptism in the Holy Spirit", but it is the experience of immersing ourselves in God and is vital in becoming close to God and benefitting from all God has for us. Baptism in the Holy Spirit is that moment we connect with God. It is the moment our spirit connects to God's Spirit. Immerse yourself in God and you are saved; dip yourselves in a tank of water and all you get is wet.

The combination of historical fact, word association, the biblical text, lack of clarity over the procedure among churches, the many ministers and theologians who agree it is not absolutely necessary and examples in contemporary life of people encountering God without having been baptised, means we can confidently say that dipping in water is not *necessary* in order to know God and to benefit from all God has for us. Anyone who wishes to know God can access God without it; and without other rituals too, wherever and whenever they like. All can be taken apart in the same way. We are the same people, sailing the same seas, whether we have the certificate in hand or not. Just as a wedding ceremony and certificate of marriage is actually a cultural procedure and does not mean anything without the relationship, so baptism means nothing without being close to God.

It is possible to connect with God and find salvation through these religious acts. We don't need to throw the baby out with the baptism water. They create a point in time for the person to know that is where and when God moved in their life — an official marking point for them to come back to in times of difficulty and questioning. Some people find these ceremonies and rituals extremely meaningful and beneficial. But they are a man-made route by which to find and know God, and they are not the *only* way to create that reality.

So, we can meet God, and God can meet us through these things, but God is not limited to meeting us this way; God does not need them or demand them. You can do it if you want to, but you don't have to.

And if that is true, then nothing of what is done in churches and in religion is necessary to know God, although it is valuable for those who wish to do it.

And if that is true, then those who wish to, can know God and experience God for themselves in lifechanging ways, without encountering church and jumping through its religious hoops. The meaningfulness of the encounter should be exactly the same for those who meet God through the Church and religion and those who meet God elsewhere.

I spent a hilarious few minutes googling alternatives to the saying, "There is more than one way to skin a cat". But many of us like cats, and not many of us would skin one. But that is the idea, that there is more than one way to find God, to find salvation. So, go happily to church and do all that it deems necessary to know God; but also know that we can find God our own way, in ways right for us, where we experience that moment in time when our spirit is awakened, that we connect with God and feel God awaken a part of our heart and soul that has long been dry.

For those who might be concerned we are saying all religions lead to God, I am not, although that is something that also ought to be explored alongside the notion that we are finding God here, not church, not Christianity and not religion. In a sense, no religion leads to God, although some use religion to find God.

The person standing on a mountain asking God for help is as valuable and welcome as the fully fledged Christian standing in church every Sunday. It does not matter how you do it as long as you do it. We can free God and ourselves from this religious quagmire. There is nothing we must to do to connect with God.

Except one.

Faith.

We stood close, our bodies pressing against each other as the afternoon sun shone brightly outside. It felt as though I had waited forever for this moment; the tingling sensation of a desire as yet unmet; the force of our passion finally able to be unleashed. His hands gently touched my neck as his lips pressed against mine. I felt his hands move towards my breasts; I had chosen a dress that I knew would ignite an irresistible desire within him; something I had longed for ever since I had first met him.

He gently touched my breasts as I could feel his erection firm against my legs. The feeling was electric as we both moved together, both wanting the same thing, both unable to resist. He slipped the strap of my dress from my slender shoulder, revealing my left breast. He continued to kiss my neck as his other hand slipped the dress fully from my shoulders. As the dress fell to the floor, his hands slipped down to my waist. He gently slipped his hands inside my silk underwear, his fingers finding the place I had wanted him to find for so long.

I wanted all of him, and I knew he wanted all of me. Our bodies moved in unison and the feeling of desire finally being met was sensational. I cared for nothing else in that moment; I did not care that people would not approve, I did not care that he had a wife and children, and I did not care that if we were found, I would be blamed, and I could be stoned to death.

His fingers endlessly pressed time and time again in just the right place as he kissed me, his lips moving between my neck and my lips, and down to my breasts. All I wanted was to feel his erection deep inside me. The feeling grew as he slipped my underwear from me, and we both responded together, falling tenderly onto the bed. We didn't want to wait; the time was right as he moved onto me, the warmth of his body against mine increasing the sense of pleasure.

Finally, he thrust himself inside me. The feeling was intense as he moved endlessly in and out, tenderly and lovingly penetrating the very heart of me. It felt wonderful, it was all I had dreamed of. The feeling of absolute pleasure grew and grew, it felt as though every part of me would feel this.

Suddenly, there was a terrible noise as a group of men broke into the room, shouting and brandishing weapons.

They instantly grabbed me, throwing a robe over me to cover me. They hit me and kicked me, shouting over and over that I was a prostitute and must be condemned. I wasn't a prostitute; I merely had fallen in love with someone who happened to be married, and they would not listen as I pleaded with them to spare me.

They did not care as I shouted back that my lover was doing this as much as I was. They pointed to him, and I looked in horror as they told him to get out and never be seen again. He was spared. I knew what they had planned to do to me; I had seen it before. It was a hard thing being a woman in this society.

They dragged me out into the street, scraping my legs on the large stones that lined the streets. They continued to hit me and drag me along, shouting insults at me as they went. There was no mercy, they wanted to kill me, to have their self-righteous moment.

They moved towards the town square as one of them shouted, 'Let us take her to Jesus! He is a religious leader, let us see if he will follow the law on this one!' The religious laws stated that if a woman had been found in the act of adultery she must be stoned to death. No one seemed to care that the man had been involved too.

They dragged me out into the square in front of the temple. I was terrified; I felt sick and faint, and no one came to help. The other people of the town stood watching, knowing they could not defend or help me. The law was the law, and it was powerful.

They dragged me to Jesus, shouting at him the accusations, telling him they had found me in that moment of passion with my lover. They stood there, loudly saying, 'What do you want to do with this woman?' Everyone knew this was not a question, it was an instruction. What should be done in this case was to stone me, right there, in an attempt to eliminate sin from the town and be an example to everyone.

I had heard about Jesus, and had watched with interest what he was doing. I had seen him do so called miracles, where people who had apparently been suffering with various diseases had been healed. There was something different about this man, something compelling. He awakened in me a spiritual desire, a desire for God. I had enjoyed his teaching and wanted to know more. But not like this. I sat before him now, my robes torn and my skin bloodied and bruised. I was humiliated and terrified. I could not look into his eyes. And yet I knew somehow it was better to be in his hands than in those of the other religious leaders.

Jesus sat, while those around waited with anticipation of what he would say and do. He silently waited, and then slowly started playfully drawing with his finger in the dust, as if he were challenging the seriousness of the moment. After several moments, he looked up at the accusers, and, looking each one in the eyes as if penetrating their very souls, simply said, 'Those who are without sin, cast the first stone.'

Those simple words struck to the very heart of every man present. Each one in turn knew that they could not claim to be any better than this woman they had accused. In that moment he challenged everything; every law, every accusation. In that moment he took the religious laws and screwed them up, discarding them forever. In that moment he made it clear that God did not care about following laws at the expense of the person. God was interested in every person, whatever shape, size, gender, character or colour. Whatever they did, did not do, or desired to do. God wanted every precious soul, not a clan of religious models who could claim to be righteous because they followed a man-made set of rules.

That moment changed everything.

One by one the crowd dispersed, as each one knew they could not accuse any longer. As the last one left, Jesus turned to me and asked where my accusers were. I said they had gone. He gently looked into my eyes, smiled, and quietly whispered to me that this relationship may not be right. I guess he was thinking of my lover's wife and family, and then he said, 'Then you too may go.'

I owed my life to that man; he had saved me. When I knew he was going to be at a dinner party with some of those same religious leaders I knew what I wanted to do. It was nothing compared to what he had done for me, but I had found a freedom and a peace I had never known before. I wanted to say thank you. So I found out where he would be that night, and took my best and most expensive perfume and went to the room where they were eating. I had to force myself in as they would never let a woman like me into their private dinner party.

I walked in, head down, not daring to look at those men. I just knew I had to do it; this feeling deep inside had compelled me to go. I knelt at Jesus' feet, and took out my perfume. His feet were dusty and dry, walking the dusty roads of Palestine in the heat took it out on everyone's feet. I wanted to show him how much it meant; what he had done for me.

I was overcome, my tears falling uncontrollably as I poured the perfume onto his feet. Then, suddenly, I realised I had not bought my silk handkerchief to rub his feet with; I had nothing with which to massage the perfume in. I had to improvise, so I used my long hair. I didn't care, this moment meant everything.

I became aware of discussion, and disapproving grunts coming from the people, but I continued. As I finished I looked at Jesus. Our eyes met, and he gave me that same compassionate and loving smile. He gently said, 'Your faith has saved you, go in peace.'

I treasured those words for the rest of my life. Jesus had said them to *me*, not to anyone else there. I was changed forever.[135]

Your faith has saved you… The concept and the words are repeated in many similar stories in the Bible, hinting that it is something we should take note of.

'Your faith has saved you, go in peace.' Those words to that precious woman changed her life, and gave her something she may have been searching for her whole life; a sense of peace and happiness. She had simply found God, and knew in her heart that was what she wanted and needed. There was no performance, no one telling her she must do several things for that faith to be genuine, no one telling her that now she had faith and was saved she must behave a certain way. No rule book to follow (the Bible didn't exist then… ☺).

I doubt her life circumstances changed much, but her mental health and sense of wellbeing would have been transformed. There are many other examples in the Bible where it is recorded that people were saved by this thing called faith, where they seemingly did nothing physical, but something happened deep down inside them, in their hearts, minds and souls.

That brave woman had faith, as did the blind man healed by Jesus, as did the man crucified alongside Jesus, and many others. They did not perform certain acts, as far as we know they did not have to pray certain prayers, read the Bible, be baptised or go to church regularly (churches did not exist then either).

So, what happened? Because if it happened that way for those people, then it can happen that way for us. And that reinforces the belief that we do not need to jump through religious hoops and perform religious rituals — if all we need is faith.

So What is Faith?

Faith is a term that can have negative connotations. Faith implies religion, but we are using it to describe the experience of connecting with God and exploring or expressing our spiritual self, and not simply conforming to a religion. Because it is a familiar term I will continue to use it in that sense. Others no doubt will develop new and better ways of describing this phenomenon of discovering and encountering God.

Faith, like the concept of God, is difficult to pin down. It is not a phenomenon you can easily give a robust definition to, and is multi-faceted. Like a chameleon, it may even change according to the person or situation. Theories include an awareness of a new dimension or spiritual realm, trust in God, a connection with God or having an inner encounter with God. For some it encompasses Church and religion.[136]

The phenomenon of faith can feel like a nudge or hunch, a compulsion, an awareness that something else is there, some kind of spiritual being. A sensation, a feeling, an impression, a spirituality, trust. A deep, inner experience of God, the inner sensation of connecting with God in some way, like the pleasure of doing something you love, or enjoying the presence of someone close. It is like the bond that holds families together, that knowledge that you and they are close and will help each other; a relationship or connection.

The problem is that faith is subjective and hard to describe, a bit like describing what air is apart from the gasses it contains. Faith is often based on experience, and people experience God in different ways. No particular theory captures this concept of being close to God and of experiencing God because we are all different, with differing faith needs and preferences, and our personal experience of this God-being will be unique. Faith is different for each of us.

The Bible describes some people as having faith — those who trusted God; that when things were hard, they knew God would pull them through. The faith that saved the woman having the affair and others in the Bible who were said to have faith but without any external religious expression suggests this idea of a heartfelt, deep inner trust or connection with God that is not dependant on any external behaviour. The hint is that God sees deep inside our hearts, minds and souls, and so when we connect with God, we connect in a deep sense, where God delves into that inner part of us, the part that might remain if we strip away our physical bodies. Our spirit connects with God, and God is able to sort out any reparative work that needs doing to make us healthy and whole.

Over the years it has been portrayed by the Church that a person must show evidence of their faith externally otherwise it is not genuine;

then faith becomes a series of religious rituals that can be confirmed as genuine by the Church. Although these religious acts have their place for those who wish to express or enhance their faith by them, they are not faith in themselves. Faith is an internal, personal thing between our inner being and God. It is this deep inner connection that makes the difference to our health and lives, not the external shell of religion.

People have debated what faith is and how we should encounter God for centuries. Yet faith in God is not as complicated as religion has made it. People for centuries have simply found God in ways personal to them, ways that do not introduce them to religion but instead transform their lives, awaken their souls, and give them an experience of God they will never forget. Faith was always meant to be a simple but incredible inner connection with God, and yet it has been made so complicated and unpleasant that it actually puts people off exploring who God is and what it might be like to know God.

Some really have moulded this incredible, heartfelt experience of God, this awesome moment our souls touch the heart of God, into religion, thus putting obstacles between people and God.

It's time to sweep away the theories and discover faith again.

All Those Who Call Out to God Will be Saved

Paul had that incredible encounter of God on the Damascus Road, and went on to experience God in awesome ways — probably even physically seeing God and Heaven. Years later, while in prison, he wrote a letter to the Christians in Rome. He said: "Everyone who calls out to God will be saved." This theme flows through the Bible and through the hearts of all those who discover how amazing God is. The essence of what we need to do to connect with God, captured in a few words which show that simple response, that simple connection, that moment of discovering God, loving what we find and shouting, 'Yes please!'[137]

It's a heart response. It's a soul response. It's a faith response.

And it's not achieved by works. This means it is not achieved by any physical thing we can do.

And this means it's not achieved by any religious act if those religious acts don't promote that heart response.

Because this is a heart response, because it is our deep inner being responding to God, it does not matter how we do it. There are no magic formulas or spells, no religious rites that will seal the deal. The faith that connects us with this God-being and that is the heart of salvation is much simpler than we have traditionally thought. All we need to do to qualify is give God a nod and a smile.

Christianity has traditionally portrayed the image that faith has to be seen to be believed. If we wanted to know God and explore our spiritual side we had to attend church, and learn how to do church and Christianity. Stripping away unnecessary religious structures and beliefs frees us all to express our faith and live our lives as we choose to.

The key to finding God is faith. The lock is our heart/soul connection to this incredible God-being; where our hearts respond, our spirits connect and our heads realise these awesome experiences are what it is about, not religion. Where our entire being finds a faith that is right for us, but that is different for everyone.

As a troubled teenager when I was walking to town one morning, feelings of sadness weighing heavily on me, a Christian song popped into my head. I quietly sang this to myself, and as I did, I felt my mood lift. I looked up to the sky and said a quick prayer, and began to feel even better. There was a leap in my stomach, and over the next few moments I felt more and more strengthened and empowered. I felt happier. I felt I'd had a moment with God, where God had reached down and helped me. This, I knew, was faith.

Whirlwind of Discovery

Faith is different for everyone, but for many it is a developing phenomenon, a dynamic process of thought and experience that gathers momentum. It often starts with a tiny inkling, a thought that something, some God-being exists; then we may have an experience that adds to this belief. This happened to Millie, the vulnerable little girl we heard of previously. She had a tiny belief that there may be a God figure that existed, but certainly didn't want to do go to church. She had an underlying, quiet belief in something but found church dull. Then a friend took her to a local new church, and as she walked in someone gave her a hug. This moved her experience and knowledge of God on tremendously as she found a loving community that accepted her. As she continued to go to church her experience and knowledge increased more and more. Yet later in life, having been a Christian for many years, her desire for church has diminished, while her connection with God has grown stronger.

Our life experiences, knowledge and beliefs merge and feed into one another, and like an ever-increasing spiral, or a snowball that gathers snow, they develop and grow. As we have more experiences, we may start asking more questions, and explore a little more. Often this happens in times of need, as we are forced to address some of the big questions of life.

We may start with a tiny nugget of belief, that there may be something in this idea of a God-being. Our life experiences, our life situation, our beliefs, desires and knowledge converge and as we add in new experiences and new knowledge our beliefs adapt, evolve and change. And so we embark on a journey, a whirlwind of discovery, like an ever-upward moving spiral that never ends. Our faith is part of us, an integral part of our being. Similar to love, it grows and changes over time. Faith grows, develops and evolves, but it is always just right for us, a thing that is solely between us and God.

We can ask others to guide and help us in our journey of discovering our faith, but we don't have to, and as much as that can be good, we may get some unhelpful answers, as beliefs vary so widely about faith and what it should look like.

Picture yourself turning towards God and wanting, wishing, imploring God to hold you close. As you wait, you sense God gently reaching out towards you, and wrapping those divine, loving and strong arms around you, holding you tight. God accepts you at that moment, looking down upon you with a gentle smile, and tells you that you are loved and understood. All your fears disappear in that second. Nothing else matters in that moment when you are face to face with God.

The thoughts of Saint Teresa of Avila, the Spanish nun from the sixteenth century who, after a phase of ill health, had a period of spiritual awakening and wrote the classic work, *The Interior Castle*, reflects the idea of the ever-increasing spiral of discovery gathering momentum with new pieces of information and experiences. Like a kaleidoscope or maze, discovering and experiencing God becomes a journey that evolves and changes. In our health chapter we took that journey inside ourselves, to explore our deep, inner self and find what lies within.

Saint Teresa found God in ever increasing intensity as she ventured into those inner places. She describes the outer rooms as a place where we might tentatively acknowledge God, maybe finding small but significant experiences, but as we travel through the rooms inside us through contemplation, the experiences of God gain in intensity until we reach the inner, central chamber, which is filled the most intense experiences with God. The further you go in the more of God you find and know. Many do not go as deeply in as they could,[138] but whatever happens and whether you find God or just find yourself in your inner being, the journey is worthwhile.

The distractions of life can pull us away from this contemplation on our inner being, but we can return as often as we wish. Spending time here can be restorative, leading to us understanding ourselves better. We are discovering ourselves as much as we discover God. Saint Teresa had a number of years where she could not pray or spend time with God, but after this she found she went deeper with God, and had experiences that were more profound. It is almost as if we are naturally led into these places when we are ready. Anyone in a dry place spiritually may have greater things to come.

For Saint Teresa, this ability to experience God is not dependant on the structures, practices and beliefs of Christianity or religion; we can perform this inner reflection alone with God at any time and in any place. In fact, the lady who wrote the preface to *Selections from the Interior Castle,* poignantly says that there would be great fear in our churches if people began to discover God for themselves. For if we do that, what will happen to all the vast structures, organisations and ceremonies of Christianity and religion?[139]

What happens indeed…

I wonder if Christianity has clung on to the feeling that we need to certify our faith by the many things are told to do; proving that we went through baptism, that we attend church faithfully, that we are seen to behave in a way acceptable to the Church, in order for Christianity and the Church to survive. The focus is on the external ritual, the shell of religion, when God is at the heart. We have churches that are neat and tidy, full of model Christians, when all along God is everywhere; out on the streets, in the mountains, hills and homes, waiting for us. If we strip away the external shell of religion, we might find ourselves standing together with God, naked, free to enjoy each other's presence in new and exciting ways.

We Cannot Fully Understand It, But We Can Feel It!

Just as we do not need to fully understand or comprehend God in order to benefit from all God has for us in our lives, so we do not need to understand the methods by which we can become close to God. It is largely inexplicable anyway; bizarre that there is a part of our being that is so difficult to determine the nature of, and that is nurtured by a God-being that is even harder to define. But the encounters speak for themselves; and leave even the most hardened atheist stunned, when face to face with God.

For those who benefit from religion, let it remain. But for the many who don't, we are free to experience God in our own way. In fact, even many faithful Christians can find church to be a hindrance, and it may be that we discover more of God outside of church or religion. We don't need to perform, in order to meet God. The shell of religion alone does not give us the health benefits and isn't the key to connecting with God. They are helpful to some, but they are not *necessary*. They are not the only key to the entrance gate to God's presence. Some may continue to insist that they are, that the centuries of Church belief and practice cannot be swept away so easily. These and many other rituals have evolved over the centuries and become so fixed into doctrine it is hard to separate them; needed by the church, but not by God.

I can eat bread and drink wine, dive into water and stand in church anytime, but I don't meet God through these any more than I do on the stunning hills of Dartmoor. No religious ritual or act is necessary, but being drenched in God's love is. All we need to do is give God a nod and a smile, a wink, a glance or a plea, and then sit back and wait, and see what God will do.

The idea of immersing ourselves in God is also an incredible one. What an amazing thing to sit covered in the presence of God and enjoy God filling us up with love and power. That day when I experienced this for the first time as opposed to faking it in church was the most incredible feeling I have ever had. Better than the best wine, the best steak and chips, the best holidays, the best sex.

There is a beautiful section of the New Testament, attributed to Paul writing to the Ephesians, but in fact written by an unknown author to an unknown audience. It is a prayer we might all wish to receive; a phenomenon we would love to see in our lives and It describes what this life with God is all about: "When I think of all this, I stand in awe before our awesome God, and I ask that from God's boundless resources, you are empowered and given inner strength through God's Spirit. I ask that God comes to dwell in your hearts and that your spiritual roots grow down into God's love and keep you strong. May you see how vast God's love is, and may you experience this love and power, though it is too great to understand fully. Then you will feel complete, with all the satisfying life and power that comes from God. God is utterly incredible, and is able through mighty power at work within us, to accomplish infinitely more than we could ever wish for."[140]

There is no indication here that God cares one tiny bit what we wear, how many tattoos we have, where we come from, where we are now, what we do or what our life preferences are; be they sexual, cultural or playful.

It is enough to cry out to God with our hearts, souls, minds or voices. We do not need to be in a particular location or building; we can be alone, or with others. God can speak to everyone, wherever they are, whatever they are doing.

So, the desperate alcoholic, the person who has lost someone close, the angry, the sad, those who turn to addiction because they want to escape from the pain they feel, God sees all of that, and wants to bring relief. Knowing God can bring relief to the stressed, the anxious, those fearful of death, the sad, the lonely, the happy and fulfilled too. Even those who do not believe in God and yet have the little question in their minds, that little doubt, that there may be *something*… If we call out to God to help us and ask God to show us more about this divine being that we have not even begun to understand yet, God will. God leaps to the aid of all those who call for help.

Anyone can come to God's awesome presence, and it does not matter what mess we are in when we get there. It does not matter what we believe, do not believe, like, or do not like. Nothing matters, except that we find God, and express that discovery in our own way. The typical image of the holier than thou Christian — those that might be more acceptable to our churches — can be blown apart by the realisation that God just simply does not care what is on the outside.

Those who wish to can take part in whatever religious performances they like, but alone, they will not save them. We can have a wonderful relationship with God and enjoy eternity in God's presence and never set foot inside a church. If the Church as an institution did not exist, we would still be enjoying being close to God, being blessed with God's presence personally. If I wish to be a hamburger, I can cover myself with lettuce and mayonnaise and sit inside a giant bread roll, but I am still not a hamburger.

Church is Not for Everyone but God Is

In some cases, churches can hinder us encountering God. Initially, my life was transformed by church, and by the people there that became my family. I loved it, I would go to the most boring meetings and be so happy. I found God there, and a family who united around their love for God and others, and so church came to mean a huge amount to me.

I attended church throughout my life from age thirteen, and when we got married we went to a Baptist church in Cambridgeshire with around a hundred and fifty people. Married life was good, but after seven years we realised something was wrong. We had been trying to have children for five years, but nothing was happening. We were also incredibly busy with jobs, renovating a house and garden, and church life; we were heading towards burnout without realising it.

The pressure you feel when you are experiencing infertility and trying for a family is immense. Month after month the disappointment grows, and the stress and pressure it puts on you is something you do not understand unless you have felt it yourself. It is an incredibly cruel and destructive thing to endure. The crux came when we had a miscarriage, and at the same time a close friend told us she was pregnant.

I lost it. I just could not get myself out of the pit of grief I was in. I wanted to stay there, just me and my grief, and not do anything or see anyone. Suddenly, the church that had been a constant support and important part of my life became a place of hurt. Filled with children, singing children's songs, celebrating pregnant ladies, everything was family centred. In addition, church friends did not understand and instead judged us. We were taken aside one Sunday and told to get over what we were feeling and get on with life; we were being immature. My close pregnant friend was always at church but I could not face seeing her, something I now know is a common reaction by many women in that same position. The last straw came on Mother's Day, when during the church service the pastor announced there were flowers for all the mothers. The children went around the hall distributing bunches of flowers to all the mothers, and one little girl came to offer me some. I said no, I could not take it, and she looked surprised, but I repeated that I could not take them, and she walked off. I was not a mother, therefore I did not qualify for the flowers.

I did not go back to church for a long time. I spent time instead at home, just me and God. The church that had been my lifeline, my Christian family, suddenly was too awful and scary to go to. Instead of finding love and support in our time of deepest need, we found judgment and exclusion. I did not want to be there, it was just not the right place for me to be. All I could do in that most desperate of times was look up to the sky and say, 'Help me, God.'

I needed to stay away from church; I wanted just me and God, alone, and this was the only thing that kept me going; in those darkest of times I had something I could hold onto. God never said anything, I never had dramatic visions or dreams, I just felt God's comforting presence there with me. My need to stay away from church shocked me and yet spoke to me profoundly at the same time. I realised that my faith in God was not dependent upon church. That it did not matter where I was, I was close to God. God was what mattered, not church.

Others experience the same. Excluded because they do not quite fit the brief. Some just dislike large groups of people, or perhaps like me, they find church too difficult a place to be, too challenging, too hard. Too downright boring!

Church is right for some. Some people thrive in that atmosphere and build their lives around it, and that is great. But for those who perhaps do not “conform” or just do not like it, do not find it a good, wholesome place to be, where instead of being built up and feeling supported we can feel judged and excluded, perhaps it is not the best place to find, and then express, our faith.

The curious thing is that Christians really do (sometimes) experience all the wonders of God, and this amazing experience of being close to God and feeling spiritually alive, makes you want to tell others so they can experience it too. If you found a fantastic drug that made you feel amazing and was legal you’d want to tell your best friends. But what we then say is that people should come to church to find that. We do not offer God, we offer church and religion, and there are a lot of people who people do not like or want church and religion.

The Church is that crazy mix of being really good, doing amazing things for many communities worldwide, enabling people to find God. There are some churches today where the presence of God fills the place and people can feel God and often see God doing wonderful things in people’s lives. In the past services have been interrupted by the awesome presence of God. Many churches worldwide have thousands of people attending each day, some travel halfway across the world to get to them because amazing things really do happen there. They carry the presence of God immensely and to attend is the most wonderful thing, although it is impractical for many people to get to them.

Yet in many churches, God gets pushed out and replaced with all the rituals we perform and all the fuss in our services; the notices, the hymns, the prayers, a long sermon. Suddenly there is no space for God. There is probably no need for God either, when we have our religions. Many do not remember the contents of a sermon and yet preachers speak for hours. There is a lingering sense in many churches that some are better than others; some can preach, others are not good enough. It is said in some churches that if you are gay you cannot lead worship or preach, you might not even be allowed in. Yet other people can lead, obviously who are deemed worthy enough — or at least ones that can hide the things they do that Christianity might consider wrong. So, we have barred some from experiencing God, and those who do come, find at the end of a service they have not quite connected with God because of all the other things they had to do. They know what time the coffee morning is but they don't know God. There are even many Christians who are getting tired of the religious performance that goes on every Sunday and questioning many of the things we do and why we do them. Many Christians are leaving their churches and expressing their faith elsewhere. In a recent survey, it was found that more and more people are reporting experiences of God, but less people are attending church.[141] People are finding God and rejecting church in droves. There's something wrong somewhere.

Even if every church were perfect, there will still be many people who would feel uncomfortable, whether the more quiet, introverted character types, those who do not like large groups of people or crowds and who just prefer to be alone, or those who simply do not have time for church services. For some people, church is just not the right place to be. Thankfully we can conclude that although church is great for some, you don't need it in order to find God.

Because it is God that is important, not religion, and not religious practices, it also suggests that it does not matter what religion you claim to be part of, or what religious practices you take part in. It does not matter what culture you are based in, what your history is, what you believe about God, the world or life in general. Anyone and everyone can turn to God and have a meaningful relationship with God. There are some who will be part of other religions who sense an emptiness in religious practice and expression and call out to God, often privately. No one may ever know you are close to God in this way, in fact for some, their lives may be in danger if others did know. But you can call out to God secretly, telling no one, and God will come quickly to your aid and help you. God is there for every single person in this world. There is no model person, no mould that we must all look like if we are to be close to God, no particular religious expression that is the key to finding God. Faith is the only thing we require, the embryo of which is found in every heart and soul. There will be people in heaven in burkas, in combat gear, in traditional clothing, and in nothing at all.

Salvation and a fulfilling life in God does not occur in Christianity or any religion, it occurs in God. Two thousand years of Church history, doctrine, theology and religion cannot make a person right with God. There will be many there in that new exciting world, enjoying that delicious roast lamb and fine wine, who never once went to church. There may also be many faithful churchgoers who will finally stand face to face with God and find they missed the brief; who are found to be a bit too religious for God.

A modern faith that is relevant to all people today and enables us all to meet God may look very different to the religious structures and beliefs of the past, as more and more people come to know God and express that in new and innovative ways. It will be hard for the churches and many Christians to watch this happening, as the old ways are questioned and perhaps even discarded or changed. But millions more will discover God as we realise we do not need to tick those tiresome religious boxes. We can have incredible encounters and awesome new lifechanging experiences as we sit, stand and play at God's feet, gazing in awe at the sight. Many stories are waiting to be told, many more barriers are waiting to be demolished. Faith is evolving, and in the process it is blasting out through the walls of our religious buildings and going where it should be; into the hearts and lives of those who wish to know God.

Chapter Nine
Connecting with God;
Discovering Our Spiritual Preferences

Where many of us have desperately needed God in our lives, all we have found or been offered is church life or religion, and often that is not what we wanted or needed. Faith has evolved over the course of two thousand years; and the results of that evolution have not always been good. Often, instead of the wonderful, lifechanging, incredible series of experiences that can enhance our lives and help us survive what life throws at us, we find a dull set of religious structures, rules and expectations, with those deemed not good enough, excluded. We have exchanged God for religion. Church is great for those who wish to express their faith that way, but tiresome rules, regulations, beliefs and practices that even faithful Christians are starting to question and dislike, means church is simply not an attractive proposition for many. Many people feel they needed God, but what they got was religion. And many aspects of religion, Christianity and the Church have become barriers to getting to know God and have obscured God from sight.

Yet we still need to nurture the spiritual aspect of our being. Our bodies and lives need us to pay attention to that part of us that we may never have explored before, a part that contributes to our overall wellbeing. We are not just physical machines, we are complex beings with multiple factors affecting us, some to the very core of our being. Allowing ourselves to explore the spiritual aspects of life and discover what we might truly believe and desire may lead to us being healthier. This does not mean finding religion, it means finding God.

Some of us dislike the idea of God because of religion, either from bad personal experience or general perception. But often we reject the image of God others have portrayed, rather than discovering it for ourselves and finding we do not like it. If you've never experienced gorgeous holidays on stunning beaches, seeing billions of stars filling every part of the night sky when there's no light pollution, that feeling when you've had your best run ever, or noodles freshly fried on the streets of Cambodia, then if people tell you these things are terrible, you may not want to try them. But we cannot reject what we do not truly know — otherwise we do not know if we are missing out on something incredible. If we taste something and still do not like it, then fine, say no. But we cannot reject what we do not know.

If I wanted to try an oyster, I would not look at a book about oysters, or explore the anatomy and physiology of an oyster, I would just go and eat one. I certainly would not reject an oyster just because someone else told me what they are like — I want to try it for myself! In the same way, if we want to know what God is like and experience God for ourselves, it is better to try that first hand, not reject it because we do not like what others say, or how others express their faith. Many have never discovered God, faith or their spiritual self because their view of these things has been tainted by religion, Christianity and church; God has been given a bad name by religion. Yet many report awesome lifechanging experiences of God that literally leave them gobsmacked. If we could buy this, the supermarket shelves would be stripped immediately.

Stripping away Church, Christianity and religion and the religious debris they leave behind, leaves us able to discover God for ourselves and express that discovery however we wish. We can tailor our faith to our own preferences. This may open the floodgates to whole new ways of doing faith.

Needed by Church, not by God

Traditionally, many will say that there are certain things a person should do in order to connect with God, such as attending church, praying a certain way, worshiping, being baptised and confessing sin. It is said we must "mature" in the faith and become more holy, as evidence that faith is real, and in order to achieve that you have to be part of a church. In reality this often means moulding ourselves to fit the ideal image of a Christian, one acceptable to our churches. It is portrayed that if we do not do these things then we are not Christian, and if we are not a genuine

Christian, we might not be saved and are heading to hell when we die. These beliefs are a key part of Christianity and are reiterated in multitudes of churches worldwide every week.

Yet many of these things are created by influential characters responding to the needs of the time, in an effort to validate faith or maintain the functioning of the Church. They represent the evolution of Church and Christianity. The Romans gave us Sunday as our holy day, church buildings, services, our leadership structure and more, and since then others have continued to shape faith as they felt it should be; heaping obstacles in the form of doctrines, beliefs and practices onto faith and knowing God. These things have become deeply embedded into Christianity and faith, and have defined and limited our encounters with God. They are needed by the Church, but not by God. They are simply man-made ways of harnessing the encounters between God and people. Our examination of the roots of these things and the meaning behind them means they are not necessary to know God, and God does not care one jot whether we do them or not. In fact, I have spoken to several influential Christian leaders recently who all believe the church functions largely to keep itself alive. The churches need our bums on seats and our money in their bank accounts, and that seems to be their priority, rather than helping people discover God. Of course, then they will indeed say that the only way to know God and experience salvation is through themselves. Their threats of hell if we do not conform keep many on those seats.

The route to discovering and encountering God has become a sticky quagmire of confusion. Like the explorers of old, we thrash through the undergrowth trying to find the way to the treasure. Sweat pours down our faces as our machetes repeatedly cut back the weeds that form the dense undergrowth. Feelings of fear and frustration grow as we try to find what we are looking for. Many of us do not wish to bother and so miss out on the awesome experiences knowing God and having a faith can bring. As we approach death, we might find we are not prepared, that we have not answered those big questions of life.

It is as if Christianity's beliefs and practices create a towering wall of weeds that hides God and prevents us discovering God and our faith. It is time to do some gardening, and strip away this religious debris. The experiences of the millions who find God in multiple ways, places and times of life tell us that our faith should be personal, flexible and that it has to be right for us as individuals, not there to suit the needs of religion. A genuine faith is not one that demands that we fit the mould of a perfect Christian, it is one that is just right for each person, and yet different for everyone.

Faith is Personal and Flexible

The missionaries of old boldly travelled far and wide to tell other cultures and people groups about God. They wanted everyone to know about this amazing God. But they inadvertently took along with them our white western version of Christianity, assuming this was right for everyone; that this was the way faith should be done and that this was what God demanded. This was sadly accompanied by colonialism, and so the Church and Christianity became involved in the decimation of cultures across the world.

One example was polygamy. Men in more exotic nations often had several wives, which was a practical arrangement, creating more children and larger family groups to look after the land and care for each other. In many societies it was a common arrangement and worked well. Western Christians came along and said that this style of living was not compatible with Christianity, and ordered families to split, the men keeping just one wife. The result was women and children being evicted from their community and home, and left in the wilderness to fend for themselves. Often, they died; without the security and support of their family group there was little hope of survival in their extreme environments. In fact, monogamy, having one wife, is a western cultural norm and when examined theologically there is no need to condemn the practice if it is right for a particular community.[142] Several Bible characters also had many wives, and had extremely close relationships with God.[143]

A whole new branch of theological study has evolved and is growing fast: contextual theology. This explores what different cultural expressions of faith looks like; a faith that is right for individual cultures and their traditions and beliefs. It rests on the belief that there is a core element that is crucial to connecting with and experiencing God, and all else is merely personal or cultural preference, or the shell of religion. Church, Christianity and religion therefore look very different from people group to people group. There is no single, correct way of doing faith. And so cultures worldwide are beginning to find faith and express it in a way right for them. This often looks very different to traditional Christianity, but what remains is the vital ingredient of us all finding God.

Just as cultures and people groups across the world find and express faith in God in their own way, so individuals must too. Contextual theology does not just stretch to the many communities of our world, is stretches deep into the hearts of every person. The key is faith, the lock is our hearts and precious souls. And it will indeed look very different for everyone.

Because our faith is our own, and has to be right for our life preferences and context, our relationship with God and our expression of that can be just what we want it to be. It must be right for us because it is ours. Our faith does not belong to the Church, it belongs to us. Church evolved the way it did because people moulded it so, but religion, Church and Christianity are not God, God is bigger and better than all our church buildings and all the reams of books that have been written, and all the sermons, and all the baptismal pools, and all the rules and regulations that have been made.

We can have a fulfilling, exciting and wonderful relationship with God and never set foot inside a church. In fact, in some cases, our relationship with God might be more exciting without church, as some struggle to keep a sense of vibrancy whilst striving to maintain orthodoxy and the religious rules and regulations the Church has created. Some people live where there is only access to a more traditional style church, which offers a more sombre representation of faith. These people may crave something that these churches seem unable to give, somewhere that allows them to experience God, not simply experience the religious structures of the Church. They want God, not Church.

The world today has changed dramatically from that of the beginning of the Church. Just the last few years have seen massive developments across the intellectual board, and also in the study of God, faith and the Bible. But while many people are questioning tradition for the sake of tradition and asking why the religious continue to do the things they do, the Church has stuck with its organisations, buildings, doctrine and rules. The Church has kept its feet in the mud while the rest of the world has gone home and cleaned its boots.

Yet people need faith and spirituality! It's part of our nature, our welfare, our health. It is an essential part of life! We need to nurture and feed our spiritual side, but instead of helping people to do this in a way appropriate for them, the Church generally has offered a dry, irrelevant and fairly judgmental scrap of faith which is not a patch on the real thing. This wonderful, life-giving, passion-creating, enlivening, amazing experience of God has been exchanged for religion, thus obscuring God. There are big hints in the Bible that in the future faith and being close to God would not consist of rules and must dos, that loving God and loving each other is all that matters. God would let each of us know if something was amiss.

Church can be a real help and support. For those who enjoy church life and religion as their expression of spirituality, let them continue. However, church is not the only way to a fulfilling relationship and life with God and to a healthy faith and spirituality. What many want is God, not church. What many need is this amazing relationship that changes our lives and puts us on a trajectory toward that perfect paradise where we finally see God face to face. A faith that is real, a faith that changes lives.

Every week, hundreds of thousands of pounds is spent producing church services, with huge amounts of effort expended, expensive buildings and expensive staff. Many of these costly weekly services serve only those who attend that particular church and follow its traditions. They are trapped by their doctrines, but as more of us question those doctrines, less are attending their services. Many seem to be slowly shrivelling up. Let's put that money and effort where God would want it to go; to the poor and needy and to helping others find God in ways right for them, rather than maintaining unnecessary religious rituals for the sake of it and calling it faith.

Faith is changing, and there will be others who suggest what that might look like in the future. But the first part of that journey of discovery is demolishing the ancient walls that obscure God, and releasing us all to a new and better faith. One that meets the needs of us today, not those of the past.

Connect with Yourself

Love God, and love those around us. Those are the only two things God tells us to do, and even this might mean different things to everyone. Yet there is one more that I believe is necessary for us today: love ourselves. In an era where we tend to give so much to so many so often, and have so little time for ourselves, we also need to prioritise ourselves. Many of us live with baggage from the past that hinders us in the present, and stops us fulfilling our potential. Many of us make decisions about our lives based on what others have told us, not what we truly believe about ourselves. Many of us never reach our full potential or achieve our dreams because someone told us we would not make it, we were not good enough, we were not clever enough. Or we have such regret about something we have done in the past that it weighs us down and causes guilt or depression. Many of us are just too damn busy or stressed to give ourselves the time we need. Many may not have even been aware of their inner self or know that this part of us needs caring for.

Follow Your Dreams…
They Might Just Be Telling You Who You Really Are

Our dreams can often tell us more about ourselves. Not only the dreams we have at night, but the daydreams, the things we find ourselves wishing we were doing. I often dream of sailing or cycling around the world, betraying my tendency for wanderlust and not being stuck in one place to long. Others dream of a career, a particular body image or lifestyle. Some wish for stability, love or kindness and acceptance.

Our dreams can tell us more about who we truly are. When we explore our desires and our dreams this can lead to us finding out more about ourselves, enabling us to make life changes that mean our dreams can at least in part become reality. Even if we cannot fulfil our wildest dreams, they help us to understand ourselves a bit better. This is part of our wellbeing journey, discovering our life preferences and doing what we can to make them happen. This journey is a bold one to take and it may involve change, but in knowing ourselves better and living according to those preferences, we will undoubtedly be happier. Ignoring our deepest desires because of the demands of life or fear of failure, the unknown or rejection can lead to inner tension, and ultimately unhappiness as we find ourselves not living according to our desires and life preferences.

Many things can affect our lives, how we feel and how much we thrive. Our feelings and emotions go deeper than many of us have ever been, and these things affect how we live, how we feel and the decisions we make. Exploring those depths, exploring what affects us, exploring hurts, exploring how we feel is part of nurturing ourselves. Just identifying hidden things we may be struggling with is the first step to freedom. These things may be spiritual questions or just simply the complexities of life. Taking time alone to explore our inner self and what makes us tick can really help us understand ourselves better, and understand our decision making and life choices.

We are all different, and have different needs and preferences, different personalities and characters that mean what suits one person will not suit another, which is why faith and our interactions with God cannot have just one expression; and why church cannot work for everyone. Even with the great variety of church styles on offer, many people do not function well in large groups, or enjoy sitting in services in their precious spare time.

Each of us can devote as much time to our spiritual health as we wish; it is not a prescription given by religious doctors. Acknowledging that there might be a spiritual aspect to our being is helpful in prompting us to explore what we truly believe about spirituality; have we ever truly explored for ourselves what our beliefs are, or do we simply reject the expressions of faith and spirituality that society, the Church and religious people present? If we could connect with God in a way right for ourselves and in a way that nurtures that aspect of our being would that be good thing for us? Would it be helpful to explore for ourselves the possibility of a higher being we are conveniently calling God, rather than rely on what others have told us? Can we experience God in a way that is right for us? When we strip away religion, the answer must surely be yes.

Franki, a psychologist, totally rejects the idea of church and religion because as a child she had a strict Catholic upbringing and this left her scarred, with a real fear and dislike of church. She certainly would never willingly attend church. But she describes herself as a spiritual person, and she says she feels that when she is walking in stunning hills and alongside trickling streams, she feels exhilarated, as though she is encountering something that makes her feel deeply alive and empowered, like an energy or a force. She does not want to call this God because she associates God with a fear of church, stemming from her church upbringing. It is a terrible thing, that some have a dislike or fear of God because of how God is portrayed by church. The Church really has got a lot to answer for.

When we strip away religion and two thousand years of the debris that has obscured God, we can re-define God. It may that what we find is very different to how God has been portrayed, and by doing this, we will undoubtedly unleash a barrage of wonderful experiences for many more millions of people that will transform lives and make the world a better place.

The idea that we have to live a certain way, change who we are, try and fit a certain image of what we think we should be like before God will accept us, is poppycock. What is right or wrong anyway when it comes to faith? Everyone seems to have different ideas. Our typical image of the holy Christian, the white, western, married, heterosexual, faithful church member with a good career and a tidy home, crumbles before our eyes. This is a man-made image, and Church, Christianity and religion are man-made ways of achieving it. But God knows us intimately and understands us and our needs and preferences, and wants to meet with us in a way right for us; to fill our lives with an orgasmic spiritual love beyond our wildest dreams that reaches to the very heart of our being.

Going Deeper

We can explore our spiritual side by testing it out and finding what works for us. As we do, we get deeper and deeper. We might wish to begin by going for a walk and talk with God, chatting to God whilst we are alone, or having a sumptuous bubble bath and glass of something nice whilst trying to meditate. Heck, a good session with a loved one in bed! As we explore our spiritual side and what works for us, we might find it gets better each time, we go a little deeper, stay for a bit longer, find we rather like the peace and the sense of connecting with this God-being. It is addictive; knowing God closely and experiencing God keeps us coming back for more. We might even find as we pray about something, we get a feeling we have been heard, and that something will be done; that there will be an answer. We might even feel peace and joy for the first time. Test it out! If we do not like it then we can stop.

The idea that we have to adopt church or religion in order to connect with God is an obstacle to finding and experiencing God. But thankfully this is not the case. There are no obstacles, except the ones we put on ourselves — and that others put on us. Because we are saying we do not need religion, Church, Christianity, or a set of rules in order to have a fulfilling experience of God and nurture our spiritual needs, there are no barriers; it is just us and God. We can strip away all the things we have ever been taught about God and find out for ourselves what is left. And I think we might quite like what we find…

It should not be difficult to connect with God and nurture the spiritual aspect of our lives, although it is common for people to say they wish they could have the spiritual experiences that some have, that they want to experience these things, but instead there can be a sense of emptiness, a void, that makes us question if it is all real or not. That is why testing it out in a way that is good for us and starting small may help. It may take a splash of optimism and boldness, and even perhaps trying something we previously thought to be nonsense just to test it out.

Because we are saying faith is personal and flexible, and that we can create our own route to finding God and tailoring that discovery to our own needs and preferences, all obstacles are gone. Our faith is our own. Our relationship with God is our own. The way we express it is up to us. God knows us intimately, and knows and understands our life preferences, and having removed the need for a religious performance before we are declared worthy enough to meet God, there is nothing we need to do except find God. Where we may previously have been rejected by Church or simply disliked it, we may find new ways to express our faith.

Stepping Out of Our Comfort Zones

I started running by signing up for the London Marathon. It was something I had always wanted to do, but for years thought that I would never be able to do it. But one day I just needed to challenge myself, so I signed up. Pushing myself in this way put me in situations where I was seriously out of my comfort zones, and really feeling as though I had to work hard and go beyond what I thought was possible in order to achieve the goal. I was even scared some days I would have a heart attack.

This act of pushing ourselves to our limits, of challenging what we think is possible, of aiming towards a goal we have always wanted but never thought we would get, changes who we are. In the process we grow, change, get rid of inhibitions and fears, and get stronger. That process is exhilarating, exciting and breath-taking, yet it is also hard; and we sometimes doubt whether we can achieve our goal. Giving up is often easier than carrying on, but the results are much greater than the difficulties of the struggle. They are worth it. We might find we need to draw on aspects of ourselves we never knew were there, in order to find the guts to achieve what we are desperate to achieve; in order to discover that inner strength that lies within, the strength that leads to success. When we look back on ourselves and our lives, those times when we stepped out of our comfort zones and smashed down the walls our inhibitions have erected, those times are the best times, times where we grow and change; and that growth and change leads to greater things.

If religion could manage to step outside if its comfort zones and smash its own self-built walls down, it may experience that same transformation.

This process of challenging ourselves is when our faith can help us achieve our non-faith related goals. Our spiritual self can help fuel our whole being to work better and achieve our life goals. This may be one reason why faith and spirituality have a key place in the definition of wellbeing. To live life to the full and to function well, we need to engage each aspect of our lives, not just the physical, although we can give differing amounts of time and energy to each aspect of wellbeing according to our preferences.

Exploring our spiritual depths and preferences is part of nurturing our inner self. When our whole self, including the physical, psychological and spiritual, is functioning as it should, we can then grow. We then have the strength and determination to achieve our goals. This is why many of us are not as healthy mentally or physically as we could be, because we do not look after the whole self. We often pay attention to the physical by looking after our bodies, without noticing the effect the psychological, spiritual, emotional, intellectual, occupational and social also have on the physical. The health of the planet also affects us, but is harder to improve. Unless we care for our whole being, we won't see our wellness goals fully met, and we may not achieve the goals we dream of.

A Pool of Strength Lies Inside Each of Us

As we take on life's challenges we have to dip into our pool of grit, determination and internal resolve to survive and see success. The more we dip into that pool of strength and determination, the bigger it gets. The more we challenge ourselves and our beliefs, the more we learn about ourselves and the stronger we get, and the more we grow. We don't even have to see success in order to grow; often the times of greatest growth are the times we mess up. The more we stretch and try and strive and push the boundaries of those comfort zones, the more we achieve. And with every attempt, however feeble or great, the bigger our reserve of grit gets. We are not then overwhelmed when we encounter really tough difficulties; we can withstand these things because we have the inner strength to do so. It is worth grasping the initiative and doing this when we feel able, because that inner strength takes time to build. It is then ready for us when we need it, to help us not only survive in difficulty, but confidently thrive.

The more we dip into our inner pool of strength and determination, the bigger that pool gets.

So let your dreams run wild! Dream big, and then go bring those dreams to reality, as far as you can. Ignoring them leaves desire waiting, leaves ambitions unfulfilled, and this leaves us frustrated, lethargic and sad. So go sign up for that marathon. Go book that trip. Go get that degree. Apply for that job. Go run, walk, swim, cycle, find your parasport. Go follow your wildest dreams. And never say you're not capable, because only you, know you. And we are capable of much more than we believe we are. So follow your dreams, they might just be leading you in the right direction.

The sense of satisfaction and achievement when we fulfil our dreams and reach our goals is incredible and will stay with us forever. When we look back on our lives, those moments of success fuel a sense of pride and achievement, elation and satisfaction. We can look back and know we managed to achieve something, giving us purpose and self-worth. It can be invigorating. Imagine reaching the end of life as we know it, and feeling a sense of satisfaction over what we achieved, and a bright hope that we are simply moving to the next phase. Death is but the second stage in something inexplicably beautiful; life.

Snowballing Beliefs That Help us Evolve

Alex, an elite runner and staunch atheist, said although he does not believe in God, he does detect a nudge, or a prod, in his mind that there might be something out there, some God-being, but he does not believe in or like God as God is portrayed. This is true for many. Alex has a small desire to explore this belief if he can do that without having to adhere to religious beliefs.

As we explore a subject, we might read about it, talk about it, think about it, perhaps experience something new related to it. We feed our minds with different ways of attempting to explore and understand something. These pieces of knowledge and experiences interact with our previous understanding, our knowledge, our ideas, and our personality. We change who we are and what we believe based on those interactions. As we develop these ideas, we receive more knowledge, more experiences, but each time slightly different, and perhaps going slightly deeper. Other life experiences will feed this evolution of belief, and our ideas and beliefs may change as these experiences and new knowledge interact with who we are. It is like a whirlwind that gathers objects in its path, or a spiral of knowledge, or like a snowball that gathers snow, this knowledge-ball gathers more and more information, experience and insight that changes us.

Beliefs can develop through culture, upbringing, influential people around us, any teaching we might receive, and our life experiences. Christians will often have beliefs nurtured by their interpretation of certain parts of the Bible and what they might hear preached from the pulpit, and what their Christian culture says is right. Where we may have firmly believed something, this can alter as we encounter new information. This revealing process never ends; we are in a constant process of interacting with the world around us and our experiences. Our beliefs evolve as we do. Even if we think we have a firm belief on something, an event might happen that changes or puts that belief in doubt. We cannot judge ourselves or others for things we may have once thought to be true but which have changed as we evolve.

Our beliefs can be so strong that when we encounter evidence that opposes them, we often cannot let ourselves change them. We do this all the time. Alex, the elite runner, totally rejected the idea of God until he realised God may be different to the ogre he had learnt about in school and church. He then realised as he developed a faith that this could be just as he wanted it; he didn't need to conform to religious ideals in order to have a vibrant faith. If we try to remain fixed in a belief on a subject despite an experience or new information that may go against that belief, we are not honouring our internal desire to grow, develop and change as new experiences and new information drop into our lives.

Faith or spirituality is a key part of wellbeing, and being open to this process of exploring faith, and allowing our ideas and beliefs to develop as we have new experiences, may be something we need. It may also be something we crave, but have been too suspicious of church to want to explore. As we discover more about ourselves, we may venture into exploring what we truly believe about God and faith, and how that might impact our lives. This journey can result in us finding God for ourselves, and finding a way of expressing this that it right for us, but this happens within the context of our whole lives, so our faith beliefs will be in line with other things we value. Alex knew he was affected by inner conflict as he was unable to let himself explore the idea of God because of his dislike of religion. This conflict affected his wellbeing.

Similarly, Mike was an atheist, disliking religion which he felt was corrupt. He found a circle of friends and together they met in the pub each week to explore faith and discuss life. This pub community developed and through it he has found a deep, inner faith that gives him mental strength and a deeper sense of who he is, which has improved his mental health.

If we firmly believe God does not exist, but there is a tiny nudge in our hearts and minds that this may not be true, it is worth exploring. If we don't, that question can hover in our minds, and those little doubts may turn to anxiety or worry, and perhaps as we approach death we may find that inner turmoil increases as we realise we have not answered those important questions.

My mother-in-law grew up in the era when people were told sugar was good for you. She maintained that belief throughout her whole life, and in old age as she was trying to lose weight, my husband, who is a doctor, would tell her sugar was actually not good and was contributing to her weight problem. Yet even in the face of modern scientific evidence, you would still hear her say, 'I've got to keep my blood sugar levels up!' In fact, her body was more than capable of keeping her blood sugar up without her taking excess sugar; but she was not shifting from her belief. Our beliefs can be powerful things. Even in the face of contrary evidence we can still maintain beliefs that may not be wholly true.

There are many who believe there is *something*, some God-being that exists, and yet dislike Church, Christianity or religion. Thankfully, exploring whether there might be a spiritual aspect to life and a being that we are calling God does not mean adhering to any religious image. The God religion has created does not exist, but something exists. The model Christian does not exist, but we exist. And there is a great desire inside each of us to live, love and thrive, fulfil our dreams and grab life with everything we have got and thoroughly enjoy it. Let us throw off everything that hinders our lives and go achieve our wildest dreams. If there are insurmountable barriers in our lives to us doing this, ask God to remove them.

God sees our inner being, and knows how and why we work the way we do, and that we are all different; this is why one way of expressing faith will not be right for everyone. God must despair sometimes, seeing people sit in dull meetings pretending to be engaged in a service but really thinking about how many other lovely things they would rather be doing! Likewise, God must hate it when people are rejected because they do not fit the Christian mould. Thankfully, the only mould God has is a love-shaped one; and love is different for each of us.

Searching for Meaning and Purpose

We all have expectations when we are young, such as finding a career, starting a relationship and having children, and perhaps exploring the world. Then we might find a home and make it our own. There is hope, expectations and goals. But we can reach a point where children may have left or never arrived at all, jobs and even careers become mundane, and life can become dull. Without goals and new things to achieve, it can be difficult to find the motivation to do anything. We thrive when we have a goal, target or something to work towards to gain that sense of achievement. It is common to encounter depression and lethargy at this time in life due to lack of direction, purpose and goals. Life often lets us down, and if and when it does, there may be nothing left to rely on. This was my experience in the depths of despair and grief with infertility. Everything — friends, church, work, relatives, money — let us down; the only thing I could hang onto was God. It is at times like this that the memories of our experiences of God have their greatest affect. Those memories and the feelings we had at those times when we met with God keep us strong in tough times. The empty shell of religion simply cannot give us that strength and help. We need that power and strength that only comes when our hearts connect with the heart of God.

Faith can give us a purpose in life, or be a way of achieving purpose. Faith enables a vision of the future, a sense of direction where there isn't just death at the end of our lives, there is an optimistic hope that we will not simply be a menu for worms, but that there is a new life with God, and where we are reunited with our loved ones. The stories we have heard and the evidence from people's experiences show there is a great chance that there is indeed something real in the idea of a God-being, and that death is merely the gateway to a glorious future life. But there are also endless spiritual depths to delve into now, with new discoveries to be made, both about ourselves and about God. Religion has not even scratched the surface.

It is common to feel there is something missing from our lives, some aspect of life we are not quite satisfying. Things such as alcohol, fun, food, sex or exercise can satisfy us momentarily but in the background we might feel we have an unmet need. That may be our spiritual self, crying out for some attention. God is there to be found, and when we look, God *always* responds.

Seek and Ye Shall Find

"If we seek God, God will be found by us."[144] The idea of us searching for God or seeking God is something that many of the Bible authors describe as their experience, and they also encourage others to do the same. It is in searching that we find; it is in the pursuit of something that we get the answer. Some may claim that God is a figment of our imagination and does not really exist, that we find what we think we will find. But the wealth of stories of people experiencing real, physical phenomenon when they encounter God shows it cannot be a figment of a fertile imagination. Something real happened to me that day when that man put his hand on my head and prayed.

The key to pursuing is never giving up. We keep searching until we find what we are looking for, just like a lover getting up to find their loved one, or hunting for treasure we believe is there. How, where and when we search is part of our personal journey. God and our own personal faith and spirituality are there to be found. God will always respond to our search, but how we search and what we find helpful in searching are up to us. We each have different preferences and abilities. Some of us love exploring the hills, mountains and seas, and certainly these are inspiring places to seek God. But some of us are lying on our sick bed, unsure of what the future holds. Some suffer depression; unable to lift ourselves from our inner pain, unable to imagine hope. We are all so different, and that is why the journey, and the search, will be different for each of us.

This pursuit is mutual; God searches also for us. There is a verse in the Bible that hints at good things to come: "God searches for us and looks after us. God rescues us and brings us to a beautiful place where we will have everything we need. God will wipe every tear from our eyes, there will be no more death, mourning, crying or pain. Just like a flock of sheep needs good, safe grazing land, God will tend to us in a good pasture; there we will lie down and rest, we will feed in a rich pasture in peace and safety. God will search for the lost and helpless, help the injured and strengthen the weak."[145] This analogy speaks of sheep; the reality is of precious lives. Paradise awaits.

The Call

God stands on the side-lines and waits in the alleyways, gesturing with wizened hands and gently whispering for us to come in. 'But,' we cry, 'I don't like you!' And so we continue our journey. The next street, the next building, we might notice God again, but this time take a quick look, seeing if God really is what we think God is. We see God again, this time sitting beside a hospital bed, lovingly holding a dying person's hand, leading them to new life. We stare a little harder because we see something we were not expecting, a vision of pure love. We glimpse God again, this time comforting the partner of the deceased, giving them hope that will keep them strong. We spot God sitting beside the depressed, the lonely, the hurting, those who have seen too many awful things, things that people should not have to endure.

As we notice God more and more, we might find ourselves searching in other places, trying to spot God; trying to catch a glimpse of what God is like. As we discover more, God lovingly pulls us closer in, showing us more about who God is and what God can do. There is a mutual response; God pulls us closer and we find we cannot resist coming, wanting more. For some it is the feeling of finding something important you have been searching for, that feeling as your heart leaps when you finally discover it. For others, it is a feeling of peace. For others still, an excitement or overwhelming joy. Who knows what experiences await us?

A Life Beyond Life

As we explore God, some will find that not only are our lives suddenly flooded with meaning and purpose and new spiritual experiences that we never thought possible, but we may catch a vision of the future, of a life beyond what we experience now, a life beyond death. Some may find this a relief, those to whom this life has not been kind. Thoughts of another realm, a new spiritual horizon, an encounter with God can bring us great comfort. Some may even find a life beyond life; a new aspect to our current lives that lifts us from our troubles, as a whole new world of potential opens up to us and we find new meaning and a new source of strength.

This journey of discovery is a bit like travelling. We live our lives based in one area of the world but if we travel, we suddenly realise there are many other ways of doing life, many vibrant cultures and a world full of new exciting experiences. Travel opens our minds to how big, complex and beautiful the world and its inhabitants are, and we are different as a result. It's all part of that whirlwind of discovery. When we experience God and all the wonderful things God has for us, we are changed. This vision of eternity and a life with God beyond this one can give us meaning and purpose, hope and expectancy. This fills us with excitement and can give us new purpose. The struggles of life suddenly do not seem quite so hard.

Experiences feed that journey of discovery, that journey of growth, that journey of discovering ourselves. Experiences matter, because there can be times when even faith may feel a bit mundane or difficult or life's struggles can steal our peace; we can then hold onto our memories of what God did for us, or others, in the past. This is why experiencing God for ourselves is so essential, because a set of religious rules or activities offers little support in tough times without that deep, inner heartfelt experience of God. This is why the Bible writers felt so keenly that they should write down what God did. Those experiences are our source of strength when things get tough. They also increase our faith about what is possible; we begin to believe that if God can help us with this problem, what else can God help us with? If God can do that, what else is possible? When running alone and that last ten miles of a marathon is full of pain and mental struggle and our legs want to give up, we have only our inner grit, and the memory of thousands cheering us on to help us continue.

Design Your Faith

Jeanette was widowed with two small children at age thirty-five. She had been bought up in a mixed faith family, with Catholic and Protestant parents, and had always been struck by how her mother's faith gave her such mental strength. Jeanette began to question the point of religion whilst growing up in that environment, whilst witnessing people seemingly using religion to hurt and kill each other. Although Jeanette has a deep faith, she believes religion is not necessary and only creates conflict. It did not take her long to leave behind her childhood religion. She was quite relieved as she finds church stale and mundane, and quite boring.

Jeanette does not read her Bible as she feels it is flawed, that people tend to believe naively what it says, and can manipulate the wording of it. She describes herself as having a scientific approach to life and that many aspects of religion do not make sense. She describes much of religion as codswallop, but she has a deep faith.

Jeanette feels that different times of our lives demand more or less reliance on faith, and that her faith beliefs change and develop according to life events. She believes there is a God-figure that exists, but she doesn't know what it is and doesn't *need* to know, in order to have faith. She does not pray or talk to this God-being, although she would not rule out talking to it in the future. Whenever she faces a situation, she asks herself, 'What is the Christian thing to do?' And this for her is to respond with love and kindness. She does not need to be religious to hold onto her faith. Jeannette rejects any pressure to attend church or seek solace in religion as that is not her preference at this time, and she feels it would distract from the many good things she is doing.

For Jeanette, God is a positive force for good, a positive momentum that inspires people to help each other. Jeanette works tirelessly for her community and known locally as one of the kindest, most loving and caring people, she quickly jumps to the aid of those in need and displays in huge volumes that ethos of "Love God and love each other". Her faith runs deep, she oozes God, and yet is not in any way religious.

We can design our faith to suit our lives, just as we would design our homes, our body image, and the food on our plates.

Steps to Discovering Our Spiritual Preferences

It can be difficult to come up with ideas of how to kick start and maintain this connection with God. Some steps to guide us may help:

1) Acknowledge the nudge. Is there a tiny nugget of a belief that there may be a God-being that exists? It is good to be honest with ourselves about what our inner beliefs regarding faith are even if we do not have concrete evidence at this point.
2) Allow ourselves to explore this nudge. We can begin this journey any way we wish, we can attend a religious building, or go for a walk and talk to God, or even dream about God; what would you like God to look like and be like if God did indeed exist?
3) Imagine what you would like your faith to look like. If anything is possible, what would you want time with God to be like? What would you want God to do for you and say to you? Would you like to experience an overwhelming feeling of God resting on your physical body, filling every fibre of your being? Or would you like to hear a quiet voice, reassuring you or guiding you? Or perhaps a deep sense of peace and happiness? Visualise what you would want God to do for you and what you would prefer time spent with God to be like, assuming anything at all is possible.
4) Challenge our thinking: do we dislike the idea of God because of how God is portrayed by others in society and because of religion, Christianity and Church? Do we know what we dislike if we do not relish the idea of God? We need to know for ourselves what God is like, not rely on the opinions of others, or how others express their

faith. We can find out by taking the first step onto that spiral of discovery.

5) If you are struggling with something, however big or small, talk to this God-being about it. Just simply throw up a quick request for help; and see what happens. It may be that your situation changes and help comes, or that you are given the strength to endure.
6) As we enter and journey on that spiral of discovery and knowledge, we begin to discover our spiritual preferences and desires. As we have new experiences or learn new information, it can be helpful to record how we feel, adding it to our bank of knowledge and experience. This is unique to us; how we find God and express that discovery is our choice and we can design our faith in whichever way we choose. A faith that is our own can then contribute to our wellbeing.
7) We may wish to share our journey and our discoveries with others, as those writers of the Bible did, and others since. Not so that we insist they do the same as us, but so that they also discover their preferences. And so we discover our own faith and how we wish to express it, and our faith and wellbeing journey evolves.

And so that tornado, that snowball, gathers momentum, and gathers experiences and knowledge. And as it does, we change, we evolve, and we grow. And when we look back in time, we discover just what a fantastic impact it has had on our lives. I don't believe we will be disappointed.

There are many ideas on how to express faith and we have some here, but some may not need ideas, wanting instead to develop our faith our own way.

Quietness and Solitude

Some find personal reflection, similar to mindfulness, beneficial. Some people benefit from a routine and so might find a short time at the start or end of the day to reflect is helpful. Others, like myself, prefer to be spontaneous, and some days you will spend more time, others less. Christians are often compelled by their churches to have a quiet time, daily time spent with God, praying or singing, or exploring some aspect of Christianity. But this idea does not suit everyone, and the result is often guilt as people's lives and preferences do not easily fit with the church's expectations. It is better to design our own faith preferences, but it can be helpful to reflect about God or talk to God if we feel unsettled, if something is bothering us but we are not sure what. This can become fluid, flexible and instinctive, and a natural part of life.

Some call this prayer. Anthony, the first monk who lived in the deserts of Egypt and was the among the first to reject church life in favour of a faith lived out in solitude, founded the first monasteries.[146] Today, people still retain this lifestyle of complete dedication to God, lived out in communities where prayer is the focus.

There is one such community on Dartmoor, at Buckfast Abbey. There is a remarkable sense of peace in this place, where entering is like encountering another world. It is as though God is somehow able to meet with people, that you can sense God's presence there. The monks describe their lives as being a journey towards understanding themselves and God. Their journey involves prayer and physical work, although they are clear in saying prayer means different things to everyone. They even blow apart traditionally held views on defining God, admitting the concept of God is far too complex for definitions. One abbot believes God is present in every aspect of the world and people, and remains open to the suggestion that we must all find what God is for us personally.[147]

There is a cave in Derbyshire that was once the home of a hermit; a person who wished also to remove themselves from society and live alone in the stunning but harsh woodlands and moorlands. As you locate this cave on the footpaths that crisscross this area and peep inside, your eyes take time to adjust to the darkness. You begin to find the marks on the walls where the hermit carved the cave by hand, a simple hollow with a platform for a bed and a nook for a candle. If there is enough light, you can begin to focus on some markings on the right-hand wall; a figure carved into the bedrock. This was the only décor, and may have meant everything to the hermit; this was a carving of Jesus on the cross. Little is known of the occupant but that this dark, damp cave was their home for several years. They probably welcomed strangers who needed shelter.[148]

We do not have to live in damp, dark caves to find God, unless we wish to. But the examples of those over the years who have stepped outside the confines of the norm and chosen their own way, chosen what is right for them according to their life preferences, show that there is no need to live our lives and our faith according to what we are told or according to the confines of religion; we can choose our own path. It may mean solitude, it may mean busyness, it may mean something entirely different. Faith is no different to any other part of our lives in that we should have it just the way we want it.

The traditional images of God can be deconstructed. As we do, religious structures and beliefs crumble and we can all find what God means to us, and our own way of expressing that discovery. The data we have on how spiritual health impacts our general health, means that we will probably all feel better for embarking on that journey of discovery.

Reflecting on our Wellbeing

Reflecting on the aspects of wellbeing; the physical, social, occupational, intellectual, emotional, spiritual and others we may find important to us, can help us identify which areas of our lives might need some attention. The idea that we can take tentative steps to explore faith and God in our own ways may be reassuring. We can stop if we wish, and return to it later. There is no rush or compulsion to perform. This journey is our own.

Going to our favourite place can be a way of spending time connecting with God. Some like to find a place in the home, but for some, a walk or cycle, or finding a special place outdoors, in a garden or a religious building of any sort, just somewhere that is special to us can be helpful. For some, a longer walk in the countryside on a day off is fuel enough for the week. For some, the wild places are church! We might wish to reflect and connect with God through writing a diary, thinking, meditating, singing or any activity we enjoy. We could even draw our inner castle.

Reflection can be calming for our souls, or can highlight aspects of our lives that are causing us distress or inner turmoil. Often it is when we have times of reflection that these things have a chance to come to the surface, and we recognise areas that may need some repair work. Some people do not make big decisions before they have sought God's help first.

Write Your Own Bible!

We can write our own Bible! The Bible is a collection of different types of writing by people who wrote down their experiences of God. It is a great resource for discovering God and God can speak to us through it if we wish to use it — as long as we use it correctly — to find God, not rules for living.

We can write down how we feel about God, life, our experiences, how our life has gone so far and what we would like to happen in the future. There might be times we felt a God-being might have been involved in something that happened to us, a time we had a strange or miraculous experience. Or putting in things we are grateful for. Gratitude and being thankful foster better mental health, and can help as part of our spiritual journey. We could combine this with scrapbooking, assembling pictures and items that tell our life story. Sometimes an object that is dear to us can help us connect with God.

Write down poems, prayers, requests, ideas. If we would like a certain experience of God but feel we have never had one, write that down — ask for it! Make it yours, draw pictures and make it colourful and creative. It is our personal communication book with God. It can be what we want it to be, and say what we want it to say. We could add verses from the "real" Bible that may mean something to us, or from other literature. We could search an online Bible resource for ideas. We can then look back in a few years and see if our experiences match up to what we wanted.

This may be difficult for those who have a high view of the Bible as the Word of God. The same is true for other ideas we have explored, such as Church and its many structures and beliefs. But the hope is it will allow those who wish to, the freedom to explore and express their faith in helpful ways. Those who disagree can maintain their beliefs as their own expression of faith but need not interfere with how others wish to express theirs. It is helpful if we can respect each other's beliefs and accept that what some find helpful may not be true for others. This is part of exploring the future of faith, together or alone. We do not have to agree in order to experience God.

We can also write our own worship songs or hymns. We can access many hymns on YouTube and other internet sites, and experiment with what is out there — there are some really good songs out there written by fantastic guys recently, and they can help us connect with God by singing along at home. But we can also write our own! They are an expression of our faith, our needs, our requests, our experiences. Those who are talented musically could massively contribute to helping others express their faith by writing some new material relevant to the journey of finding God.

Sometimes I grab a friend from the running club and we have no idea what distance or what speed we will run, we just want to be free. We might at the start say, 'What do you fancy?' and we say, a 10k? A half marathon? Shall we do road or trail? We might set off and say, 'Let's go for it, let's do a trail half!' and off we go, excitedly chatting away, exploring the countryside. It is like this with God. We might go out for a walk and talk with God, and say, 'God, what do you want to say to me today?' And God might show us some revelation, a picture, a word, or give us a desire to do something new. We grab God's hand and say, 'What shall we do today?' and God might say, 'Are you up for anything?'

When we experience God, it is something we never forget. And then when we need it most, those experiences give us the strength we need to survive, thrive and win.

Once we strip away religion, we release the opportunity to find ourselves in an exciting whirlwind of discovery.

Coffee With God

Some might be able to imagine that we are about to sit and have an hour with God now. What would we say to God? If God could do anything for us now, what would we ask for? Could we put ourselves right now, in our minds, in a place where we can talk face to face with God? What is God like? What characteristics does God have? Picture God sitting beside you now, wherever you are. This is a special time, where we can ask God anything. It's just us and God, and so we can tell God anything;

how happy we are, how angry we are, how sad we are, how hurt we are, or how we don't even know how we are because we are so numb by the complexities and troubles of life.

Stress and times of difficulty are when we need that inner grit and strength, but they can also bring us closer to God because in those times when people let us down and there is little hope, when structures of society, our friends and family, our career, our home and money might be suddenly taken away, it may be that faith in a God-being is all we have left. I find it helpful to pray in times of difficulty, and this can make us feel relieved that we have handed over the problem to someone more capable of solving it. Answers do not always come quickly. But sometimes all you can do in these difficult times is sit in God's presence and say nothing. This was my experience, and that is okay because anything is okay. How we design our faith is up to us. The sense that we are not alone in what we are experiencing is soothing. That support can be the thing that gets us through.

There are no right or wrong ways of doing this. We can sing, write, draw, talk, walk, swim or lie in the cool grass on a hot day. We can do whatever makes us happy. We can do whatever we find connects us to this incredible God-being. All it takes is a nod and a wink in God's direction, a look up to the sky or down to the earth and a wish to connect. A notion that this prod or nudge might be God saying, 'Hi.' If we want to, we will find God. And in the process we can each redefine faith for ourselves, and perhaps for others too.

Connecting with God Through Church

Some people find church structures helpful. Majestic buildings, a priest who can pray for us and minister to us, the Bible, worshipping with others and the concept of a sacred place and services where many do indeed meet God. The space for quiet reflection can be helpful for many.

Not all churches are bad; some are full of life and allow God to do what God wants each week in meetings. They create a culture where our faith can indeed be our own, and experiences of God abound. But even those churches are not for everyone, or not accessible to everyone. There are many people for whom the only nearby accessible churches are the ones that are far too religious and dull to be worth going to. So for those who either cannot get to a church that might suit them, or who just do not like church, Christianity or religion, but do fancy what *God* has to offer, they can tailor their faith to themselves.

Some like to dip in and out, finding church helpful for a certain period of their lives, or go on a whim, just for a day to find peace and space in a religious building or in a service. This is one way of connecting with God, but for many, these settings are not helpful. We know that we can connect with God alone on a mountain or on our bed as much as we can in a church, we do not have to be in a religious building or do religious things in order to connect with God and receive all the experiences God might have for us. We can buy a burger in McDonalds, or we can make one ourselves in our own kitchen.

Surf Church

But church doesn't have to look like it traditionally has done. There is a church in Portugal that meet on the beach and go surfing together. Simply called Surf Church, they have a café in a tent, and meet to have fun and chat informally about life, faith and God. They form a community of people with a common interest and church naturally happens around that. It is informal and fun, but it is church.[149] More and more groups are stepping outside the traditional model of church and religion, as more people become disillusioned and start to think outside the box. Some meet in pubs, some over sport, some as groups that have health issues in common, or careers, jobs or families in common. This gives us a freedom to think for ourselves whether there is a way we can explore life and faith together with others in a context we are familiar with. Go set up your own church (and you don't have to call it church…)!

Churches also must explore new ways of helping people discover God outside the church setting, and without expecting people to join their activities and adopt their beliefs. There is a core belief in Christianity that we must meet together as part of our faith, again based on a few Bible verses such as Hebrews 10:25: "Do not give up meeting together…" Churches tend to take this to mean meeting weekly for church services, but faith is more diverse than that. The Church's belief is reinforced by a desire to fill the seats on a Sunday and swell the church bank account; two things that are often of more importance than finding God. It would be great if churches and individual Christians could ask themselves why we do what we do, is it all necessary? Does it work? If not, let's change it.

Is This What Happens When God Finds You?'

This is the remarkable story from Jon, a professional businessman. For many years Jon had a general dislike of Christians, Church or religion, stemming from a time when at the age of seventeen, his young girlfriend, who he adored, took him along to her lively, modern church. They truly loved each other but she wished to see him become a Christian and felt that if he didn't, she could not continue the relationship. Jon describes his experience of that church as terrifying, and just could not grasp the idea of God, faith or what they were trying to achieve. Having found the church environment difficult, he certainly did not wish to go back, and wanted nothing more to do with Christians or church. He didn't mind too much as he wasn't sure of his religious beliefs, but the inevitable breakup left him hurt and feeling bitter towards Christians. Religion just didn't make any sense to him.

His life continued, and Jon had a good career and a contented and happy family life with his new wife and their three beautiful children. Jon continued to reject any idea of God or religion, even though his new wife was a strong Christian and regularly attended church. What he didn't know was that she had been praying for him.

The encounter came many years later. One evening, Jon got a notification from his employer that he would be due six months paid leave in two years' time due to long service. His thoughts wandered onto what he could do with that time, but dreams of travelling to the exotic destinations he would love to visit had to be quickly shelved, as the family had numerous debts that meant money would be tight. This was a Tuesday evening, and later that evening as he relaxed with a glass of wine, he was reading a science magazine that showed a picture of Jesus as he would have looked; not the familiar blond hair and blue eyed man often portrayed, but a man of medium height, with short dark hair and beard, brown eyes and olive brown skin.

The picture didn't have an impact on Jon at the time, but later that night he had a vivid dream. He found himself walking through a black turnstile and down some stone steps leading to an underground room. Jon stood on the sandy floor of this ancient stone room, taking in the comforting ambience from a warm orange light. He noticed he was carrying a medium sized shoulder bag that contained a large, heavy weight. He somehow knew that the heavy weight was God.

He had this same dream three times, but the third time it changed. This time, he knew he had to open the bag. As he did, his entire world changed.

The moment he opened that bag he woke up. He was suddenly filled with an overwhelming sensation that filled every fibre of his being. From his head to his feet, his entire body was encompassed by this tingling, awesome, powerful sensation. It felt erotic, but it wasn't sexual. For half an hour this powerful sensation continued as wave after wave washed over him. It felt as though every part of him was being infused by this incredible power. He lay there in awe, totally overcome by this incredible encounter.

It was five a.m., and he suddenly felt compelled to get up and go to the beach but because it was his day off, he stayed in bed. This nagging feeling continued, and so after fifteen minutes he got up. He took his dog to the beach, where, as he turned a corner beside some sandstone rocks, the sun began to rise. The colours of a glorious sunrise began to fill the sky, and his entire vision was filled with this stunning scene. The tide had just gone out, leaving that refreshing feeling of a new cycle of life, as the birds prodded their beaks into the sand searching for morsels to eat.

He was alone on the beach. His dog had wandered off, and in an attempt to entice her back, he threw a ball. It landed in the sand near some molluscs, and Jon bent down to pick the ball up. As he did, he was startled by a pattern the molluscs had drawn in the sand. There before him was a question mark. His mind was instantly cast back to his experience in bed. He realised this meant something. He found himself saying, 'Is this what happens when God finds you?'

He looked up again, and at that moment the sun crept out above the cliffs. He turned, and with a renewed energy, started walking towards it. He just wanted to carry on walking; walking towards the sun, walking towards the light. He knew God had moved powerfully in his life, and he didn't want it to end.

He had to return home, however, and as he did, his wife asked where he had been. He simply answered, 'There's some crazy s**t going on,' and told her all about it.

His wife was about to go away for the weekend but felt torn, as she did not fully understand what was happening and felt uncomfortable leaving Jon. As she prayed, she felt God say to her, 'Leave Jon with me.' She knew at that moment that because God had done this, he would be okay.

Later, as they shared this incredible story together, Jon's wife confessed to him that she had been praying for him to find God for many years. Three years before hand, she had written out a Bible verse and hidden it in his pillow. It was Matthew 14:28: "God, if it's you, tell me to come to you."

They knew the significance of Jon then having that experience of God whilst lying in bed with his head on that same pillow.

These encounters with God continued. Several times in the night Jon would find himself woken by God, filled with the Holy Spirit. Those incredible, tingling, powerful sensations continued time and time again to fill his entire body. He often found himself compelled to stand, his arms outstretched as God showed him powerful, intense and meaningful visions. He felt he could *see* God. He saw colours that are beyond description, iridescent reds and oranges that filled his vision. It was like a fiery wind was almost dancing around his mind, as if the colours were alive and almost playful. He felt the Holy Spirit pouring through his body time after time, as waves of power and love washed over him. These encounters literally changed Jon's life. Importantly, though, Jon knew he was safe. These were the most incredible experiences of his life.

These encounters had some practical outcomes. Jon's six-month leave would have started on 9th June 2019. A few months before, he was called to a meeting and informed he was being made redundant. His last day of work? 8th June 2019. Jon asked God for a certain amount for his redundancy money, and when he received his cheque, it was ten times that amount. This meant he could pay his debts, and also that he could be free in those six months to travel. As he asked God what to do with that time, he felt God show him a picture of the Golden Gate Bridge in San Francisco. He also realised God was showing him various birds, as he walked in the hills around his home. He travelled to San Francisco, and visited Bethel Church, Bill Johnson's church, where those incredible miracles regularly take place that we described in our chapter on experiencing God. He felt God say the word "Father" to him, which impacted him greatly as his own father had recently died, and Jon had also been concerned about being a good father to his own children. The birds also had significance; Jon was later offered a job working for a bird protection charity.

Jon had never read the Bible, and knew little of Christianity or church life and belief. But after this encounter, he instinctively knew about common aspects of faith such as loving others, forgiveness and benevolence. He felt God had taught him those things. He now talks to God regularly, but always while outside on his walks. He does not need to go to a building to find God. In fact, Jon says God usually finds him!

He realises the significance of what has happened, and knows it is an immense privilege to have experienced God pouring into his life in this incredible way. This has literally changed his life and he has a totally new outlook on life. He has no fear of death any more.

Jon also feels no need to get involved in religious practice, describing it as man-made nonsense. This was driven home when he did attend church with his wife a while ago, and when hoping to take communion, was turned away as he had not been confirmed. But he knew he didn't need communion, when he had encountered God in such a powerful way.[150] Let more of us experience God in such a way!

Re-Writing Faith

Many people want God. Many people need God. And the way we find God and express that discovery is changing. Walls are being demolished, blockages are being removed. God is emerging from the dust and debris of two millennia of Church and religion, and people who have disliked and rejected Church will find God in new and exciting ways. God wants to be close to us and does not care how we find that connection. The great news is that God exists outside the walls and beliefs of our churches and we can find God anywhere.

Nurturing our spiritual self is essential for overall wellbeing, but because we are all different, this will look different for each of us. We can tailor our faith and our spirituality to our own needs and preferences, just like we would for any aspect of life. To ignore this part of us because we do not like what others say God is like and how they suggest we should express our faith, could mean we miss out on an incredible encounter with God that may change our lives forever. It is worth exploring this for ourselves even if we feel we do not need it now, as there may be times in the future when we are desperate for a support that life and the world cannot give us.

What we need is God, and often what we get is religion. For too long, Church has replaced lifechanging, awe inspiring, captivating experiences of God for a dry, rather boring religion with rules, beliefs and practices we must conform to in order to be accepted. People were labelled sinners, and ordered to conform to be saved from this sinful state. God was portrayed as an ogre, ready to cast us into hell if we make a mistake.

An image of God has been created that is simply wrong, and yet many have believed it. It is no wonder many do not like the idea of God. Yet God looks with saddened, compassionate eyes at those who need and want God, those who desire freedom, life and love and a faith journey filled with incredible lifechanging experiences of God, and instead get a religious building and a set of rules, those who do not manage to find God because God stays hidden from their view, disguised by religion. Those who desire fine wine and delicious roast lamb from God's table whilst sitting in God's empowering presence, but instead get a McDonalds in the car park.

It is time to get back to experiencing God. It is time to strip away all the encumbrances two thousand years of Church history have burdened God with; all the things that obscure this God-being. It is time to sweep away the religious debris, and to nourish our spiritual appetite with this loving, powerful, life giving, lifechanging God-being.

Encountering God was always meant to be an incredible, awesome experience. It was always meant to be filled with wonder and orgasmic experiences of God filling up our lives, hearts and bodies with God's extravagant love. It is not dull, it is not boring, it is flipping incredible. And we're all invited to the party. All religious masks and preconceptions can be left on the doorstep.

When we find God, we can be safe in the knowledge that we are precious to God, and we can begin, or reignite, an incredible journey of discovery of God and all God has for us. A part of us that we might not have known existed comes to life in a way we never thought possible. The exploration of God is endless and exciting and there are many new experiences up for grabs. And one day, when we cross over from this life to the next, God will welcome us with open arms into paradise. Death therefore will not be sad or difficult, it will be the happiest day of our lives.

What do we find when we strip God of religion and break down those religious walls that have obscured God? Let's go find out for ourselves!

It's time to find faith again.

It's time to find ourselves again.

It's time to find God again.

Appendix 1
Inconsistencies

One consideration when examining how we should use the Bible is the presence of undeniable inconsistencies in the text. Here is a snapshot of some:

- In 1 Samuel 16 David and Saul meet, but by 1 Samuel 17, Saul does not seem to know who David is.
- In the New Testament, the four gospel accounts present the life and ministry of Jesus in very different ways, putting events in different orders, and sometimes contradicting one another. E.g.: In John, Jesus cleanses the temple at the beginning of his ministry, in the other gospels it is just before Jesus' arrest. Other seemingly crucial details differ.
- Details of Jesus' birth and death differ between the gospel writers.
- Judas' death differs: in Matthew 27:5 he hangs himself, yet in Acts 1:18 it says that he fell and his bowels burst from inside him.

Textual evidence from the Old Testament reveals heavy editing of the text by the authors and editors who interwove already existing texts to create another, greater story, but with the consequence that the story does not flow smoothly. This creates apparent contradictions or mistakes:

- The Noah's ark story in Genesis does not quite flow smoothly. The length of time the flood lasts in one place is 40 days and 40 nights, but in verse 24 it is 150 days. Finally, by chapter 8:13, ten and a half months later the waters dry up. One pair of every animal is taken into the boat in 6:19-20, but in a slightly clunky note in 7:2, it is seven pairs of the animals for sacrifice.
- In the creation narratives, there are two accounts that vary dramatically in detail. In Genesis one there are the well-known seven

days of creation with man and woman created on day six. In Genesis two, man is created before anything else.

- In Exodus 24, there is a bewildering account of Moses being asked to go up and down a mountain several times, often being recorded as going up when he was already up. In verse 1, it is said only Moses can gaze upon God, yet by verse nine the elders all go up, see God and eat a meal with God. They appear to gaze fully upon God, yet Exodus 33:23 says God's face must not be seen. Other accounts show people seeing God.

This is a work of creative nonfiction. The events are portrayed to the best of the author's memory. While all the stories in this book are true, some names and identifying details have been changed to protect the privacy of the people involved.

ENDNOTES

[1] Ian McCormack survived his encounter and today is a church minister in New Zealand. You can read more about his incredible encounter on his website:
https://www.aglimpseofeternity.org/.
Story Paraphrased from Testimony on Ian's website and Ian McCormack and Jenny Sharkey, *Clinically Dead*, Gospel Media, 2013. Ian McCormack has granted permission for use.

[2] Morris-Young, Amy, information and story sent in personal email to author. Permission grated by Amy Morris-Young for use.

[3] Wynne-Jones, J., 'Two Percent of Anglican Priests Don't Believe in God, Survey Finds'. *Independent* Website, https://www.independent.co.uk/news/uk/home-news/survey-finds-2-of-anglican-priests-are-not-believers-9821899.html?r=4671, 31st January 2022.

[4] Acts 2:1-4, paraphrased from the New Living Translation

[5] Acts 2: 42-47, paraphrased from the New Living Translation

[6] Hurtado, L. W., 'Christ' in Green, Joel B. et al, (eds), *Dictionary of Jesus and the Gospels,* Leicester: InterVarsity Press, 1992, 106-117.

[7] Tacitus, 'The Christians Accused By Nero' in *The Annals of Tacitus*, No. 44, p 423, work in public domain, https://www.google.co.uk/books/edition/The_annals/3DgstTVjP7sC?hl=en&gbpv=1&printsec=frontcover, accessed 15th February 2022.

[8] Hill, Jonathon, *The History of Christianity*, New Lion Handbook, Oxford: Lion Hudson PLC, 2007, 56.

[9] Open Doors, 'World Watch List 2022', *Open Door* Website, https://www.opendoorsuk.org/, accessed 17th February 2022.

[10] Godwin, Roy and Roberts, Dave, *The Grace Outpouring*, Colorado Springs: David C Cook, 2019.

[11] Hill, *Christianity*, 72.

[12] Freeman, Charles, *A New History of Early Christianity,* London: Yale University Press, 2009, 222.

[13] Encyclopaedia Britannica, 'Sunday', 'Sol Invictus', 'Christmas Day', *Encyclopaedia Britannica* Website, https://www.britannica.com/, accessed 22nd November 2021.

[14] Hill, *Christianity,* 74-77.

[15] Hill, *Christianity,* 74-77.

[16] Circumcision, including female circumcision exists in some cultures and religions. Many are fighting to eradicate female circumcision (FGM —Female Genital Mutilation) due to the trauma it causes.

[17] Encyclopaedia Britannica, 'First Council of Nicea', *Encyclopaedia Britannica* Website, https://www.britannica.com/event/First-Council-of-Nicaea-325, accessed 2/11/21, and Bruce Shelley, '325 The First Council of Nicaea,' *Christianity Today* Website, https://www.christianitytoday.com/history/issues/issue-28/325-first-council-of-nicea.html, accessed 12th December 2022.

[18] Encyclopaedia Britannica, 'Commitment to Christianity of Constantine 1', *Encyclopaedia Britannica* Website https://www.britannica.com/biography/Constantine-I-Roman-emperor/Commitment-to-Christianity, accessed 2/11/21.

[19] Gorg, Peter H., *The Desert Fathers*, San Francisco: Ignatius Press, 2008, 12-13.

[20] Hill, *Christianity*, 86-87.

[21] Augustine, *Confessions,* Book VIII, Chapter VII. 17. In public domain.

[22] Hill, *Christianity*, 90.

[23] Augustine, *Homily VII,* paragraph 8, in public domain.

[24] Hill, *Christianity,* 249-252.

[25] Weber, Kerry, 'Confession Via Phone, For a Fee', *Jesuit Review* Website, https://www.americamagazine.org/content/all-things/confession-phone-fee, 1st Feb 2022

[26] Hill, *Christianity*, 251.

[27] Hill, *Christianity,* 251.

[28] Hill, *Christianity,* 251-256.

[29] Melton J. Gordon, 'Pentecostalism', *Encyclopaedia Britannica* Website, https://www.britannica.com/topic/Pentecostalism, accessed 22nd August 2020 and Yong, Amos, *The Spirit Poured Out on All Flesh*, Michigan: Baker Academic, 2005, 176ff.

[30] Van Der Haak, B., 'Atlas of Pentecostalism', *Pulitzer Centre* Website, https://pulitzercenter.org/projects/africa-nigeria-pentecostal-christians-holy-spirit-global-religion-iconography-cartography-data-visualization, accessed 22nd August 2020.

[31] Morson, G., 'Leo Tolstoy', *Encyclopaedia Britannica* Website, https://www.britannica.com/biography/Leo-Tolstoy, accessed 15th February 2022.

[32] Sent by Anne in personal email to author. Permission granted for use.

[33] We have to be careful when interpreting the Bible. We record some stories here to illustrate the point and we discuss proper interpretive methods in a later chapter. The existence of contemporary stories that are often just as incredible adds verification to these bible stories. It seems God has throughout history been ready to do incredible things for us, some of which have been recorded for posterity.

[34] Revelation 21:3-4, 22:1-5 paraphrased from the New Living translation.

[35] Exodus chapter 2ff, paraphrased from the New Living translation.

[36] Keener, Craig, Dr., *Miracles*, Grand Rapids: Baker Academic, 2011. Story sent in personal email to author, paraphrased for use. Permission granted for use by Dr Keener.

[37] Sent by Pat in personal email to author. Permission granted for use.

[38] Sent by Anne in personal email to author. Permission granted for use.

[39] 2 Corinthians 12:1-4, paraphrased from the New Living translation.

[40] Johnson, Bill, *The Supernatural Power of a Transformed Mind*, Shippensburg: Destiny Image Publishers Inc., 2005, 29. Paraphrased. Permission granted for use by Bethel Ministries.

[41] Johnson, *Supernatural,* 36. Paraphrased. Permission granted for use by Bethel Ministries.

[42] Johnson, *Supernatural,* 49. Paraphrased. Permission granted for use by Bethel Ministries.

[43] 2 Kings 4:8-37. Paraphrased from the New Living translation. This is a story from the Bible at a time when many people had servants, something we now realise is totally unacceptable. The scars of the shameful history of slavery run incredibly deep for many.

[44] Morris-Young, Amy, story and information sent in personal email to author and in 'What I Saw When I Died', *National Catholic Reporter*

Website, https://www.ncronline.org/news/spirituality/what-i-saw-when-i-died, accessed 24th Feb 2022. Paraphrased. Permission given for use by Amy Morris-Young.

[45] Packer, J. I., 'John Wesley', *Christian History* Website, https://www.christianitytoday.com/history/people/denominationalfounders/john-wesley.html, accessed 23rd August 2020.

[46] Psalm 63:1, paraphrased from the New Living translation.

[47] Eads, Lauren, 10 of The World's Most Disgusting Foods, *The Drinks Business* Website, https://www.thedrinksbusiness.com/2018/10/10-of-the-worlds-most-disgusting-foods/, accessed 9th January 2023.

[48] Scott, Richard, 'Viewpoint: Religion Benefits health', *British Journal of General Practice*, 2014, 64, (624):353.

[49] Garrison, Andrew, 'Religion, Health, and Questions of Meaning', *WebMD/Medscape Health Network* Website, https://www.ncbi.nlm.nih.gov/pmc/articles/PMC1681650/?report=reader#__ffn_sectitle. Accessed 22nd August 2020.

[50] Fisher, Nicole, 'Science Says: Religion is Good for your Health', *Forbes* Website, https://www.forbes.com/sites/nicolefisher/2019/03/29/science-says-religion-is-good-for-your-health/#64c495943a12. Accessed 22nd August 2020.

[51] Koenig H. G. et al, cited in Bunn, A., and Randall, D., 'Health Benefits of Christian Faith', *Christian Medical Fellowship Website*, https://www.cmf.org.uk/resources/publications/content/?context=article&id=25627. Accessed 22nd August 2020.

[52] Philippians 4:6-7, paraphrased from the New Living translation.

[53] Philippians 4:11-13, paraphrased from the New Living Translation.

[54] Koenig, Harold, 'Religion, Spirituality and Health: The Research and Clinical Implications', *ISRN Psychiatry Journal*, 2012, 278730, https://www.ncbi.nlm.nih.gov/pmc/articles/PMC3671693/#sec2title. Accessed 22nd August 2020.

[55] Sims, Andrew, *Is Faith Delusion?,* London: Continuum, 2009, xi-24.

[56] Julia, sent in personal email to Author. Permission granted for use.

[57] Lee, Matthew T., Poloma, Margaret M. and Post, Stephen G., *The Heart of Religion*, Oxford: Oxford University Press, 2013.

[58] E. G. Agarwal, A. K., 'Religion and Mental Health', Editorial, *Indian Journal of Psychiatry*, (1989) 31, (3), 185-186, and Bunn, A., and Randall, D., 'Health Benefits of Christian Faith', *Christian Medical Fellowship Website*, https://www.cmf.org.uk/resources/publications/content/?context=article&id=25627. Accessed 22nd August 2020.

[59] John 9:39.

[60] Kelly, Annie, 'Gross National Happiness in Bhutan: The Big Idea From a Tiny State that Could Change the World', *The Guardian* Website, 21st August 2020, https://www.theguardian.com/world/2012/dec/01/bhutan-wealth-happiness-counts.

[61] Ura, Karma, et al, *An Extensive Analysis of GNH Index,* Thimphu: Centre for Thimphu Studies, 2012.

[62] World Health Organisation, 'Constitution', *World Health Organisation* Website, https://www.who.int/about/who-we-are/constitution. Accessed 20th August 2020.

[63] Hettler, B., 'The Six Dimensions of Wellness', *National Wellness Institute* Website, https://nationalwellness.org/resources/six-dimensions-of-wellness/. Accessed 26th August 2020.

[64] Hettler, 'Wellness'.

[65] Bunn, et al, 'Benefits'.

[66] Teresa of Avila, *Selections from the Interior Castle*, Harper Collins Spiritual Classics, Emilie Griffin (Ed), San Francisco: Harper San Francisco, 2004.

[67] Health and Wellbeing Information, Coordination and Education Australia (HWBE), 'Six Dimensions of Wellbeing', *HWBE* Website, https://hwbe.com.au/about-us/. Accessed 3/11/21.

[68] Koenig, 'Religion'

[69] Romans 15:13, paraphrased from the New Living translation.

[70] Romans 5:3-5, paraphrased from the New Living translation.

[71] Rachel McDermott, email to author, used with permission.

[72] Boston, P., et al., 'Existential Suffering In The Palliative Care Setting: An Integrated Literature Review', in *Journal Of Pain And Symptom Management*, Vol. 41, Issue 3, March 2011, p604-618.

[73] Philippians 4:6-7, paraphrased from the New Living translation.

[74] Hutchesson, Beryl M., 'Jesus Is Lord', Testimony written for *Burrswood Herald*, Summer 1986, Quarterly paper of Burrswood Christian Centre. Reprinted with the kind permission of The Dorothy Kerin Trust and the family of Beryl Hutchesson. All rights reserved.

[75] Middleton, Ant, *The Fear Bubble*, London: HarperCollins Publishers, 2019.

[76] Morris-Young, comment sent in personal email to author, used with permission from Amy Morris-Young.

[77] Sections of Revelation 21-22 and Ezekiel 47, paraphrased from the New Living translation.

[78] Klein, W.W., et al., *Introduction to Biblical Interpretation*, Nashville: W Publishing Group, 1993, 27.

[79] 2 Corinthians 12:1-7, paraphrased from the New Living translation.

[80] The Author.

[81] Isaiah 25:6, paraphrased from the New Living translation.

[82] Revelation 22:1-2, paraphrased from the New Living translation.

[83] Diane. Story sent in personal letter to Author. Permission granted for use.

[84] Scriven, Joseph, 'What A Friend We Have in Jesus', 1855, Public Domain.

[85] Bradley, Julie, *Escape from the Ordinary*, USA: Close Reach Publishing, 2018. Paraphrased, permission for use given by Julie Bradley.

[86] E. G. Psalm 36:7, 136:26, Romans 8:39, Ephesians 2:4.

[87] E.G. Psalm 42:8 and 85:12.

[88] The World Counts, 'People Who Died From Hunger', *The world Counts* Website, https://www.theworldcounts.com/challenges/people-and-poverty/hunger-and-obesity/how-many-people-die-from-hunger-each-year/story, accessed 2/11/21.

[89] Luke 15:3-7, paraphrased from the New Living translation.

[90] Haggai 2:19, paraphrased from the New Living translation.

[91] Wilking, S. and Effron, L., 'Snake Handling Pentecostal Pastor Dies From Snake Bite', *ABC News* Website, 24th August 2020, https://abcnews.go.com/US/snake-handling-pentecostal-pastor-dies-snake-bite/story?id=22551754.

[92] Barton, John, *A History Of The Bible*, Milton Keynes: Penguin Random House, 2019, 239-259.

[93] Barton, *Bible*, 239-259. For example, the type of paper they were written on was different to the special scrolls reserved for writing ancient scripture on, and when New Testament authors used Old Testament texts they would say 'It is written' or 'Scripture says'. They did not do this when using texts from their fellow New Testament authors.

[94] Klein, W.W., et al., *Introduction,* 40-41.

[95] Burgon, John W., *Inspiration and Interpretation*, 1861, p89, in public domain.

[96] McGrath, Alister, *Christian Theology*, 4th Ed, Oxford: Blackwell Publishing, 2007, p134ff.

[97] Hill, *Christianity*, 68.

[98] Barton, *Bible,* 239-263.

[99] Barton, *Bible*, 403-404.

[100] Jude 1:9. Barton, *Bible*, 228.

[101] Barton, *Bible*, 449.

[102] Christianity Today, 'William Tyndale,' *Christianity Today* Website, https://www.christianitytoday.com/history/people/scholarsandscientists/william-tyndale.html, Accessed 2/1/2023.

[103] E.G.: Gryboski, Michael, *Christian Post* Website, 'Latest NIV Bible translation clearer on homosexual sins, says theologian', https://www.christianpost.com/news/latest-niv-Bible-translation-clearer-on-homosexual-sins-says-theologian.html, Accessed 3/11/21.

[104] Tindal, Matthew, *Christianity as Old as The Creation*, London, 1730, p186, in public domain.

[105] The Junia Project, 'Who Was Junia?' *Junia Project* website, https://juniaproject.com/who-was-junia/ accessed 17th Fenruary 2022.

[106] Barton, *Bible*, 406-407.

[107] Dalley, Stephanie, *Myths From Mesopotamia*, Oxford: Oxford University Press, 2000, xv ff.

[108] Livius, 'Nabonidus, Cylinder From Sippar', *Livius* website, https://www.livius.org/sources/content/nabonidus-cylinder-from-sippar/, accessed 1/11/21.

[109] British Museum, 'Culture', *British Museum* Website, https://www.britishmuseum.org/collection/object/W_1851-0902-509, accessed 2/11/21

[110] London School of Theology, 'Cosmos, Humanity and Myth', in *Old Testament Theology In Context*, MA Workbook, 1-9.

[111] London School of Theology, 'Celestial Court', in *Old Testament Theology In Context*, MA Workbook

[112] Comparisons are surprisingly similar. You can find the full text here: The Electronic Text Corpus of Sumerian Literature website, https://etcsl.orinst.ox.ac.uk/section4/tr4051.htm, accessed 14th November 2021.

[113] Again, remarkably similar to many Bible texts. See here for full text: Digital Egypt for Universities, 'Belief in One God in Ancient Egypt', *Digital Egypt for Universities* website, https://www.ucl.ac.uk/museums-static/digitalegypt/amarna/belief.html, accessed 14th November 2021.

[114] Charles Wesley, 'And Can It Be', 1738. Public Domain.

[115] Crowder, 'Ghost,' *New Release Today* Website, https://www.newreleasetoday.com/lyricsdetail.php?lyrics_id=110981, 18th January 2022.

[116] Dalley, *Myths, xvi.*

[117] As yet there is no archaeological or geological evidence of a worldwide flood. This article by Benjamin Radford takes us through the many problems the story faces: https://www.livescience.com/44442-noahs-ark-true.html. Accessed 20/11/21.

[118] Dalley, *Myths*, 7.

[119] Mark, Joshua, 'Enuma Elish, The Babylonian Epic of Creation', *World History Encyclopaedia* Website, https://www.worldhistory.org/article/225/enuma-elish — -the-babylonian-epic-of-creation — -fu/?visitCount=2&lastVisitDate=2021-4-12&pageViewCount=2, accessed 2/11/21.

[120] Chadwick, Henry, *Augustine, A Very Short Introduction*, Oxford, Oxford University Press, 1986, 12.

[121] Hill, *Christianity,* 68-71.

[122] Barton, *Bible,* 353.

[123] Origen, *Commentary on John* book 10, 10:14, c226-229 CE. In public domain, cited in Barton, *Bible*, 350.

---

[124] Klein, et al, *Introduction*, 26-35, 337.

[125] Jeremiah 31:31-34, paraphrased from the New Living translation.

[126] Isaiah 1:11-17, paraphrased from the New Living translation.

[127] E.g. Exodus 17:14, Deuteronomy 32:7, Jeremiah 30:2. Remembering what God did in the past is a strong theme in the Bible. This enables us to celebrate what God has already done but also know that God can do anything for us in the future.

[128] Paraphrased from McCormack, Ian and Sharkey, Jenny, *Clinically Dead,* free download e-book and Ian's testimony https://www.aglimpseofeternity.org/ website (Permission granted for use by Ian McCormack), Revelation 1, 21-22 (New Living translation) and Morris-Young, Amy, comment sent in personal email to author, used with permission from Amy Morris-Young.

[129] Hill, *Christianity*, 91.

[130] Encyclopaedia Britannica, 'Council of Trent', *Encyclopaedia Britannica* Website, https://www.britannica.com/event/Council-of-Trent, Accessed 3/11/21.

[131] Niles, Randall, 'Mikveh, Qumran', *World History Encyclopaedia* website, https://www.worldhistory.org/image/7489/mikvah-qumran/, accessed 3/11/21, and Taylor Farnes, Alan, 'John the Baptist and the Qumran Connection', *Studia Antiqua* Journal, Vol. 9, no. 1, April 2011.

[132] Dunn, J. D., 'Baptism', in Marshall, I. H. et al (eds), *New Bible Dictionary*, 3rd Ed., Leicester, Inter-Varsity Press, 2004, 120-122.

[133] Dockery, D. S., 'Baptism', in J. B. Green et al (eds), *Dictionary of Jesus and the Gospels*, Leicester: InterVarsity Press, 1992, 55-58.

[134] Thayer and Smith. 'Baptizo', *The NAS New Testament Greek Lexicon*, website, https://www.Biblestudytools.com/lexicons/greek/nas/baptizo.html. Accessed 7th September 2020.

[135] John 8:1-11 and Luke 7:36-50, paraphrased from the New Living translation.

[136] Dulles, Avery, *The Assurance Of Things Hoped For,* Oxford: Oxford University Press, 1994, 170-180.

[137] E. G. Luke 7:50, 8:50, 18:42, Acts 2:21, 2:47, 16:31, Romans 10:9-10, 10:13, Ephesians 2:8-10.

[138] Encyclopaedia Britannica, 'St Teresa of Avila', *Encyclopaedia Britannica* website, https://www.britannica.com/biography/Saint-Teresa-of-Avila, accessed 3/11/21 and Teresa of Avila, *Selections From The Interior Castle*, Harper Collins Spiritual Classics, translated by Kieran Kavanaugh and Otilio Rodriguez, HarperSanFrancisco, New York, 1979.

[139] Hampl, Patricia, 'Foreword', in Teresa of Avila, *Selections from The Interior Castle, Harper Collins Spiritual Classics*, San Francisco: 2004.

[140] Ephesians 3:14-21, paraphrased from the New Living translation.

[141] Hay, David, *Something There*, London: Darton, Longman and Todd Ltd., 2006, part one and two.

[142] Newson, Debbie, Essay submitted debating polygamy towards BA in Theology London School of Theology, 2012.

[143] E.G. Old Testament characters such as Jacob, David and Solomon.

[144] E. G. Deuteronomy 4:29, Proverbs 8:17, Jeremiah 29:13, Matthew 7:7, Luke 11:9.

[145] Ezekiel 34:11-16 paraphrased from the New Living translation.

[146] Gorg, Peter H., *The Desert Fathers*, San Francisco: Ignatius Press, 2003.

[147] Buckfast Abbey media presentation as seen at Abbey display, August 2021.

[148] Derbyshire Heritage, 'Cratcliffe Hermitage', Derbyshire Heritage Website, https://derbyshireheritage.co.uk/curiosities/cratcliffe-hermitage/, accessed 3/11/21.

[149] Surf Church, *Surf Church* website, https://surfchurch.pt/en/. Accessed 7th September 2020,

[150] Jon, Story given to author in interview and written by author. Used with permission.

Bibliography

Agarwal, A. K., 'Religion and Mental Health' Editorial, *Indian Journal of Psychiatry*, (1989) 31, (3), 185-186.

Atkinson, David J. et al, (eds), *New Dictionary of Christian Ethics and Pastoral Theology*, Nottingham: Inter-Varsity Press, 1995.

Augustine, *Confessions,* Book VIII, Chapter VII. 17. In public domain.

Augustine, Homily VII, paragraph 8, in public domain.

Baker, Heidi, *Compelled By Love*, Lake Mary: Charisma House, 2008.

Barton, John, *A History Of The Bible,* Milton Keynes: Penguin Random House UK, 2019.

Bosch, David J., *Transforming Mission*, Maryknoll: Orbis Books, 2014.

Boston, P., et al., 'Existential Suffering In The Palliative Care Setting: An Integrated Literature Review', in *Journal Of Pain And Symptom Management*, Vol. 41, Issue 3, March 2011, p604-618.

Boyd, Gregory A. and Eddy, Paul R., *Across the Spectrum*, Grand Rapids: Baker Academic, 2002.

Bradley, Julie, *Escape from the Ordinary*, USA: Close Reach Publishing, 2018.

Bradley, Julie, *Crossing Pirate Waters*, USA, Close Reach Publishing, 2020.

British Museum, 'Culture', *British Museum* Website, https://www.britishmuseum.org/collection/object/W_1851-0902-509.

Buckfast Abbey media presentation as seen at Abbey display.

Bunn, A., and Randall, D., 'Health Benefits of Christian Faith', *Christian Medical Fellowship Website*, 1st July 2020, https://www.cmf.org.uk/resources/publications/content/?context=article&id=25627.

Burgon, John, *Inspiration and Interpretation*, 1861, in public domain.

Chadwick, Henry, *Augustine*, Oxford: Oxford University Press, 1986.

Chadwick, Henry, *The Early Church* (Revised Ed), London: Penguin Books, 1993.

Christianity Today, 'William Tyndale,' *Christianity Today* Website, https://www.christianitytoday.com/history/people/scholarsandscientists/william-tyndale.html.

Crowder, 'Ghost,' *New Release Today* Website, https://www.newreleasetoday.com/lyricsdetail.php?lyrics_id=110981.

Dalley, Stephanie, *Myths From Mesopotamia*, Oxford: Oxford University Press, 2008.

Derbyshire Heritage, 'Cratcliffe Hermitage', Derbyshire Heritage Website, https://derbyshireheritage.co.uk/curiosities/cratcliffe-hermitage/.

Digital Egypt For Universities, 'Belief in one God in Egypt', *Digital Egypt For Universities* Website, https://etcsl.orinst.ox.ac.uk/section4/tr4051.htm.

Dockery, D. S., 'Baptism,' in J. B. Green et al (eds), *Dictionary of Jesus and the Gospels*, Leicester: InterVarsity Press, 1992.

Doerksen, Brian, 'Refiners Fire', Vineyard Churches Website, https://www.vineyardchurches.org.uk/songs/refiners-fire/.

Dulles, Avery, *The Assurance of Things Hoped For,* Oxford: Oxford University Press, 1994.

Dunn, J. D., 'Baptism', in Marshall, I. H. et al (eds), *New Bible Dictionary*, 3rd Ed., Leicester, Inter-Varsity Press, 2004.

Eads, Lauren, 10 of The World's Most Disgusting Foods, *The Drinks Business* Website, https://www.thedrinksbusiness.com/2018/10/10-of-the-worlds-most-disgusting-foods/.

Encyclopaedia Britannica, Various articles, *Encyclopaedia Britannica* Website, https://www.britannica.com/.

Electronic Text Corpus of Sumerian Literature, Enlil In The E-kur, *Electronic Text Corpus of Sumerian Literature* website, https://etcsl.orinst.ox.ac.uk/section4/tr4051.htm.

Fisher, Nicole, 'Science Says: Religion is Good for your Health', *Forbes* Website, 23rd March 2020, https://www.forbes.com/sites/nicolefisher/2019/03/29/science-says-religion-is-good-for-your-health/#64c495943a12

Freeman, Charles, *A New History of Early Christianity*, London: Yale University Press, 2009.

Garrison, Andrew, 'Religion, Health, and Questions of Meaning', *WebMD/Medscape Health Network* Website, 2nd April 2020, https://www.ncbi.nlm.nih.gov/pmc/articles/PMC1681650/?report=reader#__ffn_sectitle.

Gill, D. W., 'Hope', in *New Dictionary of Christian Ethics and Pastoral Theology*, David Atkinson et al., (eds), Nottingham: Inter-Varsity Press, 1995, 455-457.

Godlee, Fiona, 'What is Health?' *The British Medical Journal*, 2011; 343.

Godwin, Roy and Roberts, Dave, *The Grace Outpouring*, Colorado Springs: David C Cook, 2019.

Gorg, Peter H., *The Desert Fathers,* San Francisco: Ignatius Press, 2008.

Green, Joel B. et al, (eds), *Dictionary of Jesus and the Gospels,* Leicester: InterVarsity Press, 1992.

Grudem, Wayne, *Systematic Theology*, Nottingham: Inter-Varsity Press, 1994.

Gryboski, Michael, *Christian Post* Website, 'Latest NIV Bible translation clearer on homosexual sins, says theologian', https://www.christianpost.com/news/latest-niv-Bible-translation-clearer-on-homosexual-sins-says-theologian.html.

Hampl, Patricia, 'Foreword,' in Teresa of Avila, *Selections from The Interior Castle, Harper Collins Spiritual Classics*, San Francisco: 2004.

Hawks, Steven, 'Spiritual Wellness, Holistic Health, and the Practice of Health Education', *American Journal of Health Education*, Jan/Feb 2004, Vol. 35, No. 1.

Hawthorne, Gerald F. et al, (eds) *Dictionary of Paul and his Letters*, Leicester: InterVarsity Press, 1993.

Hay, David, *Something There*, London: Darton, Longman and Todd Ltd., 2006.

Health and Wellbeing Information, Coordination and Education Australia (HWBE), 'Six Dimensions of Wellbeing', *HWBE* Website, https://hwbe.com.au/about-us/.

Hettler, B., 'The Six Dimensions of Wellness'' *National Wellness Institute* Website, 26th August 2020, https://nationalwellness.org/resources/six-dimensions-of-wellness/.

Hill, Jonathon, *The History of Christianity*, New Lion Handbook, Oxford: Lion Hudson PLC, 2007.

Hillsong United, 'Oceans', *Hillsong* Website, https://hillsong.com/lyrics/oceans-where-feet-may-fail/.

Hurtado, L. W., ‘Christ’ in Green’, Joel B. et al, (eds), *Dictionary of Jesus and the Gospels,* Leicester: InterVarsity Press, 1992.

Hutcheson, Beryl, ‘Jesus Is Lord’, Testimony written for *Burrswood Herald*, Summer 1986, Quarterly paper of Burrswood Christian Centre. Reprinted with the kind permission of the Dorothy Kerin Trust and the family of Beryl Hutchesson. All rights reserved.

Hvidt, N. C., ‘Faith Moves Mountains—Mountains Move Faith: Two Opposite Epidemiological Forces in Research on Religion and Health’, Journal of Religion and Health (2017), 56:294-304. https://www.ncbi.nlm.nih.gov/pmc/articles/PMC5222926/pdf/10943_2016_Article_300.pdf.

Idler, Ellen, ‘Religion, a social determinant of mortality? A 10-year follow-up of the Health and Retirement Study’, *Plos One* Journal, December 20th 2017, https://www.ncbi.nlm.nih.gov/pmc/articles/PMC5738040/pdf/pone.0189134.pdf

Johnson, Bill, *The Supernatural Power of a Transformed Mind*, Shippensburg: Destiny Image Publishers Inc., 2005.

Junia Project, ‘Who Was Junia?’ *Junia Project* website, https://juniaproject.com/who-was-junia/.

Juskiene, Vaineta, ‘Spiritual Health as an Integral Component of Human Wellbeing’, De Gruyter, Applied Research in Health and Social Science: Interface and Interaction, Vol. 13, No. 1, 2016, *ResearchGate* Website, 7th September 2020, https://www.researchgate.net/publication/312403100_Spiritual_Health_as_an_Integral_Component_of_Human_Wellbeing.

Keener, Craig, Dr., *Miracles*, Grand Rapids: Baker Academic, 2011.

Kelly, Annie, ‘Gross National Happiness in Bhutan: The Big Idea from a Tiny State that Could Change the World’, *The Guardian* Website, 24th August 2020, https://www.theguardian.com/world/2012/dec/01/bhutan-wealth-happiness-counts

Klein, W. W. et al., *Introduction to Biblical Interpretation*, Nashville: W Publishing Group, 1993.

Koenig H. G. et al, cited in Bunn, A., and Randall, D., ‘Health Benefits of Christian Faith,’ *Christian Medical Fellowship Website*, https://www.cmf.org.uk/resources/publications/content/?context=article &id=25627

Koenig, Harold, 'Religion, Spirituality and Health: The Research and Clinical Implications,' *ISRN Psychiatry* Journal, 2012, 278730, https://www.ncbi.nlm.nih.gov/pmc/articles/PMC3671693/#sec2title

Lee, M. T. et al., *The Heart of Religion*, Oxford: Oxford University Press, 2013.

Livius, 'Nabonidus, cylinder from Sippar', *Livius* website, https://www.livius.org/sources/content/nabonidus-cylinder-from-sippar/.

London School of Theology, 'Old Testament Theology in Context', MA workbook.

Ma, Julie C., and Ma, Wonsuk, *Mission in the Spirit*, Oxford: Regnum Books International, 2010.

MacGillivray Nicol, Donald, 'Constantine I', *Encyclopaedia Britannica* Website, https://www.britannica.com/biography/Constantine-I-Roman-emperor

Mark, Joshua, 'Enuma Elish, The Babylonian Epic of Creation', *World History Encyclopaedia* Website, https://www.worldhistory.org/article/225/enuma-elish — -the-babylonian-epic-of-creation — -fu/?visitCount=2&lastVisitDate=2021-4-12&pageViewCount=2.

Marshall, I. H. et al, (eds), *New Bible Dictionary*, 3rd Ed., Leicester: Inter-Varsity Press, 2004.

McCormack, Ian, 'Ian's Testimony', *A Glimpse of Eternity* Website, 15th September 2020, https://www.aglimpseofeternity.org/.

McGrath, Alister, *Christian Theology*, 4th Ed, Oxford: Blackwell Publishing, 2007.

Melton J. Gordon, 'Pentecostalism', *Encyclopaedia Britannica* Website, 3rd May 2020, https://www.britannica.com/topic/Pentecostalism

Middleton, Ant, *The Fear Bubble*, London: HarperCollins Publishers, 2019.

Miller, Donald E. and Yamamori, Tetsunao, *Global Pentecostalism*, Berkeley: University of California Press, no date.

Morris-Young, Amy, 'What I Saw When I Died', *National Catholic Reporter* Website, 2nd April 2020, https://www.ncronline.org/news/spirituality/what-i-saw-when-i-died

Morris-Young, Amy, 'When the Spirit Moves', *National Catholic Reporter* Website, 2nd April 2020, https://www.ncronline.org/blogs/ncr-today/when-spirit-moves

Morris-Young, Amy, Information sent in personal email to author, permission granted for use.

Morson, G., 'Leo Tolstoy', *Encyclopaedia Britannica* Website, https://www.britannica.com/biography/Leo-Tolstoy.

National Wellness Institute, 'Six Dimensions of Wellness', *National Wellness Institute* website, 22nd August 2020, https://nationalwellness.org/resources/six-dimensions-of-wellness/.

Newson, Debbie, Essay submitted debating polygamy towards BA in Theology London School of Theology, 2012.

Niles, Randall, 'Mikveh, Qumran', *World History Encyclopaedia* website, https://www.worldhistory.org/image/7489/mikvah-qumran/

Nolland, John, *Luke 1-9:20*, Word Biblical Commentary Series 35a, Dallas: Word Books, 1989.

Nolland, John, *Luke 9:21-18:34*, Word Biblical Commentary Series 35b, Dallas: Word Books, 1993.

Nolland, John, *Luke 18:35-24:53*, Word Biblical Commentary Series 35c, Dallas: Word Books, 1993.

Open Doors, 'World Watch List 2022', *Open Door* Website, https://www.opendoorsuk.org/.

Origen, *Commentary on John* book 10, 10:14, c226-229 CE. In public domain.

Oxford Poverty and Human Development Initiative, 'Bhutan's Gross National Happiness Index', *OPHI* website, 24th August 2020, https://ophi.org.uk/policy/national-policy/gross-national-happiness-index/

Packer, J. I., 'John Wesley', *Christian History* Website, 23rd August 2020, https://www.christianitytoday.com/history/people/denominationalfounders/john-wesley.html

Patalsky, Kathy, 'Defining Wellness: Hettler's Six Dimensions. Live Well,', *Healthy, Happy Life* Website, https://healthyhappylife.com/defining-wellness-hettlers-six/.

Peterson Sparks, Elicka, *The Devil You Know*, New York; Prometheus Books, 2016.

Radford, Benjamin, 'The Ark: Could Noah's Tale be True?' *LiveScience* website, 7th September 2020, https://www.livescience.com/44442-noahs-ark-true.html.

Scott, Richard, 'Viewpoint: Religion Benefits health', *British Journal of General Practice*, 2014, 64, (624):353.

Scriven, Joseph, 'What A Friend We Have in Jesus', 1855, Public Domain.

Sharkey, Jenny, *Clinically Dead*, Gospel Media, 2013, Kindle Edition.

Shelley, Bruce, '325 The First Council of Nicaea,' *Christianity Today* Website, https://www.christianitytoday.com/history/issues/issue-28/325-first-council-of-nicea.html,

Sims, Andrew, *Is Faith Delusion?,* London: Continuum, 2009.

Strohecker, James, 'A Brief History of Wellness,' *HealthWorld* Online Website, 7th September 2020, http://www.mywellnesstest.com/certResFile/BriefHistoryofWellness.pdf.

Surf Church, *Surf Church* website, http://surfchurch.pt/en/.

Tacitus, 'The Neronian Persecution', in *Documents of the Christian Church*, Bettenson and Maunder, (eds), Oxford: Oxford University press, 1999, 64.

Tacitus, 'The Christians Accused By Nero', in *The Annals of Tacitus*, No. 44, p 423, work in public domain, https://www.google.co.uk/books/edition/The_annals/3DgstTVjP7sC?hl=en&gbpv=1&printsec=frontcover

Tate, Randolph, W., Handbook For Biblical Interpretation, Michigan: Baker Academic, 2006.

Taylor Farnes, Alan, 'John the Baptist and the Qumran Connection,' *Studia Antiqua* Journal, Vol. 9, no. 1, April 2011.

Teresa of Avila, *The Interior Castle*, Harper Collins Spiritual Classics, Emilie Griffin (Ed), translated by Kieran Kavanaugh and Otilio Rodriguez, San Francisco: HarperSanFrancisco, 2004.

Thayer and Smith. 'Baptizo', *The NAS New Testament Greek Lexicon*, website, https://www.Biblestudytools.com/lexicons/greek/nas/baptizo.html.

The World Counts, 'People Who Died From Hunger', The world Counts Website, https://www.theworldcounts.com/challenges/people-and-poverty/hunger-and-obesity/how-many-people-die-from-hunger-each-year/story.

Thiselton, Anthony C., *Hermeneutics, an Introduction*, Cambridge: W. B. Eerdmans Publishing Co., 2009.

Tindal, Matthew, *Christianity as Old as The Creation*, London, 1730, p186, in public domain.

Torres, Beulah R., 'The Scope and Challenges of the Wellness Activities of the Older Adults', *ResearchGate* Website, https://www.researchgate.net/publication/323084807_The_Scope_and_Challenges_of_the_Wellness_Activities_of_the_Older_Adults/link/5a7ee52aa6fdcc0d4ba929b2/download.

Townend, Stuart, 'Vagabonds', *Stuart Townend* website, 23rd August 2020, https://www.stuarttownend.co.uk/song/vagabonds/.

Unterrainer, H. F. et al, 'Religious/Spiritual Wellbeing, Personality and Mental Health: a Review of Results and Conceptual Issues', *Journal of Religion and Health*, 2014: Apr; 53 (2): 382-92, *National Library of Medicine* Website, https://pubmed.ncbi.nlm.nih.gov/22965652/.

Ura, Karma et al, *An Extensive Analysis of GNH Index*, Thimphu: Centre for Bhutan Studies, May 2012, http://www.grossnationalhappiness.com/wpcontent/uploads/2012/10/An%20Extensive%20Analysis%20of%20GNH%20Index.pdf

Van Der Haak, B., 'Atlas of Pentecostalism', *Pulitzer Centre* Website, 29th July, 2020, https://pulitzercenter.org/projects/africa-nigeria-pentecostal-christians-holy-spirit-global-religion-iconography-cartography-data-visualization.

Vanhoozer, Kevin J. et al, (eds), *Dictionary for Theological Interpretation of the Bible*, Grand Rapids: Baker Academic, 2005.

Vine, W. E., Vine's Expository Dictionary of Old and New Testament Words, Nashville: Thomas Nelson, 1997.

Weber, Kerry, 'Confession Via Phone, For a Fee', *Jesuit Review* Website, https://www.americamagazine.org/content/all-things/confession-phone-fee.

Wesley, Charles, 'And Can It Be', Public Domain.

Wright, Christopher, J. H., *The Mission of God*, Downers Grove: InterVarsity Press, 2006.

Wilking, S. and Effron, L., 'Snake Handling Pentecostal Pastor Dies From Snake Bite', *ABC News* Website, 24th August 2020, https://abcnews.go.com/US/snake-handling-pentecostal-pastor-dies-snake-bite/story?id=22551754.

World Health Organisation, 'Constitution', *World Health Organisation* Website, 20th August 2020, https://www.who.int/about/who-we-are/constitution.

Wynne-Jones, J., 'Two Percent of Anglican Priests Don't Believe in God, Survey Finds', *Independent* Website, https://www.independent.co.uk/news/uk/home-news/survey-finds-2-of-anglican-priests-are-not-believers-9821899.html?r=4671.

Yong, Amos, *The Spirit Poured Out on All Flesh*, Michigan: Baker Academic, 2005.

Zarei, Nooshin et al., 'The Impact of Spirituality on Health', Shiraz E. Medical Journal, June 2016, *ResearchGate* Website, 23rd August 2020,
https://www.researchgate.net/publication/304456467_The_Impact_of_Spirituality_on_Health